LGBT PEOPLE AND THE
UK CULTURAL SECTOR

LGBT People and the UK Cultural Sector

The Response of Libraries, Museums, Archives and Heritage since 1950

JOHN VINCENT
The Network, UK

ASHGATE

Published by
Ashgate Publishing Limited
Wey Court East
Union Road
Farnham
Surrey, GU9 7PT
England

Ashgate Publishing Company
110 Cherry Street
Suite 3-1
Burlington, VT 05401-3818
USA

www.ashgate.com

British Library Cataloguing in Publication Data
A catalogue record for this book is available from the British Library

The Library of Congress has cataloged the printed edition as follows:
Vincent, John, 1948-
  LGBT people and the UK cultural sector : the response of libraries, museums, archives and heritage since 1950 / by John Vincent.
    pages cm
  Includes bibliographical references and index.
  ISBN 978-1-4094-3865-6 (hardback)—ISBN 978-1-4094-3866-3 (ebook)—
ISBN 978-1-4724-0331-5 (epub) 1. Libraries and sexual minorities—Great Britain.
2. Museums and minorities—Great Britain. 3. Sexual minorities—Archives. 4. Sexual minorities—Great Britain. I. Title.
  Z711.92.S49V56 2013
  027.6'30941—dc23

2013024822

ISBN 9781409438656 (hbk)
ISBN 9781409438663 (ebk – PDF)
ISBN 9781472403315 (ebk – ePUB)

MIX
Paper from
responsible sources
FSC
www.fsc.org
FSC® C013985

Printed in the United Kingdom by Henry Ling Limited, at the Dorset Press, Dorchester, DT1 1HD

Contents

About the author

John Vincent has worked in the public sector since the 1960s, primarily for Hertfordshire, Lambeth and Enfield library services. In 1997, he was invited to become part of the team that produced the UK's first review of public libraries and social exclusion (from which The Network originated).

John now runs courses and lectures, writes, produces regular newsletters and e-bulletins, and lobbies for greater awareness of the role that libraries, archives, museums, and the cultural and heritage sector play in contributing to social justice.

He is particularly interested in supporting the work that libraries do with LGBT people, young people in care, older people and 'new arrivals' to the UK.

Preface

Here, I want to set out some of my background and what I hope this book will achieve in order to answer the question, 'Why did I want to write this book?'.

My background

I realised that I was 'different' quite early on but, in the 1950s, could not put a name to what this might be. Growing up in Welwyn Garden City then too meant that there was a limited number of role models available.

Secondary school was mostly a nightmare. This was primarily because I was bullied and then ostracised – boys in my year recognised that I was gay even before I fully had – but also because I came to loathe the elitist, old-fashioned grammar school views that ran through much of the school and teaching (thank goodness for a handful of sympathetic teachers – one being the teacher in charge of the school library – who provided some alternative voices).

I left school in 1966 and, at college (the then North Western Polytechnic, now part of London Metropolitan University), became passionate about library services for children and young people and about different ways of looking at education (thanks to some inspired teaching by Eleanor von Schweinitz and Brian Alderson), particularly via the writings of US critics such as John Holt (1969a, 1969b, 1972) and George Dennison (1969), plus, nearer to home, the children's rights movement as exemplified by the struggle over – and eventual closure of – Risinghill School (Berg, 1968).[1]

---

1 Even in one of the titles about children's rights (Adams *et al.*, 1972) which was, overall, impressive, there was an extremely negative passage: 'The devices the adolescent uses to convince himself of his homosexuality are most interesting. Wherever the mother-figure was dominant and the mother-fixation was quite obviously the strongest element in a person's life, he will repress his mother-figure and the incest wish will be overlaid by a sexual attraction to a father-figure, i.e. a male-figure of the same sex on a masturbation fantasy basis. The adolescent would then pronounce himself a born homosexual and signal to his environment this fact, however distressing to himself, by effeminate gestures, a mincing gait, fluttering his eyelids, and using the comments of his school friends on his behaviour-pattern as confirmation of his inborn homosexuality ...we have to differentiate here between the sincere depth of the homosexuality of Michelangelo, of Shakespeare, with the meaningless superficiality, the bogus feminization of the "gay boy"' (Ollendorff, 1972: 117-118).

At the same time, I was struggling with coming out. Although, as I noted above, boys in my year at school were quicker off the mark than I was in recognising that I might be gay (or a 'poof' as they termed it on the blackboard), nevertheless I had also had some inkling that I might be sexually attracted to other boys. Before 1967 in the UK, sexual relations between two men were still illegal, and, of course, there were very, very few positive images of lesbian, gay, bisexual and trans (LGBT) people, or even sources of reliable information, never mind role models. One of my retreats from school (apart from counting down the days until I could leave!) was working in the local public library as a Saturday Assistant – there, people took me for who I was and treated me as an adult, and I also had access to the (limited) information available about LGBTs.

After 'library school', I went back to Hertfordshire, firstly as a Librarian, then a Children's Librarian. I gradually came out to close friends, and felt generally supported, especially by the 'tone' of the service, set particularly by Lorna Paulin, Joan Butler and Ann-Marie Parker.

However, the prolonged bullying (combined with timidity about the 'outside world') took its toll, and, whilst at college, I started to suffer from panic attacks – and became quite agoraphobic. I was referred by my General Practitioner (GP) to the local hospital, and then to a psychotherapeutic group, in which I started to explore who I was – and eventually came out. Combined with some reading – as much as I could find – and quite a bit of 'self-help', I gained confidence.

In 1974, I left Hertfordshire for the London Borough of Lambeth, partly because I wanted to work in a different sort of library service – and, under Janet Hill, the children's library service in Lambeth was exciting and innovative – and partly because I felt that Welwyn Garden City was not somewhere where I could comfortably explore being gay.

In 1976, I had my first, and almost only, taste of just how negative the medical profession could be. At the beginning of the year, I caught flu – except that it lingered for a couple of months. Concerned about my health, and unbeknown to me, my mother went to see my GP about my condition, and he, apparently, told her that she was fussing unnecessarily, that it was my father (who had also had flu) that she should be worrying about, and that the real problem with me was that I was gay. She and I were furious, especially as it turned out that this was a warning sign of a serious, lifelong health condition.[2]

I stayed in Lambeth from 1974 until 1996, moving jobs from Assistant Borough Children's Librarian – via Children's Librarian and Principal Librarian – to becoming head of service. I had decided to come out at my initial job interview in 1973: probably, looking back, quite a brave choice, but, at that time, there was considerable negative coverage of LGBT people in the press (especially in relation to working with children), and I decided that Lambeth should know from the start what they were taking on!

---

2   Sideroblastic anaemia (see Great Ormond Street Hospital for Children National Health Service (NHS) Foundation Trust, 2007).

The interview panel took this in their stride, and I was appointed. This set the tone for the next 22 years: apart from some whiffs of discrimination – which were never fully articulated – when I applied for some senior posts, I never faced discrimination or hostility (and, indeed, from 1979 onwards, took my partner to social events where he was welcomed by staff at all levels).

The only area where there was a slight problem was the view that, as an out gay man (and one of the most senior in the authority), I must have a view on any and every sex-related issue, so was asked, for example, what should be done about men having sex in a sports centre changing-room!

In 1995-1996, Lambeth underwent a major restructuring and a number of senior managers lost their jobs. I was made redundant: after some initial nervousness about leaving local government after so long, I embraced a different life!

I was invited to become part of the research team working on the Library and Information Commission-funded project, published by the then Resource in 2000 as *Open to All?* (Muddiman *et al.*, 2000a; Muddiman *et al.*, 2000b; Muddiman *et al.*, 2000c), to which, amongst other papers, I contributed a Working Paper on LGBT issues (Vincent, 1999).

As a further development of this project, I was a founder-member in 1999 of 'The Network – tackling social exclusion in libraries, museums, archives and galleries', regularly running courses and conferences, speaking at events, and producing a monthly newsletter and regular ebulletin. Some of the comments that have been made about my coming out on courses are included later in the book. Particular areas of interest in terms of my training and writing are developing provision for: LGBT people; young people, especially looked-after children; new arrivals; and older people – and these have all informed this book.

Growing up 'different'

My secondary school experience left an enormous scar which it took years to repair; I finally put the matter to rest by – as a one-off – going to a school reunion and meeting some of my peers as adults, with my being out and comfortable with it.

Struggling with 'difference' is a theme that has also come through strongly in some of the interviews for this book. For example, as Adrian Whittle says:

> I came to London in 1988, married and with two small children. I came out two years later. It was an extremely difficult process and the working environment I was in was not supportive. Staff working for me gossiped not just with each other (to be expected) but also with members of the public, some of whom were quite happy to share their opinion of me to my face in front of other customers. There were other gay men in the management structure but I have to say they were not supportive being relatively closeted themselves – although people knew that they were gay, there was something of a 'don't ask don't tell' approach to

things. I was lucky enough to have a couple of supportive friends in the service and of course, one gains confidence over time. I was also lucky enough to be able to progress to a senior level in local government, and to some extent this protects one from overt homophobia – although not entirely. When I worked in Hackney, the other senior managers at my level regularly played five a side football together. I was later told I was never invited because they were worried I might look at them in the changing room. That's a bit sad for a group of men who had worked in a so called left-wing authority for several years and still held this view. (Whittle, A. 2013)

Lorne has described growing up gender variant:

I think the biggest thing to be aware of about young people who present outside of the gender binary, or as gender variant in their appearance, clothing, mannerisms etc is that we are hyper-sensitive and conscious of how the outside world may be perceiving us. When I was a teenager and young adult I was so self conscious of how I looked that I became extremely anxious, quiet and shy. I have seen this in trans and gender queer or gender questioning young people that I have worked with and heard similar stories from friends as an adult. This meant that when I went places, looking for information or representation of the LGBTQ world, I would rarely speak to people or ask for help (for example in a library looking for a particular book ...)

I guess the issue goes beyond feeling 'at home' or just welcomed into a library or museum etc. When as a young person I felt extremely uncomfortable in myself, I was anxious and embarrassed all the time. The issue was about never feeling 'at home' within myself and therefore anyone looking at me, was, for me, a mirror being held up to the fact that I looked, and in my mind *was* 'weird' or 'different'. I didn't want people to see me, because then I would have to see me and in some way acknowledge me, I wasn't ready to do this until I was about 20 years old. (Lorne, 2012)

David Murray (in answer to a question about whether he had ever faced hostility/homophobia) replied:

Only once – when I went for a job interview as a senior manager in a County and it was clear they were very perplexed by the man without a wife and [with] a shaven head. I think I got to the decision not to go there long before they did, but the sense of burning anger that anyone dare exclude me on the grounds of who I slept with remains with me. (Murray, 2012)

What I hope this book will achieve

The reason for describing some of my background is so that I can demonstrate my 'take' on being gay, and to set out the aims of this book.

Whilst I recognise that young (and not-so-young) people may well find it easier to come out today – and, indeed, the necessity to have life framed by coming-out stories may be fading – nevertheless we know that many people still struggle and still have to face hostility, threats, even violence. One of the motivators for much of my work (writing, running courses, talking to people about being gay and the issues we still face) is to try to improve the situation for those who 'come after' me, to try to prevent more young people being bullied and feeling so overwhelmed that they self-harm or take their own lives.

I think that the cultural sector can play a huge part in this by providing safe, informed (and informative) spaces where people can explore who they are – and be who they are too. However, not all the cultural sector understands this – or wants to play this role – so this books is intended to make visible the needs and demands of LGBT people, and to demonstrate the good practice that parts of the cultural sector have developed, as well as identifying gaps where this is not happening.

John Vincent
February 2013

Acknowledgments

My thanks to everyone who has contributed so generously to this book. I have been heartened by the enthusiasm and goodwill shown by all the people I have talked to, written to and emailed, and interviewed – I am enormously grateful. My thanks go particularly to the following:

- the interviewees (many of whom also contributed all the way through the process of writing the book): Elizabeth L. Chapman, Rachel Hasted, Jacky Logan, Lorne, David Murray, Kathryn Rooke, Adrian Whittle;
- the people who generously gave time to meet me and discuss aspects of the book: Andrew Flinn, Lesley Hall, Jon Newman, Richard Sandell, Matt Smith, Oliver Winchester;
- friends and contacts who have so generously shared their thoughts, ideas, writings and personal archives; and/or who have made comments on various drafts: Jane Allen, Susan Blishen, Gabrielle Bourn, Helen Carpenter, Sean Curran, Mark Dunton, Colston Hartley, Katie Herzog, Bernard Horrocks, Rebecca Howell, Wolfgang Kaiser, John Lindsay, Oliver Merrington, Izzy Mohammed, Ross Parry, John Pateman, Jan Pimblett, Jonathan Platt, Sue Regan, Avril Rolph, Sue Sanders, Norena Shopland, Di Stiff, Richard Ward, Stephen Welsh, Helen Wilkinson;
- all those people who have kindly responded to emails, sent information about their work and generally supported this project;
- the libraries, museums and archives that have supported me and helped with my many enquiries, including: the British Library; the information team at CILIP; the staff of Devon County Library Service; Hannah Little and Laura Stevens at the Glasgow Women's Library; Stefan Dickers and the staff at the Lesbian & Gay News Archive, Bishopsgate Institute; Sue Donnelly and the staff of the Archives at the London School of Economics; the Museums Association; Elizabeth James and staff at Senate House Library, University of London; Mark Dunton and the staff of The National Archives; Sonia and the staff of the Women's Library;
- Stonewall for their LGB history timeline (Stonewall, 2011c) which has been invaluable in planning this book.

Finally, I should like to thank Ashgate (especially Dymphna Evans) for agreeing to my proposal for this book – and all their subsequent support; the EndNote team for all their help with technical queries; and last, but certainly not least, Robert for all his support, comments and help during a long writing process.

Glossary and abbreviations

Glossary – LGBT terms

Bisexual describes sexual and/or romantic desire for men and women.

Gay was originally applied to men and women, but now generally applies to sexual and/or romantic desire between men.

Gender 'refers to the socially constructed roles, behaviour, activities and attributes that a particular society considers appropriate for men and women' (World Health Organization, 2012).

Intersex 'is a general term used for a variety of conditions in which a person is born with a reproductive or sexual anatomy that doesn't seem to fit the typical definitions of female or male' (Intersex Society of North America, 2008).

Lesbian is the commonest English language term for describing sexual and/or romantic desire between women.

Queer (which was originally a derogatory term) has been reclaimed to mean either anyone who is not heterosexual or people who do not identify with one particular gender. It is also used to describe people whose sexual orientations or activities place them outside the mainstream.

Questioning refers to people who are questioning their gender, sexual identity, sexual orientation or all three.

Sexual identity refers to how people think of themselves in terms of whom they are sexually and romantically attracted to.

Sexual orientation refers to the general attraction people feel towards people of one sex or another (or both).

Transgender 'is an all-encompassing term for people that cross gender boundaries, permanently or otherwise' (Women's Resource Centre, 2010: 1).

Glossary – LGBT terms, organisations, activities

BIG – Burning Issues Group

CHE – Campaign for Homosexual Equality, a campaign group that has been in existence since 1969 (Campaign for Homosexual Equality, 2012)

GALOP – Lesbian, Gay and Bisexual Anti-Violence and Policing Group

GIRES – Gender Identity Research and Education Society

GLF – Gay Liberation Front

GLG – Gay Librarians Group

IDAHO – International Day Against Homophobia and Transphobia. The date of 17 May was chosen to commemorate the World Health Organization's decision to remove homosexuality from the list of mental disorders in 1990 (Wikipedia, 2011b)

LGB – Lesbian, gay and bisexual

LGBT – Lesbian, gay, bisexual and trans

LGBTQI – Lesbian, gay, bisexual, trans, queer/questioning, intersex

LiL – Lesbians in Libraries

LLGC – London Lesbian and Gay Centre

Abbreviations

AAL – Association of Assistant Librarians

AIDS – Acquired Immune Deficiency Syndrome

AM – Member of the National Assembly for Wales

BAME – Black, Asian and Minority Ethnic people

BME – Black and Minority Ethnic people

CILIP – Chartered Institute of Library & Information Professionals

CNN – Cable News Network

CPS – Crown Prosecution Service

DCMS – Department for Culture, Media and Sport

DHG – Diversity in Heritage Group

DTI – Department of Trade and Industry

EHRC – Equality and Human Rights Commission

ESRC – Economic and Social Research Council

FA – Football Association

GLC – Greater London Council

GNP – Gross National Product

GP – General Practitioner

HIV – Human Immunodeficiency Virus

HLF – Heritage Lottery Fund

ILEA – Inner London Education Authority

IPUP – Institute for the Public Understanding of the Past

JRF – Joseph Rowntree Foundation

KGB – The main security agency for the Soviet Union

LfSC – Librarians for Social Change

LGA – Local Government Association

MLA or MLAC – Museums, Libraries and Archives Council

NHS – National Health Service

PAT – Policy Action Team

RFC – Rugby Football Club

SEU – Social Exclusion Unit

TNA – The National Archives

TWM – Tyne & Wear Museums
V&A – Victoria & Albert Museum
WiL – Women in Libraries

Chapter 1

Introduction

The potential role of the cultural sector[1] in working and contributing towards social justice is immense. This book is going to look at one aspect of this – the relationship between the cultural sector and LGBT people in the UK since 1950.

There are some superb recent publications which focus on LGBT people and the cultural sector, but none reflecting life in the UK and none with exactly the perspective this book hopes to bring. Of particular note are: *Out Behind the Desk* (Nectoux, 2011), which includes interviews with LGBT library workers; *Serving Lesbian, Gay, Bisexual, Transgender, and Questioning Teens: A How-to-do-it Manual for Librarians* (Martin and Murdock, ca. 2007); and *Serving LGBTIQ Library and Archives Users* (Greenblatt, 2011a) – this book builds on previous work by Ellen Greenblatt (Gough and Greenblatt, 1990) and brings the assessment of provision into the twenty-first century, including the role of the Internet and Web 2.0.

Also of major historical importance is the pioneering work by Norman G. Kester, who gathered together the stories of some 30 librarians, focusing on the impact of their sexuality, *Liberating Minds* … (Kester, 1997); and by Sanford Berman, 'radical librarian … known for promoting activist librarianship in which personal ideals entailing social justice are part and parcel of professional work' (Wikipedia, 2012i) and who did so much to champion LGBT-friendly Library of Congress subject headings (see Johnson, 2007).

It has been a conscious decision not to include a chapter on LGBT history – especially world history – prior to 1950, as this is now well covered elsewhere (see: Aldrich, 2006; Stonewall, 2011a).

Terminology

Some basic definitions of the terms used in this book are listed in the Glossary, and there is further discussion of some of the more complex issues in Appendix 1.

As the term 'LGBT' is in common usage in the UK at present, this is the term used throughout the book ; however, there are strong arguments (again, please see Appendix 1) for changing or widening the terminology, particularly to the less-divisive and all-embracing 'queer' (see Curran, 2012a).

---

1   Rather than constantly referring to libraries, museums, archives and cultural and heritage organisations, this book will use the term 'cultural sector'.

There is also something of a debate currently about whether we should call people from the past 'gay' or 'LGBT' – or even apply terms retrospectively at all. As this book starts in the 1950s (when same-sex relationships were being identified as such – whatever the name they were given), it does seem appropriate to use the term 'LGBT'.

This book is also aiming to avoid unnecessarily complex language generally, and to be readable and approachable. As Christina Patterson has recently commented wittily:

> You could plough through some exhibition catalogues, and some visual arts criticism (which often doesn't seem to be all that critical) and look at some galleries' websites, and wonder how it was that people who are often quite young learnt to speak the kind of language that would have gone down very well on a cultural studies course in the 1970s, but which seems very, very, very old-fashioned now. (Patterson, 2013)

Finally, the 'new museology' is fascinating and important – it is critical that people are challenging what a 'museum' is and does and exploring the complexity of 'museums' – but this book is going to take a more pragmatic approach, looking at the role that museums (and the cultural sector) have played and can play to meet LGBT people's needs.

The LGBT 'community'

People frequently describe LGBT people as a 'community'. Whilst this is an easy shorthand, it may also bring its own problems – for example: some people may not want to be positioned in an LGBT community because of their particular gender or sexual identity; the term could itself contribute to stereotypes; and, similar to the concept of a 'Black community', for example, there is no universal LGBT community, but, rather, people who may ally over certain issues and not over others (Formby, 2012).

Presenting LGBT history

This book is arranged chronologically. Within each time period there is a brief background of social and political history (and also LGBT history), which is intended to help set the scene for the responses by the cultural sector. History is always contested, so this is meant only as a personal, introductory take on the period, not a definitive, analytical text.

One dilemma that anyone writing about LGBT history faces is how to present it. Robert Mills's analysis (Mills, 2010) of some of the issues facing museums, galleries and archives as they attempt to reflect LGBT history in their collections, exhibitions and events begins to identify the problem with taking a simple linear-progress approach: it tends to over-simplify and does not necessarily reflect the experiences of all LGBT people, for example along race or class lines. The constant focus on representative[2] 'out' individuals (exacerbated by casting a very wide net, historically, so that we end up with a list of people who might have once had a gay 'fling') misses the real complexities of people's lives – the occasions when we decide not to come out, the people we are 'out' with and those we are not.

Robert Mills argues strongly that, to contest the usual approach:

> Linear-progress narratives will be abandoned in favour of stories that take as their point of departure sexual intensities, tastes and roles, gender dissonances, dispositions and styles, queer feelings, emotions and desires. Queer-history exhibitions will adopt a style of presentation partly modelled on scrapbooks and collage; in place of the representative 'object', they will appropriate fragments, snippets of gossip, speculations, irreverent half-truths. (Mills, 2010: 86)

In addition, in terms of deepening our understanding of the range of people who may identify as LGBT, artist and activist Ajamu[3] argues:

> Many projects aimed at our BME LGBTQ communities emerge from within the wider LGBTQ voluntary organisations run mostly by and serving white people. These are formally constituted organisations, 'the sector'. The lack of Black presence is approached as a problem to be fixed, and a box to be ticked. These initiatives to reach the so-called 'hard to reach' arise quite often from within institutions where Black communities are simply not understood, or are perceived in stereotypical ways …
>
> Well meaning individuals and organisations parachute in and out quickly without developing long term mutually beneficial relationships and rarely do they consistently include the communities in ongoing community engagement processes. The complexity of the work is under-estimated and relatively large organisations put aside paltry pots of funding for the task in hand. (Ajamu X., 2011: 74)

These themes have also been taken up by Oliver Winchester who emphasises the need to deepen the representation of LGBT people in museums (and, by extension, the rest of the cultural sector). Complicating factors include 'the inherent tension

---

2   Robert Mills cites Judith Halberstam's work which highlights the pitfalls of the 'representative individual' model of minority history, which is not likely to explore 'intersections between gender, sexuality, race, and class' (Halberstam, 2005: 44-45; Mills, 2010: 85).

3   Ajamu has described himself as 'an artist who has created an archive' (Ajamu, 2012).

that lies at the centre of the gay liberation movement and its legacy – the desire to eradicate discrimination whilst enshrining difference …' (Winchester, 2012b: 143)

In addition, he asks how museums can 'play "catch up" without producing reductive and overly simplistic stories of gradual transition from repression to liberation over the course of history …' (Winchester, 2012b: 143). In an interview with me, Oliver suggested that a good museum gives you 'opportunities to make up your own mind', whilst, at the same time, showing something of its 'inner workings', its 'underbelly', and not trying to simplify everything into a straightforward presentation (Winchester, 2012a).

This book aims (if possible) to take a line between these two approaches: it will take a linear approach, but this is deepened by the responses (by LGBT people, the wider community, and the cultural sector) to what is happening at the time.

Finally, there is also the danger that LGBT people present themselves or are viewed as victims (the 'wounded' LGBT person); again, whilst acknowledging issues that have faced – and continue to face – LGBT people, this book attempts not to fall into the victim mentality.[4]

Coming out

Coming out is a never-ending process of telling people that you are LGBT: Will they think of you differently? Will they be hostile? And, in the past at least, was coming out a threat to your job? One interviewee talked about never coming out in the 1960s and 1970s – 'you were frightened to' – and Rachel Hasted said:

> I got my first job in a museum … in September 1976. I came out as a lesbian to my friends in 1984, but I did not speak about that at work. I was too frightened. There was no legal protection for LGBT people in employment (or anywhere else) and I was worried that it would affect my career. (Hasted, 2012)

Coming out is still an issue in 2012. As columnist Owen Jones says: 'But the very fact that coming out – whether you're a TV anchor, pop star, teacher or train driver – remains such an event shows how far the struggle for equality has to go … (Jones, 2012); and, in an interview at the end of 2011, author Stella Duffy emphasised the continuous process: 'You tell people all the time. Even booking a hotel for myself and my wife now, I still have to come out. Generally, the world assumes that you're straight. It's a process of coming out, annoyingly, exhaustingly, daily' (Williams, 2011b).

Yet not everyone now thinks that coming out is important or necessary – for example, there is a growing view amongst younger people that their sexual identity is irrelevant (and possibly too defining).

---

4   This issue was explored more fully in a paper by Sally Munt at the 'Brave New World?' conference in February 2013 (Munt, 2013).

This book will take the stance outlined by Schools OUT:

> We need to make LGBT people visible. A phobia is an irrational fear. It's a fear
> of the unknown. When we are hidden and invisible people don't trust us. When
> we are in the media, in the family and in the community we are known and the
> fear subsides …
>
> It is essential … to assert the sexual orientation of lesbian, gay and bisexual
> people in history … Otherwise children will assume they are not and that renders
> us invisible. Worse, if and when they find out the truth they may wonder why
> we didn't tell them. Thus by not informing them we are feeding homophobia.
> (Fenwick and Sanders, 2012: 16)

LGBT people and the cultural sector

The starting point for work on social justice is that we know that the cultural sector
tends to be under-used by people who are socially excluded. This may be people
who have visited once but not found what they wanted, and/or were not made to
feel welcome; people who have used our services but have found them wanting;
and people who have no real idea of what the cultural sector offers. Our work
must therefore involve assessing who is not using our services and finding ways of
meeting them to make some sort of 'offer' – with the aim that, of course people do
not have to use us, but their decision not to should be a conscious one, rather than
because they do not know or understand what we do.

We know that some LGBT people do use our services (do we actually know
how many?), but what about the people who do not? Were they made to feel
'different' or unwelcome? Did their experience of visiting/using us show them
that we do not have anything to offer?

A fascinating – but also depressing – revelation is how many of the interviewees
have said that libraries, museums and archives provided no support for them
during their growing-up. For example: 'There was absolutely nothing. Growing
up in the rural north east, and in the 70s, any sense of "gay lib" passed me by.
And of course, in those days, Durham enforced the "don't use the adult section til
you're 14" very strictly' (Murray, 2012):

> I did visit museums and was a voracious reader hooked on library books. I never
> found anything about gay culture deliberately (remember this is the 1950s and
> 1960s.) I did finally find the complete works of Oscar Wilde in the school library
> and read it from cover to cover. I also used to read the library copies of the
> Sunday papers which were busy 'outing' the Bloomsbury group at that time
> – very educational. However, I always bought my contemporary feminist and
> lesbian books, I realise I never expected to find them in a library.
>
> I adored museums because they were weird and full of unrelated and bizarre
> things that suggested there was much more to life than anyone was letting on.

However, I felt they were very 'establishment' and I was not surprised that they didn't tell me anything outside the accepted mainstream of culture. I went to the counter-culture for that: most of my enlightenment came from reading the sexist but entertaining *Oz* and *IT*, followed later by *Spare Rib*. You didn't get them at the library. (Hasted, 2012)

I used public libraries all the time as a child and as a teenager – I loved libraries and I loved reading (and still do). However, I never looked for anything LGBT-related as I didn't become aware of my sexuality until I was at university. Nonetheless, I think it's quite telling that despite my voracious reading habits, I never came across anything LGBT-related by chance – I was growing up during the 1980s and 1990s, when Section 28 was in force, and there was a big silence around the issue. The first LGBT book that I remember reading was *Oranges Are Not The Only Fruit*, which my favourite teacher recommended to me when I was doing A-levels. It has now been read so many times that it's falling to pieces! (Chapman, 2012b)

However, we also need to remember that the cultural sector can provide support:

For many queer and questioning people in the process of coming out, the public library has often been the first source for information. Likewise, university holdings and GLBTQ archives have been crucial repositories for the restoration and reconstruction of hidden queer history. Both kinds of institutions remain vital sources for accurate information and for facilitating research into the history and culture of sexual minorities. (Pettis, 2009)

The intended audience for this book

This book is intended to be readable, practical and understandable. It is aimed at:

- practitioners, especially people working in frontline positions (and as volunteers);
- cultural sector students;
- people with an interest in the cultural sector;
- people with an interest in LGBT/queer studies;
- people who may not know about the historical background to the relationship between LGBT people and the cultural sector;
- the general reader.

Chapter 2
The 1950s and 1960s

The social background

The 1950s was a decade of recovery, culminating in material prosperity for some – Harold Macmillan's 'most of our people have never had it so good' (BBC Home, 2008a) – but, at the same time, the discovery of what have been called the 'hidden poor'; Arthur Marwick has described this period as 'the incredible shrinking social revolution' (Marwick, 1968: 387).

It was also, in Andrew Marr's words, 'the last decade of "olde Britain" – when women were housewives, men smoked pipes and schoolboys sported caps and shorts' (Marr, 2007).

There was no doubt that Britain was changing. Post-war, there were several waves of immigration, starting with the new arrivals on the 'Empire Windrush', in 1948, and followed by people from India and Pakistan, and later, Kenyan Asians. However, Britain could not be described as a multicultural society, and tensions came to a head with the anti-Black riots in Nottingham and London in 1958. As Peter Fryer put it: 'Between 1958 and 1968 black settlers in Britain watched the racist tail wag the parliamentary dog' (Fryer, 1984: 381).

Driven in part by the economic boom, consumer spending rose; access to television became more common-place; and, by the end of the 1950s, teenagers had become a recognised separate group (no longer just 'adults-in-waiting'), with their own fashions, music and desire to change the conservative and cosy 1950s.

These trends continued into the 1960s, with low unemployment and rising wages; increased consumerism; the burgeoning of pop music and teen culture; mass access to the wider world through television and the beginnings of holidays abroad; even major changes to the UK diet.

Yet, as Dominic Sandbrook has described for The National Archives:

> despite the much-discussed stereotype of the 'permissive society', popular attitudes to moral and sexual issues remained strikingly slow to change. For all the excitement surrounding the landmark *Lady Chatterley's Lover* trial in 1960, or the liberalisation of the divorce, abortion and homosexuality laws later in the decade, most people held similar attitudes to their parents; in this respect, the generation gap was a media invention. (Sandbrook, n.d.)

How should we look back on the 1960s? Perhaps they should not be singled out as the decade when everything changed: 'In the end the sixties were not "good" or "bad", neither "swinging" nor "cautious", neither better nor worse than the fifties, seventies or eighties' (Donnelly, 2005: 196).

LGBT background

In the 1950s, the differences between the experiences of men and women, rich and poor (and middle-class), urban and rural were perhaps even more striking than they are today. 'This was the fifties. Women didn't have a sexuality of their own, so it wasn't like, "she's gay like me" it was "oh we like each other" but we didn't have a name for it, we didn't have a label on it, we just knew we liked each other' (Diane, c2008: 10).

The 1950s saw a burgeoning 'gay scene', in London particularly, but also in Brighton, Cambridge, Edinburgh and elsewhere (Cook, 2007a: 150-156); there was also a developing lesbian bar 'scene' in places such as Brighton, Manchester and London (Jennings, 2007). For example:

> For the many who did venture onto the scene in the fifties and sixties, Brighton offered a seemingly vast array of clubs and pubs, catering to every class and lifestyle. Venues ranged from the lavish Regina Club in North Street and the very select Argyle Hotel in Middle Street to the Belvedere and Fortune of War pubs on the seafront. (Brighton Ourstory, 2001a)

In some places, it was more underground: 'When I started to have a relationship with 'J' we went to the folk club and there were friends of 'J's' and suddenly there's this whole wide world of gay women and gay men' (Sheila, c2008: 5). However, it was still extraordinarily difficult for LGBT people to meet each other, primarily because for fear of being found out and facing violence, the law and disgrace (Porter, K. and Weeks, 1991).

In many ways, the 1950s were dominated by the Cold War (and, in the USA, McCarthyism),[1] and the 'hardest and most bitterly fought confrontation ... was on the espionage front' (Knightley, 2011), which had a tremendous impact on life in the UK. As H. Montgomery Hyde described it: 'The drive against homosexuals proceeded on a relatively minor scale until 1951, when it suddenly began to be intensified as the result of an incident of international proportions which occurred in [May] of that year' (Hyde, 1970: 213).

---

1   US Senator Joseph McCarthy (1908-1957) 'used his position as chairman of the Committee on Government Operations and its Permanent Subcommittee on Investigations to launch investigations designed to document charges of Communists in government; censured by the Senate on December 2, 1954, for behavior that was "contrary to senatorial traditions"' (Senate Historical Office, c2005).

This 'incident of international proportions' was the defection of the spies Guy Burgess and Donald Maclean.[2]

At the same time, the newspapers made gay men (particularly) into a headline-grabbing problem. For example, in 1952, the *Sunday Pictorial*, according to an article in Wikipedia:

> ran a three part series entitled 'Evil Men' promising an 'end to the conspiracy of silence' about homosexuality in Britain. 'Most people know there are such things – "pansies" – mincing, effeminate, young men who call themselves queers [...] but simple decent folk regard them as freaks and rarities.' The *Sunday Pictorial* compared homosexuality to a 'spreading fungus' that had contaminated 'generals, admirals, fighter pilots, engine drivers and boxers'. (Wikipedia, 2011e)

The same newspaper called Guy Burgess and Donald Maclean 'sex perverts' and suggested that gay men were 'bad security risks' (Sunday Pictorial, 1955) – it was what Keith Howes described as 'the Red Queens under the bed scares of the post-Second World War period' (Howes, 1993: first page of Preface).

Sheila Kerr concluded her biography of Guy Burgess with: 'Burgess's defection had a devastating impact during the Korean War. Whitehall floundered in this unpleasant scandal of espionage, sex, and conspiracy ... The revelations (like those of W.J. Vassall later) did much to prolong and accentuate repressive attitudes to homosexuality' (Kerr, 2011).

The case of John Vassall[3] (noted in passing above) had an impact that was to last for years; Vassall was entrapped by the KGB:

> He became acquainted with a Pole named Mikhailsky, who worked for the Embassy, and who introduced him to the homosexual underworld of Moscow. In 1954, he was invited to a party, where he was encouraged to become extremely drunk, and where he was photographed in compromising positions with several men. (Wikipedia, 2012e)

Following threats to publicise the photographs, Vassall was persuaded to spy for the Soviet Union – which reinforced the view prevalent at the time that LGBT people were a security risk.

Similarly, the *News of the World* reported regularly on court cases – some of these saw an approach by a gay man as justification for assault and murder (News of the World, 1950; cited in: Wikipedia, 2012d).

---

2   Burgess and Maclean were part of the Cambridge Five spy ring, who passed information to the Soviet Union.

3   William John Christopher Vassall (1924-1996), British civil servant (Leitch, 1996).

In addition, the then Home Secretary, Sir David Maxwell Fyfe,[4] started a clamp-down on gay men,[5] which led, for example, to what was called 'The Great Purge' of autumn 1953, 'in which nearly five thousand men were arrested on charges of either gross indecency … solicitation, or sodomy' (Summerskill, C., 2012: 47).

There was also a series of high-profile prosecutions, for example of the actor Sir John Gielgud;[6] the author Rupert Croft-Cooke,[7] and, perhaps most famously,[8] Lord Montagu,[9] Michael Pitt-Rivers[10] and Peter Wildeblood.[11] As Colin Spencer noted, these trials 'sent tremors of terror and panic through British homosexuals' (Spencer, 1996: 360).

The newspaper reports suggested that, in Matt Cook's terms, the issue was: 'the predatory homosexual and his insidious networks of vice, and also the idea of a valiant police force and judiciary doing their best to combat the threat' (Cook, 2007a: 169).

This theme was continued in relation to court cases involving the Guards, in which 'the War Office constituted the Guards as virtuous normal men exploited by vicious queers' (Houlbrook, 2005: 229); however, if authors such as John Lehmann were to be believed, for some young guardsmen this was simply a way of earning some extra money, without sin or exploitation having much to do with it (Lehmann, 1976, 1985).

However, as Colin Spencer suggested:

> Junior policemen rose in the ranks on the number of convictions they secured, so homosexuals were easy prey for an ambitious policeman. Convictions for male soliciting rose to an average of about forty a month in the West End of London in the early 1950s … between 1945 and 1955, the number of annual prosecutions

---

4   David Maxwell Fyfe, 1st Earl of Kilmuir (1900-1967), politician, lawyer and judge.

5   This period was captured by Rex Batten in his fictionalised account, *Rid England of this Plague* (2006), and also in his interview with Clare Summerskill (Summerskill, C., 2012: 51-53).

6   John Gielgud (1904-2000), actor (see Internet Movie Database n.d.).

7   Rupert Croft-Cooke (1903-1979), writer (see Brown, E. 2002).

8   According to an article in the *Daily Mail* (2007): 'In the summer of 1953, Lord Montagu offered Wildeblood the use of a beach hut near his country estate. Wildeblood brought with him two young RAF servicemen, Edward McNally and John Reynolds. The foursome were joined by Montagu's cousin Michael Pitt-Rivers. What happened next depends on whose testimony you believe. The airmen attested to dancing and "abandoned behaviour". Wildeblood said it was "extremely dull". Montagu maintains that it was all remarkably innocent, saying: "We had some drinks, we danced, we kissed, that's all"'.

9   Edward Douglas-Scott-Montagu, 3rd Baron Montagu of Beaulieu (1926-), politician and founder of the National Motor Museum (see Wikipedia, 2011d).

10   Michael Pitt-Rivers (1917-1999), landowner (see Wikipedia, 2011c).

11   Peter Wildeblood (1923-1999), writer and gay rights campaigner. Author of *Against the Law* (1955), an exposé of the then criminal justice system, which led to campaigns for prison and LGBT reforms.

for homosexual behaviour rose from under 800 to just over 2,500 of whom over 1,000 were given custodial sentences. (Spencer, 1996: 360)[12]

Nicholas de Jongh saw the 'witch-hunts' in the USA as a 'response to the political anxieties of the Cold War' (de Jongh, 1992: 51) and suggested that the persecution of LGBT people was taken up enthusiastically in the UK by people similarly politically driven; for example, he quotes Lord Hailsham as saying: 'Homosexual practices are ... contagious, incurable ... Homosexuality is ... as much a moral and social issue as heroin addiction' (de Jongh, 1992: 54).

As a result of all this persecution: 'old cases were dredged up again, married men committed suicide, some had their reputations ruined and their businesses failed, others endured years of being blackmailed and reduced to misery and penury because of it' (Spencer, 1996: 360-361).

Incidentally, it was not just LGBT people that were the focus of attention; according to Alan Sinfield:

> in the 1950s there was suddenly a swathe of social problems – juvenile delinquents, unmarried mothers, latch-key children, the elderly; there were shortages of housing, teachers, nurses, engineers; there was gambling, divorce, prostitution and the colour bar. It is not that there were suddenly more problems ... But as a way of apprehending social instability it was suddenly central to the self-understanding of social democratic societies in the post-war period. (Sinfield, 1999: 238)

In 1954, the Government appointed a Committee, chaired by John Wolfenden:[13]

> to review 'homosexual offences' alongside prostitution, after a number of high profile court cases revealed both the harsh nature of the existing laws against sex between men, and their uneven application. No openly gay men or lesbians were asked to serve on the committee, although it did interview individuals whose lives had been affected by the laws. (Kollman and Waites, 2011: 184)

Despite considerable opposition, for example from the Law Society, the Wolfenden Report (Committee on Homosexual Offences and Prostitution, 1957) was published: 'It said society and the law should respect "individual freedom of actions in matters of private morality" and stressed it was neither condoning nor condemning homosexual acts. Ultimately, private morality or immorality was "not the law's business"' (BBC Home, 2008b).

---

12   The statistical information cited by Colin Spencer was taken from Antony Grey (1992).

13   John Wolfenden (1906-1985), educationalist (see Wikipedia, 2012b).

However, the Government did not act on the parts of the report relating to homosexuality, and it was only after intense lobbying by the Homosexual Law Reform Society, established in May 1958, (and a change of Government) that the Act was passed in 1967 (Great Britain, 1967).

One significant influence was the film, *Victim*:

> Homosexuality was the last 'social problem' to be explored in detail. Made in the wake of the publication of the Wolfenden Report, *Victim* (1961) depicted two onscreen acts of heroism: the first by the barrister Melville Farr (Dirk Bogarde) in being prepared to reveal his sexual orientation at a time when homosexual acts were illegal, in order to break up a blackmail ring, and the second by Bogarde himself, the first major star to play an explicitly gay character in a British film. (BFI. Screenonline, 2012)

The 1967 Act excluded Scotland, Northern Ireland, the Channel Islands and the Isle of Man; the laws were not reformed there until 1980 (Scotland), 1982 (Northern Ireland), 1983 (Channel Islands) and 1992 (Isle of Man).

Whilst the change in the law was clearly progress, it was still limited. As Colin Spencer noted:

> If this was a victory it was a severely limited one. It soon became clear that the change in law was unpopular with the police, for indecency and importuning offences increased. Clubs where men danced together were raided and fined for gross indecency. Plain-clothes policemen were still used as decoys in public lavatories, public parks and open spaces. (Spencer, 1996: 367)

This outline may make it appear that the law was the only threat to LGBT people in this period, but, sadly, this was not the case.

Another major threat was the view that LGBT people could be 'cured' by some form of medical intervention:

> The end of the 19th century saw the advent of the concept of homosexuality as a pathological medical or psychological condition ... which legitimised treatments to change it ... Though sexual behaviour in private between adult men was decriminalised in Britain in 1967, treatments to change homosexuals into heterosexuals peaked in the 1960s and early 70s. (Smith, G. *et al.*, 2004)

Treatments included electric shock aversion therapy; induced nausea (when looking at images of men or women);[14] oestrogen treatment; and religious and/

---

14   '1965: United Kingdom: Dr C. Barker reports on the development of new aversion therapy methods to "treat" homosexuality in the British Journal of Psychiatry. Barker claims his method – injecting drugs every two hours for six days and nights to produce dizziness

or psychoanalytical therapy.[15] The major study reported in the *BMJ* concluded firmly that:

> Homosexuality was removed from *ICD-10* (*International Classification of Diseases*, 10th revision) only in 1992. Our study shows the negative consequences of defining same sex attraction as a mental illness and designing treatments to eradicate it. It serves as a warning against the use of mental health services to change aspects of human behaviour that are disapproved of on social, political, moral, or religious grounds. (Smith, G. *et al.*, 2004)

One of the most high-profile cases (which still reverberates today) was that of Alan Turing:[16]

> It all went wrong for Turing in the 1950s after he picked up a boy at the Regal Cinema on Oxford Street (now the Dancehouse Theatre) and took him home. The boy allegedly tried to blackmail Turing, and the mathematician went to the police. When they discovered that there had been a (then illegal) homosexual relationship between the two men they turned the tables on Turing and prosecuted him for gross indecency. His conviction led to the removal of his security clearance at a time of public anxiety about spies and homosexual entrapment by Soviet agents. He was forced to take hormones to 'cure' him of his sexual leanings which made him grow breasts, and on 8 June 1954 Turing's cleaner found him dead. The cause was established as cyanide poisoning. (New Manchester Walks, 2012)

For women too, there were the threats of 'cures' – and suspicion about their interests: 'Revealed: How RAF tried to "cure" lesbian recruits … and ordered officers to be on lookout for women who enjoyed cricket' (Drury, 2011). Women were also pushed back into a role that some had refused during the Second World War and were threatened and made to feel guilty:

> During the years of WWII, the freedom to explore lesbian lives was extended to women of all classes aided by the temporary absence of men and the increased geographical mobility of women engaged in war work. The return of men after 1945 pressured women into returning to a domestic, heterosexual lifestyle under

---

and nausea in the patient while he views pictures of nude males – is highly effective in helping gay men achieve "recovery"' (Rush, n.d.-b).

15   There is a brief discussion of some of these methods – and their brutality – in *The Radical Therapist* (Landerson, 1974).

16   Alan Turing, 1912-1954, British mathematician, logician, cryptanalyst, and computer scientist (see Wikipedia, 2012m). In 2009, the then Prime Minister Gordon Brown gave an apology for the 'appalling' way in which Alan Turing was treated (BBC News, 2009), and, at the time of writing, a campaign to grant Turing a pardon has gone to the House of Lords (BBC News Manchester, 2012).

the threat of confiscation of their children, with lesbians forced to live lives in which they repressed their sexuality and suffering agonies of guilt about their alleged 'depravity'. (Birmingham LGBT, 2011)

Nevertheless, it was not complete gloom!

The Sixties, as well as being a time of hedonism, were also noted for their head-expanding movements, with a proliferation of single-issue campaigns and the beginnings of grass-roots politics. Many people, emboldened by the change in public attitudes towards gay men and lesbians, formed self-help groups ... The Minorities Rights Group was one such organization which had been set up as early as 1963 by Esme Langley[17] and Diana Chapman[18] ... notable for being the first explicit and dedicated lesbian social and political organization. (Jivani, 1997: 154)

The magazine for lesbians *Arena Three* was published from 1963 to 1972 and led to the setting up of meetings and social groups to support lesbians (Hamer, 1996: 166-190; Jennings, 2007: 152-158).

However, given this background, it is not surprising that, for young (and not-so-young) people in the 1950s and 1960s, there were very few LGBT role models – perhaps the most outstanding example was the inclusion in mainstream Sunday lunchtime radio programming of *Beyond our Ken* and *Round the Horne*, with, particularly, 'Julian and Sandy';[19] these were hilarious characters, but they also traded on stereotypes.

According to Keith Howes's superb encyclopaedic survey (Howes, 1993), LGBT issues were raised in *Woman's Hour* from 1946 onwards (and Keith notes that this programme had regular LGBT contributors, such as Godfrey Winn,[20]

---

17   Esme Langley (ie Dr Esmé Ross-Langley), 1919-1991, 'British writer who made a major contribution to the social evolution of women in Britain' (Wikipedia, 2012a).

18   Diana Chapman, along with Jackie Forster (1926-1998) and Ceri Ager, had been involved in the founding of the Minorities Research Group, and the beginnings of the first lesbian magazine, *Arena 3* (which ran from 1963 to 1972) (Traies, 2009: 50).

19   'One of the most popular sketches was Julian and Sandy, featuring [Hugh] Paddick and [Kenneth] Williams as two flamboyantly camp out-of-work actors, speaking in the gay slang Polari, with [Kenneth] Horne as their comic foil. They usually ran fashionable enterprises in Chelsea which started with the word bona, for example Bona Pets, or in one episode a firm of solicitors called Bona Law – a play on the name of Prime Minister Bonar Law – and their claim "We've got a criminal practice that takes up most of our time" at a time when homosexuality was illegal' (Wikipedia, 2011a).

20   Godfrey Winn (1906-1971), journalist, writer and actor (see Wikipedia, 2012f).

Beverley Nichols[21] and Nancy Spain,[22] in the 1950s); and in radio soaps: *The Dales* in the 1960s and *Waggoners' Walk* in the 1970s.

However, references to LGBT lifestyles were covert or pieced together from hints and 'knowing winks'; for example the mainstream magazine *Films & Filming*, published in the UK from 1954 to 1990, included pictures of naked and near-naked men and women, and also 'was alert to the needs of men in need of flat-shares and hobby-shares in big cities through its personal ads page' (Howes, K., 1993: 258). Similarly, Gavin Butt (2005) has explored just how discussions of LGBT issues took place in the Cold War USA – but equally applicable in the UK – emphasising the important part played by gossip and rumour.

In addition, talking about LGBT people in film:

> For years Hollywood, on screen, has tried to deny the very existence of homosexuals ... The liberated 60s brought on a slow revolution, but until relatively late in the history of film-making, gays and lesbians were pictured as psychotics, vampires, serial killers, child molesters, or as misfits on the verge of either suicide or emotional breakdowns. (Porter, D. and Prince, 2010: 2)

There were some films with LGBT themes or undercurrents, for example *Some Like It Hot* (USA, 1959), *A Taste of Honey* (UK, 1961) and *The Pumpkin Eater* (UK, 1964).

Nevertheless, there was an enormous void: Could the cultural sector help to fill it?

Libraries

'A central tenet of professional librarianship holds that "libraries change lives". Certainly in the case of the lesbigay population, the meaning of that statement is literally true, for through reading, many lesbigays first find confirmation of their identity and learn that they are not alone' (Carmichael, 1998: 1).

This was particularly true in the 1950s and 1960s. Books with lesbian or gay themes[23] were starting to appear more regularly from the 1940s onwards, particularly in the USA (but also in the UK), for example: Mary Renault, *The Friendly Young Ladies* (1944); Denton Welch's short story, 'When I was Thirteen'

---

21   Beverley Nichols (1898-1983), author, playwright, journalist, composer, and public speaker (see Wikipedia, 2011h).

22   Nancy Spain (1917-1964), writer and broadcaster (see Golden Age of Detection Wiki, ca. 2006).

23   For further information, see, for example Ian Young's round-up of USA gay paperbacks (Young, I. n.d.) and Aaron Rush's *Queer Heritage* timelines (Rush n.d.-a, n.d.-b).

(1944, 1948); Gore Vidal, *The City and the Pillar* (1948, 1949);[24] James Barr, *Quatrefoil* (1950, 1953); Donald Webster Cory, *The Homosexual in America* (1951); Fritz Peters, *Finistère* (1951); Mary Renault, *The Charioteer* (1953); James Baldwin, *Giovanni's Room* (1956, 1957); John Rechy, *City of Night* (1963); and Mary Renault's *The Last of the Wine* (1956) also appeared in paperback – to a far bigger audience – in 1963 (Renault, 1963) and, a bit later, the 'Dave Brandstetter' series by Joseph Hansen.[25] Many of these were stocked by libraries in the UK too, and I remember seeing and looking at many of them in my local public library, although they did not entirely overcome the impression described so well by Barbara Gittings (the gay rights activist and co-founder of the ALA Gay Task Force) as 'the lies in the library, books that were "strange to us", cruelly clinical ... and always bad' (Gittings, 1998: 82).

Books can, of course, have a major impact, as Simon Callow recalled: 'There was a depressing Penguin book by D.J. West on homosexuality.[26] It described the awfulness of being homosexual, the constant shame and weird narrow life you'd lead – I was scared by that, I thought I don't want my life to be like that' (Williams, 2011a: 23).

However, even for avid readers, libraries offered very little of LGBT relevance: 'I tried to find out things from libraries but there was absolutely nothing. There wasn't a gay switchboard, there wasn't a lesbian line, there was nothing' (Sharley, cited in Summerskill, C., 2012: 143):

> I did visit museums and was a voracious reader hooked on library books. I never
> found anything about gay culture deliberately (remember this is the 1960s). I did
> finally find the complete works of Oscar Wilde in the school library and read it
> from cover to cover. I also used to read the library copies of the Sunday papers
> which were busy 'outing' the Bloomsbury group at that time – very educational.
> (Hasted, 2012)

'Pre-Stonewall era coming out stories often describe furtive searches through indexes and card catalogs under the heading "homosexuality" only to find one's intuitive sense of self distorted through vocabularies of perversion and criminality.

---

24   '*The City and the Pillar* sparked a public scandal, including notoriety and criticism, not only since it was released at a time when homosexuality was commonly considered immoral, but also because it was the first book by an accepted American author to portray overt homosexuality as a natural behavior' (Wikipedia, 2012c).

25   'Dave Brandstetter' was a gay private detective: Joseph Hansen was one of the earliest writers to take LGBT themes into genre fiction. The sequence started with *Fadeout* (Hansen, 1970, 1972) – all the titles have subsequently been published in an omnibus edition (Hansen, 2006).

26   This title (West, 1960) was widely available as one of the few published by a 'reputable' publisher.

Despite this, many found comfort in the knowledge that they were not alone' (Pettis, 2009).

Museums and archives

Whilst we know that there would have been activity in museums and archives – certainly LGBT museums and archives staff would have seen to that – it would have been limited by the legal and social situation of the time, and, so far, nothing appears to have been recorded about this period. This highlights the urgent need for more research into our cultural heritage past.

Chapter 3
1969-1976: Stonewall – the start of something

The social and political background

The early 1970s are sometimes remembered as a slowing-down after the 'swinging sixties'. However, as Dominic Sandbrook argues, echoing Mark Donnelly, cited above (Donnelly, 2005: 196), the idea of the 1960s being liberated and 'swinging' was something of a myth:

> In fact, the lazy stereotype of the permissive, self-indulgent 1960s is enormously misleading. The landmark reforms of the era, such as the abolition of capital punishment and the legalization of homosexuality, were passed in defiance of public opinion and remained deeply controversial: when the magazine *New Society* conducted an extensive poll on public attitudes in 1969, 'easier laws for homosexuality, divorce, abortion, etc.' was ranked as comfortably the most *unpopular* change of the decade. (Sandbrook, 2011: 424, his emphasis)

In addition, he describes the years under the Conservative Prime Minister Edward Heath's government (1970-1974) in the UK as:

> a period of extraordinary cultural and social flux, when immigrants were transforming the cultural landscape of Britain's cities, feminists and homosexuals were testing the boundaries of conventional morality, teenagers were growing their hair and defying their parents, and environmental campaigners were questioning the assumptions behind the great post-war boom. (Sandbrook, 2011: 12)

Indeed, the period from the 1950s to the 1980s saw the development of a series of social movements: these included, for example, CND from the 1950s (Campaign for Nuclear Disarmament, ca. 2010); Anti-Apartheid (Action for Southern Africa, n.d.) and anti-racism[1] from the 1970s; and, in the forefront, was the growth of the Women's Liberation Movement from the late 1960s onwards (Byrne, 1994).

---

1   As noted in chapter 2, there was increasing awareness of and anger towards (what was later described as) institutional racism, and this intensified from the 1970s onwards (see Coard, 1971; Milner, 1975; Smith, D.J., 1977).

Over 27 and 28 February and 1 March 1970 women's groups from around the country met at the first National Women's Liberation Conference at Ruskin College, Oxford to discuss the challenges facing women and the liberation movement and to work out a series of demands. Later in 1970 the newly formed Women's National Co-ordinating Committee announced the resulting four basic demands:

> *Equal pay*
> *Equal education and job opportunities*
> *Free contraception and abortion on demand*
> *Free 24-hour nurseries.* (British Library, n.d.: their italics)

In 1974, these demands were extended with calls for:

- financial and legal independence for women;
- a woman's right to a self-defined sexuality and the ending of discrimination against lesbians. (Byrne, 1994)

Finally, at the National Women's Liberation Movement conference in 1978, the seventh demand was added: 'Freedom for all women from intimidation by the threat or use of violence or sexual coercion regardless of marital status; and an end to the laws, assumptions and institutions which perpetuate male dominance and aggression to women' (Feminist Archive North, 2006).

In addition, the 1970s saw the UK hit by a wave of strikes, and, as *Social Trends* suggests, 'the three day working week and winter of discontent became potent symbols' (Social Trends, 2010). As Mark Garnett argues, the 1970s (leading into the 1980s) were significant for the struggle between the UK Left (for example via a number of high-profile industrial disputes) and a combination of 'the police, the courts and the Freedom Association' (Garnett, 2008: 8), and could be headlined as a period of anger and fear (the latter coming through particularly in responses to LGBT issues).

These heady times seemed right for the development of a LGBT movement too – what happened?

LGBT background

As noted in chapter 2, in the UK, the Homosexual Law Reform Society had been founded in 1958, complemented by the work of the Albany Trust,[2] also founded in 1958. In 1963-1964, the Minorities Research Group (MRG) was formed, providing 'isolated lesbians with resources and information about female homosexuality

---

2   The Albany Trust still operates today as 'a specialist counselling service promoting sexual well being and healthy sexual relationships' (Albany Trust, 2012).

and the opportunity to meet other women' (LAGNA, 2012). Following a dispute within the MRG, Kenric was established in 1965, 'the only lesbian organization dedicated to bringing women together socially on a nationwide basis' (Jennings, 2007; Kenric, 2010).

There was also a regional organisation, the North West Committee for Homosexual Law Reform, which started in 1964[3] and which went on to become the Committee for Homosexual Equality in 1969 (and Campaign for Homosexual Equality, CHE, in 1971) (Campaign for Homosexual Equality, 2012b).

In the USA, LGBT people had started to meet and organise from the early 1950s onwards, with, for example, the setting up of the Mattachine Society, one of the very early gay rights organisations in the USA (OutHistory, 2008, 2012) and the Daughters of Bilitis, the first lesbian civil rights organisation in the USA (Gallo, 2005). There were small demonstrations and pickets in the mid-1960s, for example at the White House and the Pentagon; and the Oscar Wilde Memorial Bookshop opened in 1967 (the first US bookstore to stock LGBT books) (Lahusen, ca. 2001; Oscar Wilde Bookshop, 2009). There were also active gay rights groups at universities such as Cornell and Columbia in the late 1960s (Beemyn, 2003).

At the same time, some writers were beginning to make the link between different liberation struggles: to take just one example, the 'black feminist lesbian mother poet' (as she described herself), Audre Lorde[4] – who was also a librarian – was deeply involved in and also wrote about Black, lesbian and feminist struggles (Kulii, 2012; Sullivan, n.d.).

And then:

> Something unremarkable happened on June 27, 1969 in New York's Greenwich Village, an event which had occurred a thousand times before across the U.S. over the decades. The police raided a gay bar.
>
> At first, everything unfolded according to a time-honored ritual. Seven plain-clothes detectives and a uniformed officer entered and announced their presence. The bar staff stopped serving the watered-down, overpriced drinks, while their Mafia bosses swiftly removed the cigar boxes which functioned as tills. The officers demanded identification papers from the customers and then escorted them outside, throwing some into a waiting paddy-wagon and pushing others off the sidewalk.
>
> But at a certain point, the 'usual suspects' departed from the script and decided to fight back. A debate still rages over which incident sparked the riot. Was it a 'butch' lesbian dressed in man's clothes who resisted arrest, or a male drag queen who stopped in the doorway between the officers and posed defiantly, rallying the crowd?

---

3   One of the founders was Allan Horsfall (1927-2012), who went on to be the founder and Life President of CHE.

4   Audre Lorde (1934-1992).

> Riot veteran and gay rights activist Craig Rodwell says: 'A number of incidents were happening simultaneously. There was no one thing that happened or one person, there was just … a flash of group, of mass anger'. (Wright, L., 1999).[5]

This explosion of anger started a whole political movement:

> In the wake of the riots, intense discussions took place in the city's gay community. During the first week of July, a small group of lesbians and gay men started talking about establishing a new organization called the Gay Liberation Front. The name was consciously chosen for its association with the anti-imperialist struggles in Vietnam and Algeria … During the next year or so, lesbians and gay men built a Gay Liberation Front (GLF) or comparable body in Canada, France, Britain, Germany, Belgium, Holland, Australia, and New Zealand. (Wright, L., 1999)

Stonewall also initiated a very different phase of LGBT politics, as John D'Emilio explained:

> Two aspects deserve emphasis. One is the notion of 'coming out', which served both as a goal and a strategy. Coming out became a profoundly political step that an individual could take … Coming out also became the key strategy for building a mass movement. Gay men and women who came out crossed a critical dividing line. They relinquished invisibility, made themselves vulnerable to attack, and became invested in the success of the movement. Visible lesbians and gay men, moreover, served as magnets that drew others to them …
>
> A second critical feature of the post-Stonewall era was the emergence of a lesbian movement … The almost simultaneous birth of women's liberation and gay liberation propelled large numbers of lesbians into liberation politics. Lesbians were active both in early gay liberation groups and in feminist organizations. By 1970 the experience of sexism in gay liberation and of heterosexism in women's liberation inspired many lesbians to form organizations of their own … Lesbian–feminism pushed the analysis of sexism and heterosexism beyond where either the women's or gay movement ventured and so cogently related the two systems of oppression that sectors of the women's movement and gay movement had to incorporate lesbian-feminist analysis into their political practice. (D'Emilio, 1991: 466-467)

---

5   To add to the context, it is worth remembering that one of the best-selling books of 1969 was David Reuben's *Everything You Always Wanted to Know About Sex… But Were Afraid to Ask* (Reuben, 1969, 1970) in which the author described gay men's encounters as usually involving only impersonal toilet sex – and that all gay men were like that! (Tobias, 1999).

Inspired by these developments in the USA, Bob Mellor and Aubrey Walter called the first UK GLF meeting, which was held at the London School of Economics on 13 October 1970. GLF very much saw itself as a revolutionary organisation, linked to the counter-culture movement,[6] according to Jeffrey Weeks (Weeks, 1990: 190). In addition, GLF launched its magazine, *Come Together*, and, between November 1970 and Summer 1973, 16 issues were published.[7]

Jeffrey Weeks has identified that GLF recognised three external types of oppression: persecution, discrimination and 'liberal tolerance'; plus self-oppression (Weeks, 1990: 190); and, in October 1971, GLF published its *Manifesto*, which included the following:

> We have therefore drawn up the following list of immediate demands:
>
> • that all discrimination against gay people, male and female, by the law, by employers, and by society at large, should end;
> • that all people who feel attracted to a member of their own sex be taught that such feelings are perfectly valid;
> • that sex education in schools stop being exclusively heterosexual;
> • that psychiatrists stop treating homosexuality as though it were a sickness, thereby giving gay people senseless guilt complexes;
> • that gay people be as legally free to contact other gay people, through newspaper ads, on the streets and by any other means they may want as are heterosexuals, and that police harassment should cease right now;
> • that employers should no longer be allowed to discriminate against anyone on account of their sexual preferences;
> • that the age of consent for gay males be reduced to the same as for straight;
> • that gay people be free to hold hands and kiss in public, as are heterosexuals. (Gay Liberation Front Manifesto Group, 1971: 16)

To pursue some of these aims, the first GLF pamphlet addressed *Psychiatry and the Homosexual* (Gay Information, 1973).

In 2010, Peter Tatchell looked back at the founding of GLF, and highlighted its political stance:

> Our idealistic vision involved creating a new sexual democracy, without homophobia, misogyny, racism and class privilege. Erotic shame and guilt would

---

6   'If you want to know what is happening among your intelligent and mysteriously rebellious children, this is the book. The generation gap, the student uproar, the New Left, the beats and hippies, the psychedelic movement, rock music, the revival of occultism and mysticism, the protest against our involvement in Vietnam, and the seemingly odd reluctance of the young to buy the affluent technological society – all these matters are here discussed' Alan Watts (1969) reviewing *The Making of a Counter Culture* (Roszak, 1970).

7   A collected edited version of the magazine was published in 1980 (Walter, 1980).

be banished. There would be sexual freedom and human rights for everyone – gay, bi and straight. Our message was 'innovate, don't assimilate' …

We saw queer oppression as a consequence, at least in part, of the way many LGBT people deviated from the socially prescribed gender roles of traditional masculinity and femininity …

We sought a cultural revolution to overturn centuries of male heterosexual domination and thereby free both queers and women. (Tatchell, 2010)

The first GLF march was held in London in August 1971, and 1972 saw the first full Gay Pride week, culminating in a march in London on 1 July.[8] Activity was not confined to London:

The Sussex Gay Liberation Front (SGLF) was established in February 1971 by a group of Sussex University students and lesbians and gay men from the town, including some of those who queued outside the Co-op Hall to see the Forty-Two Club shows. They organised the first gay demonstration in Brighton in October 1972 and the first Brighton Gay Pride march in July 1973. Only a tiny minority of the town's gay population was ready to take to the streets however, and there was not another Brighton Pride until 1991. SGLF organised the first openly gay dances and hundreds came to prestigious venues like the Royal Albion Hotel and the Royal Pavilion. (Brighton Ourstory, 2001a)

There was an active GLF in Birmingham, which began in 1972 and ran until 1977 (Knowles, 2009), with Birmingham hosting the GLF annual conference in 1972 at Birmingham University Guild of Students (Birmingham LGBT Community Trust, 2008).

GLF also organised a number of social/political events – for example: 'In January 1971 we held the first GLF Ball at Kensington Town Hall – the very first gay event of its kind in the UK' (Brown, D.M., 2010: 21).

However, this period also saw growing divisions within GLF – women within GLF formed an autonomous organisation, and, according to Jeffrey Weeks, '[t] he conflicts within the ranks came to a head during gay pride week itself, and revolved around how the marchers should dress or behave' (Weeks, 1990: 204).

In Brighton, for example, a similar split occurred which 'led to a separation from GLF and CHE, which were regarded as having no interest in lesbian issues, and a focus on issues affecting women generally – campaigns against male violence, e.g. the peace movement, Women's Aid, and Rape Crisis' (Brighton Ourstory, 2001a).

---

8 Interestingly, libraries were used as meeting places by GLF, for example Minet Library (London Borough of Lambeth) for the South London GLF in 1972 (Gay Liberation Front, 1972: 1); and by CHE, who showed films in the hall at Kensington Library in the early 1970s (Jenny quoted in: Summerskill, C., 2012: 101). The campaign to establish a gay club in Burnley in 1971 used Burnley Library as a meeting place (Fairweather, 2013).

Sheila Jeffreys (2003: 16-18) and Lisa Power (1995) identified some of the key issues for women as being: the growing importance of lesbian feminism; sexual practice (and the focus by many men on this in lieu of politics); and the adoption by some men of drag.

There were further splits, broadly along the lines of whether the movement should be radical or reformist, and/or political or part of the counter-culture.

Again according to Jeffrey Weeks, 'GLF itself was based on the illusion that there was a mass force of revolutionized homosexuals willing and able to follow its lead; it was an illusion born of euphoria which turned out to be sadly wrong' (Weeks, 1990: 204).

In addition, 1972-1973 saw the demise of most of the underground and counter-culture, accompanied by the growth in the commercial scene from the 1970s onwards, although there were still major barriers for parts of the 'community', for example for trans people, and there was an ongoing issue about what to do about paedophilia.[9] In addition, there were continuing battles over employment rights that brought LGBT work-related issues to the fore, with a number of key cases in the mid-1970s (Gay Rights at Work Committee, 1980).[10]

In the period after the demise of *Come Together*, there were broadly three types of journal/newspaper:

- Gay liberation papers, for example *Gay Marxist* (1973-1974); *Gay Left* (1975-1980),[11] *Sappho* (1972-1981),[12] and those published by local groups.
- Newspapers (primarily *Gay News* from 1972).
- Pin-ups (e.g. *Jeffrey*,[13] *Play Guy*).

By 1974, GLF had disbanded 'with considerable bitterness' (Cook, 2007b: 182) and, whilst many of its aims remained unachieved, nevertheless it left a strong legacy which flourishes today, including Lesbian and Gay Pride (and its spin-offs across the UK); the London Lesbian and Gay Switchboard (London Lesbian

---

9   Many of these issues continued to be debated into the 1980s and 1990s, particularly lesbian separatism, S&M (sadomasochism), paedophilia, and just how far the LGBT 'movement' was aware of race and disability issues.

10   The Gay Rights at Work Committee pamphlet was put together by a group that included librarians, and, in its section 'Things you can do', it included contacting libraries, 'Enlist the help of sympathetic library workers' (Gay Rights at Work Committee, 1980: 17).

11   Issues of *Gay Left* are available online (Gay Left Collective, c2007).

12   *Sappho* was 'established in 1972 to cater for lesbians with Jackie Forster as editor. Sappho organised meetings in the Chepstow public house with speakers including Anna Raeburn, Mikki Doyle from the *Morning Star*, Maureen Duffy who read her poetry, and the barrister Elizabeth Woodcraft who spoke on the rights of lesbian mothers. It was wound up in 1981 as a result of declining readership, falling subscriptions and criticism that it was not sufficiently political' (Grassroots Feminism, 2009).

13   *Jeffrey* had been preceded by the short-lived *Jeremy*, which was published from 1969-1972 (Burston, 2008).

& Gay Switchboard, 2009) and other switchboards across Britain; plus: 'theatre companies like Bloolips and Gay Sweatshop, and particularly the groups that were to structure the campaigns over Acquired Immune Deficiency Syndrome (AIDS) such as Body Positive, Jewish AIDS Trust … and IceBreakers, Outrage! and Stonewall which were all founded by ex-GLFers' (Robinson, 2003: 8); as well, of course, as a new spirit of self-determination amongst LGBT people, developed, for example, via work-based organisations such as the National Union of Students, which held its first-ever Gay Rights Conference at Bristol University in October 1973 and launched a Gay Rights Week of Action in May 1976 (Mooney, 2012: 9-10); other regional LGBT groups, such as GayWest, which grew from the Bath Gay Awareness Group, established in 1971 (GayWest, n.d.-a; Howes, R., 2011); and the large number of London-based LGBT groups, some of which are still operating today (Walton, 2010). Interestingly, CHE also survives today (see Campaign for Homosexual Equality, 2012a).

The cultural sector

So, what was the response of the cultural sector?

Libraries

I started working full-time in public libraries in 1969 (having worked as a part-time Library Assistant since 1963). The library world – and the world of work – then was very different from how it is today; for example, quite apart from the labour-intensive manual processes which drove libraries, there were policies in place from a bygone era:

- Library staff had to dress appropriately, men in jackets, women in skirts! Although the following comment was made about 1952, it could equally well apply to the 1960s: 'soon after I started work in the West Riding HQ, I took my jacket off one day, and Mrs B. quietly told me that … the County Librarian expected male staff always to wear a jacket; the women from Chief Assistant down wore green or brown dust-coats' (Hartley, 2012).
- Paperbacks were thought to be too flimsy for public library purchase and not really 'proper' books to be stocked – unless they were treated/re-bound to turn them, effectively, into hardbacks.
- Emphasis was on 'quality' reading, especially for children (books by Enid Blyton were frowned upon!).
- Many public libraries purchased heavily from academic and US publishing houses.

In addition, and of particular relevance to this book, public libraries often purchased titles that were subsequently thought to be too 'risqué' to be available on the public shelves – these were available 'on request', if the reader knew they were there! Titles included were frequently about sex, which was an additional barrier to ready access to LGBT-related material.[14]

During the late 1960s and the 1970s, many libraries began to make a real effort to provide a wider range of material to reflect the needs of more of the community; this work was captured in a burst of publishing in the late 1970s and early 1980s (and later), and some examples include: Black and Minority Ethnic (BME) communities (Alexander, 1982; Vincent, 2009); community language-speakers (Gundara, 1981; Simsova, 1982; Simsova and Chin, 1982); disabled people (Marshall, 1981; Pearlman, 1982; Strom, 1977); older people (Kempson and Dee, 1987; Turock, 1982); prisoners, ex-prisoners and their families (Wright, B.C., 1987); unemployed people (Barugh and Woodhouse, 1987); single homeless people; and LGBT people.[15]

There were certainly books with LGBT themes available – both fiction and non-fiction – but some libraries had problems with them; writing in 1973, Sean Aubrey commented:

> Quite clearly the increasing volume of gay writing poses problems for the library profession, or, I should say more correctly, for some sections of it. You can't go on with that quaint little habit you have of classifying our kind of love in the shelf headed 'sexual deviation' because the new writing isn't about your idea of deviation: it's about our central life experience … And it would be nicer still if I and my gay friends were able to find the books we want to read proudly displayed in an extensive gay studies section. (Aubrey, 1973)

The Gay Librarians Group

The idea that LGBT people within different professional groups might link – and gain strength from each other – started to take off, with the establishment of new groups for, for example, 'radical' psychologists with the formation of the London Counter-Psychology Group in 1971 (Weeks, 1990: 198); teachers in 1974 (Schools Out, ca. 2011); and, later, police officers in 1990 (Gay Police Association, 2010), and doctors and dentists in 1995 (GLADD, n.d.).

In the USA, a Task Force on Gay Liberation was founded in 1970 (within the American Library Association (ALA) Social Responsibilities Round Table); this was the start of what has now become the Gay, Lesbian, Bisexual and Transgender

---

14 The first issue of *Librarians for Social Change* included an article (Colwell, 1973) about 'censorship' in one London public library service; amongst titles available only on request were *Sex and the over-fifties* (Chartham, 1969); *Sex and the single girl* (Brown, H.G., 1963) ; and Anthony Storr's classic *Sexual deviation* (1964).

15 I compiled a brief introduction (Vincent, 1986a), which also looked back at experience from the 1960s and 1970s.

Round Table – one of the ALA's key professional groups (American Library Association, 2012; Moore, 2011).

In the UK in 1973, Bob Elbert announced the setting up of a new group 'for homosexual men and women in the profession' (Elbert, R.J., 1973b), which received a very mixed reaction. For example, S.E. Munisi wrote to say that: 'It must be made clear that even though homosexuality between consenting adults is legal, this does not absolve it from being immoral' (Munisi, 1973a).

Jane Gunton wrote, anti the idea of a group, but pro making material available: 'Surely a man's, or woman's, sexual inclinations are totally irrelevant to his or her profession ... I feel it is the task of *all* librarians to use whatever influence they have to ensure that the literature on sexuality, or indeed any other subject, is presented without bias or bigotry' (Gunton, 1973, her emphasis).

There was a couple of other letters which seemed to assume that Bob Elbert's letter was 'soliciting': 'I do think that the columns of one's professional journal are not the place in which letters soliciting contacts for non-professional activities should be published' (Hoyle, 1973):

> I cannot help but feel that the RECORD is not the proper place for this sort of thing ... If this is to be an added benefit to be gained from my subscription, perhaps you'd be kind enough to note in your columns that I am a heterosexual librarian and lady librarians with the time and the inclination can get in touch with me at the address below. (Lindley, 1973)

There were some letters of support, however. T.G. Locke wrote:

> The appearance of negative letters in the RECORD is evidence enough that homosexuals are discriminated against, even though their preference in relationships is a normal variation within our society. If 'sexual inclinations' were totally irrelevant to the profession, why then these 'anti' letters? Why the secrecy among homosexual librarians? The reference to its 'immorality and heinousness [by S.E. Munisi] is enough to promote homosexuality to a fairly important place in our professional ethics. If those who appoint, promote or dismiss homosexual librarians can hold such opinions, the need for such a group within the profession must surely be self-evident. (Locke, 1973)

Angela Eserin also wrote (1973), protesting at the publication of S.E. Munisi's letter; all these responses drew the following reply from S.E. Munisi: 'it would appear that the word "heinousness" in the sense in which it has been used is correct. It simply means sin (immorality) or shocking evil' (Munisi, 1973b).

At this point, the editor of the *Library Association Record* closed the correspondence.

Meanwhile, there was a parallel debate going on within the pages of the *Assistant Librarian*. Bob Elbert published a letter in June 1973 (Elbert, R.J., 1973a) which also received some pro and anti letters in response, including: 'homosexuality is a form of abnormality be it psychological or physical' (Guinard, 1973) (and this letter went on to challenge how it could be proven that homosexuals are 'treated as a group apart' or that LGBT people are discriminated against because they are LGBT). On the plus side:

> I maintain that if a reader comes into a library wanting 'a book on homosexuality', and that if there are two on the shelves, one containing provable untruths and the other being more accurate, the librarian has a duty to guide the reader to the more accurate book. (Goodwillie, 1974)

At this point, the *Assistant Librarian* editor closed this correspondence.

After all this huffing and puffing in the professional press, the first meeting of the Gay Librarians Group was held in London on 7 October 1973 (with proposed topics including gay bibliographies; and should the GLC discourage the provision of 'anti-homosexual works'?) (Elbert, B., 1973).[16]

This was followed by a Gay Librarians Group (GLG) meeting at the CHE Annual Conference (held in Malvern in May 1974), at which topics included drafting a leaflet on improving library provision; and sex education books for children (Quirke, 1974). By October 1974, the GLG was supporting Gay Switchboard; writing articles; preparing an annotated bibliography; proposing a literature search and information retrieval system covering the whole field of sexual politics; and discussing a pamphlet for public librarians and a pamphlet for gay organisations on activism they could direct towards the library (Greater London Council, 1974).

The GLG became strongly linked with Librarians for Social Change (LfSC), the magazine of which was founded by John Noyce in 1972 (LfSC, 1972); LfSC later produced a basic sexual politics reading list (Librarians for Social Change Collective, 1975).

The tensions between, for example, gay men and lesbians, and 'radicals' and 'revolutionaries', noted earlier also arose within LfSC, compounded by differing views on librarianship. As John Lindsay noted, in 1979:

> Shortly after publishing Radical Librarianship [(Lindsay, 1979)], John Noyce and I decided to change the name of Librarians for Social Change to Information Systems and Social Change. It seemed to us that the role of the computer had become so significant that it was going to be the systematising of the processes of information which was where the political action was going to lie. And that action would not necessarily be in a libertarian or socialist, or pro poor direction.
>
> Shortly afterwards, John decided to move to Australia. I had joined the International Socialists, now the Socialist Workers' Party, and for right or for wrong, it had been decided that after Thatcher's defeat of Labour and then the

---

16 Amongst founder members were Bob Elbert, John Lindsay and John McKay (Lindsay, 2005).

failure of a fight back, that the SWP had to concentrate on holding itself together and pull in activities. This meant I withdrew from putting resources into keeping either LfSC or Gay Rights and Work and the Gay Librarians' Group functioning. Either there was no one else, or the ideas had run out of steam. (Lindsay, 2003)

This effectively signalled the end of the first GLG.

Positive images

From the late 1960s onwards, library staff (and writers, publishers, teachers, community workers) had become increasingly aware of the need to promote positive images of all kinds of young people: this was partly the result of the work of children's librarians (especially Hill, J., 1971); partly because of a number of lobby groups and individuals that challenged the traditional ways in which books for children were written, produced and sold, including the Children's Rights Workshop, CISSY and Bob Dixon (Dixon, 1977a, 1977b); and partly the result of a subtle change in what was being published – for example, 1969 saw the publication in the USA of the first novel with a LGBT theme for young people, John Donovan's *I'll Get There ...*, published in the UK in 1970 (Donovan, 1970).[17]

The Children's Rights Workshop went on to set up the annual 'Other Award', through which it had a real influence on writing, publishing, reviewing and bookselling – and on stock selection in libraries – and which, during its lifetime, 1974-1987, moved from being a 'fringe' event to becoming a part of the annual children's book world calendar (for a summary, see Stones, 1988). Spin-off articles also appeared in the library press, including critiques of the portrayal of LGBTs in sex education books for young people (Vincent, 1976). I was a member of the 'Other Award' team.

As a result of all this activity, many libraries introduced stock selection policies as part of their selection process for children's (and, later, adult) books. These policies were used to encourage the presentation of positive images (of, for example, gender, race, sexuality, disability) and also to form the basis for rejecting material which perpetuated stereotypes and other negative images. In some cases, these stock selection guidelines formed part of a wider, cross-service set of guidelines, such as those developed in Lambeth, which included in the aims of the Library Service:

> To respond particularly to the needs of people who experience discrimination or lack of access to services and to encourage and support initiatives to help them to overcome this. These groups, covered within the Council's Equal Opportunity Policy or defined as being 'usually excluded' from involvement in Council and

---

17   This was certainly a pioneering title – but also began a trend that lasted for far too long, where LGBT characters (or, in this case, their pet dog) die (see Hanckel and Cunningham, 1976).

local affairs, are: Black people, women, people with disabilities, elderly people, single parents, homeless people, children and young people, unemployed people and others on low incomes, lesbians, gay men, linguistic and cultural minorities and people with mental health problems. (Lambeth Environmental Services, 1994)

In addition, some librarians worked closely with publishers, writers and booksellers to help them produce appropriate materials to meet these growing demands. There is more on books and information materials for children and young people in chapter 5.

Museums and archives

Sadly, and similarly to the 1950s and 1960s, we know that there would have been activity, but no records appear to survive, and I have not been able to find anyone who can recall any specific LGBT activities or events until after 1988. Again, this points out the need for urgent research.

Chapter 4

1977-1987: Small steps …

The social and political background

The late 1970s and early 1980s saw large increases in social division and social exclusion; as social commentator Alwyn Turner said of 1979: 'The society [Margaret Thatcher] inherited was so torn by division and conflict, so racked by crises' (Turner, 2010: xiv).

A major cause of this was unemployment: according to *Social Trends*, unemployment stood at around 1.4 million in 1979, and the Conservative party swept to power on the message that 'Labour isn't working'. However, during the early 1980s, unemployment rose further still, topping 3 million in 1982 (Social Trends, 2010); in addition, the length of time that some people were unemployed was considerable. At the same time, there was an increasing 'them-and-us' attitude, with some people starting to dabble in stocks and shares and others buying their own homes (under the right-to-buy legislation) which had previously been local-authority owned.

The 1980s saw a number of riots across the UK – for example in Toxteth, Liverpool in 1981(Neild, 2007); Brixton, south London, in 1981 (McFarnon, 2011) and 1985 (BBC Home, 2008b); and Tottenham in 1985 (Runnymede Trust, 2012) – which grew out of a history of racism, unemployment, and heavy-handed and sometimes racist policing. Andy McSmith argues that the apparently indifferent response to the New Cross fire (in which 11 young Black people died immediately) was also a trigger (McSmith, 2011: 91-93).

To sum up this period in terms of politics and economics:

> The election of Margaret Thatcher in 1979 marked the end of the post-war consensus and a new approach to economic policy, including privatisation and deregulation, reform of industrial relations, and tax changes. Competition policy was emphasised instead of industrial policy; consequent deindustrialisation and structural unemployment was more or less accepted. Thatcher's battles with the unions culminated in the Miners' Strike of 1984. (Wikipedia, 2013)

After a period of relative stability in the Second World War and the early post-war period, the British coal industry (nationalised in 1947) had undergone a massive contraction from 700,000 employed in 1957 to 300,000 by 1970, as alternative fuels were used to produce energy (Lyddon, n.d.). There was then a period of further stability in the 1970s, but the economic recession of the early 1980s showed up the less productive pits. When, in 1984, five pits were announced for closure, official strikes were called and endorsed by the National Union of Miners (NUM); as a result, 'The government used its limitless resources (particularly the deployment of police on a national stage) to defeat the miners ... ' (Lyddon, n.d.). In many ways, this action also hastened the decline of the Trade Union movement altogether (see Schifferes, 2004).

However, at the same time, links were forged between LGBT activists and the striking miners and their families (Clews, 2012a, 2012b): 'strong ties developed between Lesbians and Gays Support the Miners (LGSM), Lesbians Against Pit Closures and the mining communities they supported. Even when the strike concluded, the ties remained and ultimately led to one of the biggest political breakthroughs for the LGBT community' (Clews, 2012b).

Another major focus for political activity was the Greenham Common Women's Peace Camp, which ran from 1981 to 2000:

> On the 5th September 1981, the Welsh group 'Women for Life on Earth' arrived on Greenham Common, Berkshire, England. They marched from Cardiff with the intention of challenging, by debate, the decision to site 96 Cruise nuclear missiles there. On arrival they delivered a letter to the Base Commander which, among other things, stated: 'We fear for the future of all our children and for the future of the living world which is the basis of all life'. (Hipperson, n.d.)

The numbers living in poverty in the UK 'grew from 5 million in 1979 to just under 14 million in 1993/94' (Walker, A., 1997: 3) – and inequality was welcomed in some quarters as 'an engine of enterprise' (Walker, A., 1997: 5). The impact of and harm caused by this growth in inequality and social exclusion has been covered in depth elsewhere (see: Hills, 1995; Hutton, 1995; Townsend, 1979; Walker A. and Walker, C., 1987); for this book, suffice it to say that this general background dictated the direction in which the UK generally, LGBT people and the cultural sector all travelled.

Writing in the aftermath of the revelations about the cover-up of the Hillsborough disaster, novelist Kevin Sampson recently described the 1980s:

> But it's enough, for now, to note that the style of government [Margaret Thatcher] fostered brought a confrontational atmosphere to everyday life ... Anyone who bucked against the Tories' values was deemed a 'wrecker'. The play-out to the Tom Robinson Band's 1979 song Power In The Darkness lists a catalogue of 'wreckers' including 'football hooligans, juvenile delinquents, lesbians and left-wing scum'. (Sampson, 2012)

LGBT background

As noted in chapter 3, some progress in attitudes towards LGBT people was being made in the early 1970s. However, just as voices for LGBT liberation and rights were getting louder, so too were those of the opposition!

In 1977, *Gay News* was successfully prosecuted for blasphemy – a law which had not been invoked since the 1920s – by Mary Whitehouse,[1] for publishing a poem, 'The love that dares to speak its name', by the writer James Kirkup.[2] It seems clear that Mary Whitehouse was looking for a suitable case to bring, and this dealt a blow to the LGBT cause – although, as Brett Humphreys wrote (2002):

> If Mary Whitehouse hoped to damage *Gay News*, she failed. According to the paper's Literary Editor, Alison Hennegan, staff estimated the value of free publicity resulting from the trial and its aftermath at £1½ million. What was already 'the world's largest circulation newspaper for homosexuals' reached many new readers who had previously been unaware of its existence, and in later years its average sales exceeded 18,000 ...
>
> If Mary Whitehouse hoped to dampen the ardour of the gay community, she failed. Her action gave new focus to a movement that was drifting somewhat after the first flush of gay liberation in the early 1970s. A rally held in Trafalgar Square, London, on 11 February 1978 – the Saturday preceding the Appeal Court hearing – was the largest gay rights demonstration the country had ever seen. The blasphemy case gave rise directly to the short-lived Gay Activists Alliance and indirectly to the more durable Gay Humanist Group, which continues to thrive as the Gay and Lesbian Humanist Association. (Gay and Lesbian Humanist Association, 2009)

There had been a focus on books and magazines for some time: for example, it was claimed that overseas post to *Gay News* was regularly opened by HM Customs & Excise (Guardian, 1978); the magazine *Him Exclusive* was raided four times in three months (de Jongh, 1977); there were raids on the Zipper and Him bookshops in 1979 and again in 1984; and this continued with a raid ('Operation Tiger') on the London bookshop, Gay's the Word, in April 1984, in which:

> Customs and Excise officers walked into Gay's the Word bookshop in London, told its customers to leave, and seized all imported titles. Officers also raided the houses of the bookshop's directors. In November 1984 Gay's the Word was charged with the conspiracy to import indecent literature. (Bryant, 2009)

---

1   Mary Whitehouse, 1910-2001, was 'an English social activist known for her prominent opposition to social liberalism and the mainstream British media, both of which she accused of encouraging a more permissive society. She was the founder and first president of the National Viewers' and Listeners' Association, through which she led a longstanding campaign against the British Broadcasting Corporation' (Wikipedia, 2012g).

2   James Kirkup, 1918-2009, poet, translator and travel writer (Pursglove and Brownjohn, 2009).

'Operation Tiger' represented a massive assault on Gay's the Word. The raid on the bookshop itself had led to around one third of its stock being removed. They were also advised that a further £12,000 of stock had been seized in transit. And in October they received a further 20 seizure notices detailing 144 titles, many of which were standard academic texts. (Clews, 2012c)

However, when, in June 1985, the case was brought to court, the judge dismissed it, and Customs and Excise dropped the charges. Whilst this was good news, the overall message was still that there was something illicit about handling LGBT materials.

Parts of the media continued to look for 'news stories' which reflected their particular world-view. For example, in 1978:

> ... lesbians managed, like it or not, to hog headline after headline. Hardly had one story run its course than another would begin. The three major stories, intertwining and overlapping throughout the year were: the sexuality of Maureen Colquhoun,[3] then member of Parliament for the Labour Party; lesbians becoming mothers through artificial insemination; and the feminist schoolteacher who tried to teach her class to question sex-role stereotyping. (Hemmings, 1980: 157)

In the late 1970s and early 1980s, there was a shift in many local authorities towards a focus on equal opportunities, and this grew to include LGBT rights too; this work[4] had an enormous impact on the cultural sector, especially libraries. One growth area, often supported by local authorities, was in community publishing (see London Lesbian Line, 1987). The GLC also, of course, made an immense impact, especially with its funding of LGBT-related activities: 'By 1984, the GLC had spent some £300,000 on grants to gay & lesbian groups, and earmarked £750,000 for a London Lesbian and Gay Centre' (Brooke, 2011: 238); and publishing a Charter for Gay and Lesbian Rights (Greater London Council/GLC Gay Working Party, 1985).

However, during the later 1980s, particularly in London and other metropolitan areas, opposition grew to what were seen as some of the over-indulgences of 'Old Labour', and also to these equality policies; at the same time, the Government embarked on a campaign to attack, ridicule and reduce the powers of local authorities.[5] They were joined in this work by some of the media, so that a campaign built to vilify Labour Councils and their activities as 'loony lefties' (see: Bennett, 1995; Daily Mirror, 1986; Rais, 1986). As Terry Sanderson said: 'The

---

3   Maureen Colquhoun, 1928- , Britain's first openly lesbian MP.

4   Davina Cooper has analysed just how well this worked (or did not) during this period, particularly in Haringey and Islington (Cooper, 1994).

5   David Marquand suggests that this was part and parcel of the neo-liberal 'crusade' (Marquand, 2004).

use of homosexuality to make political capital gained momentum in right-wing newspapers in the early 1980s. The creation of moral panics, using one of the last remaining minority groups which it was socially acceptable to abuse, helped the papers to set the political agenda' (Sanderson, 1995: 52).

Also:

> Gradually, as more and more London boroughs elected radical Labour councils, a whole mythology was constructed ... Gays were prominent subjects of this mythology. A glance at some of the 'loony left' stories would soon leave the casual reader imagining that half the rate precept was being spent on lesbian and gay initiatives. (Sanderson, 1995: 95)[6]

Research by the Economic and Social Research Council (ESRC) (Cooper, 2005: 4) concluded that:

> The 1980s had a profound impact of [sic] lesbian and gay equalities work, both laying the groundwork for later developments and provoking opposition from the Right, which is still being felt in some quarters. Work in this area was seen as an electoral liability, following media furores in several localities concerning municipal lesbian and gay initiatives and fears about being labelled 'loony left'. Work continued to be sensitive in some areas, so that, for example, support for initiatives was sometimes withdrawn prior to local elections. Lesbian and gay work was an issue that could be played to populist prejudice via press misrepresentation and the scape-goating of key individuals and authorities.

One of the tools which the media (and the Government) employed was to pick up the negative usage of 'political correctness' and to run series of stories criticising local authorities for their 'politically correct' stance.[7] To give just one example, journalist Rachel Tingle wrote an article mocking the concept of heterosexism and courses for 'teachers, librarians and so on designed "to examine how through the curriculum, existing materials promote heterosexism"' (Tingle, 1986).

In addition, LGBT people were cast by the media as a threat to the family, for example the story in the *Daily Mail* – and cited by Simon Watney (Watney, 1987: 83) – that the London Borough of Lambeth had decided that 'family is a sexist word'.

---

6   Some of these stories were analysed by the Association of Labour Authorities in their report, *It's the Way They Tell 'Em: Distortion, Disinformation and Downright Lies* (Association of Labour Authorities, 1987).

7   For more discussion of 'political correctness', see, for example, my background paper for *Open to All?* (Vincent, 2000a).

HIV/AIDS

Nowhere was the negative attitude of parts of the media more evident than in their treatment of human immunodeficiency virus (HIV)/acquired immune deficiency syndrome (AIDS) stories.

Simon Watney summed up the media coverage when he wrote: 'I am not aware of a single article in the mainstream British press which pays serious attention to the situation of the two million or so gay men in the UK who are currently living through this crisis' (Watney, 1987: 86).

Media-commentator Terry Sanderson also felt the strength of anti-gay feeling: 'The wave of anti-gay revulsion which AIDS released during the 1980s was frightening and depressing' (Sanderson, 1995: 205).

This 'panic' grew: 'The delivery of the [AIDS awareness] leaflets to all British homes ... had the intended effect: AIDS was now a household word in Britain. However, it also had another effect. It characterized gay men as being plague bearers' (Jivani, 1997: 188):

> The AIDS backlash had led to a hardening of public attitudes towards gay men and lesbians, as evidenced by the *British Social Attitudes Survey*. In 1983, sixty-two per cent of respondents had said they did not approve of homosexual relationships. The proportion of people who espoused this attitude increased steadily through the Eighties, rising to sixty-nine per cent in 1985 and to seventy-four per cent in 1987. (Jivani, 1997: 195)

In addition, *Social Trends* reported that:

> nearly four in ten (38 per cent) adults aged 18 and over in Great Britain felt that there should be definitely or probably a legal right for employers to dismiss employees with AIDS. Just under a third (31 per cent) felt that there should be definitely or probably a legal right for doctors and nurses to refuse treatment to AIDS sufferers and just under a quarter (24 per cent) felt that there should be definitely or probably a legal right for schools to expel children with AIDS. (Social Trends, 2010)

However:

> The advent of AIDS seemed likely to endanger the fragile tolerance ... Commentators predicted (some gleefully) the end of gay male lifestyles, but they proved to be wrong. AIDS, on the contrary, stimulated a new sense of resistance among gay men ... [which] revealed a political energy in the gay male community that had seemed possibly absent and certainly on the wane. (Cant, 1988: 8)

Exactly what the impact of this negative media portrayal was will be explored further in the next chapter.

Libraries

By the mid-1980s, some library services were developing good, positive provision for LGBT people, yet this was still small-scale. Writing in 1986, I said: 'Librarians are a key resource in helping overcome some of these areas [of discrimination]. Yet, very little has been done in the way of providing services to lesbians and gay men, and, indeed, there are still battles in some authorities over providing magazines' (Vincent, 1986a: 22).

There was some work to promote LGBT stock and services, for example:

- Hackney (Hackney Leisure Services, 1984)
- Haringey (Haringey Libraries, 1985)
- Islington (Islington Libraries, 1985)
- Lambeth (Lambeth Amenity Services, 1987a, 1987b)

However, a lot of this was carried out in the face of continued criticism. For example, as recorded in *Branchlines* (the newsletter of the then Library Association London & Home Counties Branch): 'The first issue of *Branchlines* carried an article about a gay publishing exhibition mounted in Camden. This publicity has resulted in many enquiries to the author ... It has also resulted in the criticism that this newsletter gave too much prominence to gays' (Library Association London and Home Counties Branch, 1986)

There were also continuing struggles to have public libraries subscribe to *Gay News*: for example, it was not until September 1981 that it was made available in the main libraries in Bath, Bristol and Weston-Super-Mare (GayWest, n.d. -b).

The media too were looking for examples they could use against the implementation of equalities policies, for example from 1986, commenting on *Jenny Lives with Eric and Martin* (Bösche, 1983): 'Gay sex book is "vice lure" – police chief hits at peril in libraries' (House, 1986).

Writing in 1987, Richard Ashby summed up developments by saying that, despite the Association of Assistant Librarians (AAL) having adopted an equal opportunities policy which includes sexual orientation:[8]

> Within the profession the issue has been almost totally ignored. There seems to be no literature, with the exception of a page in John Vincent's recent AAL Pointer *Community Librarianship* [(Vincent, 1986a)]; there have been no professional meetings, and the Library Association Library can come up with nothing more than a handful of requests from librarians asking what other librarians have done. (Ashby, 1987: 153)

---

8   The AAL had established a Lesbian and Gay Working Party to help create this equal opportunities policy (Lesbians in Libraries, 1986: 1).

Richard Ashby continued:

> If we are going to take seriously our Equal Opportunities obligations we have
> to take a number of positive steps. Although considered from the point of view
> of services to gay people, the topics which follow apply equally to all areas in
> which such a policy might be implemented. In this sense there is nothing special
> about a service to gay people, it is the sort of service we should be giving to all
> we serve. (Ashby, 1987: 154)

These steps should include:

- staff training and awareness
- drawing up a comprehensive materials selection policy
- using the materials selection policy to shape an effective materials selection practice
- helping 'gay people find their way around our libraries'
- talk to 'lesbian and gay people and their groups' (taken from: Ashby, 1987: 154).

Finally, Ashby concluded:

> In any discussion of library service to gay and lesbian people it is important to be
> aware of the political implications. Recent attacks on the 'loony left' especially
> in some London Boroughs, have centred on their positive action on Lesbian
> and Gay issues. Some politicians think that the issue is a vote winner (or loser
> depending on which side you are on), others are taking advantage of the AIDS
> scare to promote their own authoritarian views. It is hinted that where politicians
> cannot dismantle Equal Opportunities Policies they would at least try to remove
> sexual orientation from the list of prohibited discrimination.
>
> Librarians must counter such arguments by a renewed commitment to the
> principle of free and equal access to libraries and information. (Ashby, 1987:
> 154-155)

Women in Libraries

In 1974, Librarians for Social Change (LfSC) published a 'special' issue of the
journal devoted to their Feminist Group (Librarians for Social Change Collective,
1974); however, this group was short-lived, and there was little focus on feminism
and sexual politics within librarianship until the formation of the Feminist Library
Workers Group (following a meeting held in September 1980) – this in turn led
to a conference, held in February 1981, during the plenary session of which the
group, Women in Libraries (WiL), was formed.

As Avril Rolph noted:

Once *Women in Libraries* was formed, the ten or so of us who had organised the conference, plus a few more interested women formed the planning group to take *Women in Libraries* forward. Of that group at least two of us identified as lesbians although at that point, and for some time afterwards, lesbian issues had a very low profile. (Rolph, 2000: 199, her italics)

At the time, however: 'There was, perhaps not surprisingly, much ridicule and hostility directed towards *Women in Libraries*' (Rolph, 2000: 199, her italics).

Avril Rolph cited WiL member Jane Little's comment: 'The group has also made an impact in the professional press; and judging by the jibes in the [*Library Association Record*] and New Library World, some men in the field are feeling very threatened by the idea of women getting together to challenge this male-dominated profession' (Little, 1982: 21).

WiL certainly did have an impact, and, as well as organising events and conferences (Jespersen, 1982; Women in Libraries, 1987), it produced a regular newsletter, *WiLPower*, and also formed regional and local sub-groups.[9]

Lesbians in Libraries

In 1984, a number of lesbians responded to an enquiry about setting up a group to explore the specific issues faced by lesbians in libraries, and, on 19 November 1984, the first meeting of Lesbians in Libraries (LiL) was held at A Woman's Place; the report of this meeting challenged WiL members to recognise: 'the oppression of lesbians, and queried how much heterosexual feminist librarians were doing to make lesbians visible (through book selection, by support to co-workers, by attitudes to library workers for example)' (Rolph, 2000: 200).

As Avril Rolph noted:

Once *Lesbians in Libraries* was formed, however, the luxury of being able to discuss only those issues of particular relevance to us quickly gave us the impetus to try to make a definite impression, both on *Women in Libraries* and the wider library profession. At a relatively early stage we decided we needed our own leaflet – a brainstorming session produced the text for 'Why *Lesbians in Libraries*' which concluded with *LiL*'s four aims:

- pressurise librarians and library authorities
- pressurise library suppliers
- provide book lists
- promote these issues within *Women in Libraries*.

9　There is more information about the early years of WiL available (Rolph, 1984).

The pressurising referred to was in relation to the provision of lesbian materials in libraries which we saw (and which I still see) as vitally important. (Rolph, 2000: 201, her italics)

LiL organised and took part in a range of activities, including:

meetings with Onlywomen Press [10] to discuss how to improve distribution of their output through library suppliers. Also, letters to library suppliers about their failure to provide any books with positive lesbian images, and letters to feminist and 'alternative' publishers about the lack of books portraying any aspect of the lives of children with lesbian mothers.

They produced an occasional newsletter, and also held well-advertised regular meetings at the London Women's Centre – these resulted in 'visitors from Spain, Denmark and Holland turning up, as well as librarians and library users from London and the rest of the UK' (Rolph, 2000: 202).

Arguably the most important piece of work that LiL undertook was the publication of their annotated booklist, *Out on the shelves: lesbian books into libraries* (Allen *et al.*, 1989), a listing of 226 books, periodicals, booklists and organisations (together with information on sources for ordering LGBT materials for libraries).

... one of our concerns at this point was, obviously whether [the Association of Assistant Librarians] would carry on with publishing *Out on the shelves*. There was presumably some debate within AAL, or more widely, about whether to do so, but they decided to go ahead, adding the Library Association's own brief on the implications of the Act as an appendix ... [11]

By including this brief as an appendix to *Out on the Shelves* the Library Association was clearly saying that librarians should not be frightened by Clause 28 into not providing the kind of stock we were suggesting. The official view of the profession was thus that librarians had an obligation to provide relevant material for lesbian and gay readers as part of their wider remit of a comprehensive library service. (Rolph, 2000: 204-205)

Avril Rolph herself had doubts as to the impact of *Out on the Shelves*:

Whether *Out on the Shelves* did achieve the breakthrough in awareness we hoped for is doubtful. Apathy, believing 'there are very few or no lesbian users in my library', or that including such stock would only alienate 'normal' people, as well as fear of falling foul of Section 28, remained all too common, but we

---

10   Onlywomen Press has been in existence since 1974 (Onlywomen Press, c2011).

11   The then Library Association had published this brief (Library Association, 1988) as clarification and support for libraries that were receiving challenges under the Act.

were pleased that the 'official' library profession, under the auspices of the AAL, had produced the book in spite of Section 28. And we felt, and I think I still feel, that it did serve to put lesbian issues firmly into the professional arena. (Rolph, 2000: 206)

However, it undoubtedly raised the profile of sexuality in general and lesbians in particular at a time when there was a danger of this area of libraries' work being forced back underground.

LiL continued with other activities after the publication of *Out on the Shelves*, including running a workshop at a conference organised by AAL, 'Section28: a year on', and contributing to a book on lesbian history produced by the Lesbian History Group (Lesbians in Libraries, 1989). 'at some stage during the early 1990s *LiL* quietly wound down, largely I think as those of us most fully involved became more involved in other activities' (Rolph, 2000: 206).

The Lesbian and Gay Librarians Group

A 'new' Gay Librarians Group was formed in 1985, primarily in response to the impounding[12] by HM Customs of material destined for Gay's the Word bookshop; it quickly became the Gay and Lesbian Librarians Group (Gay Librarians Group, 1985). Its first event was a fringe meeting at the 'Information 85' Conference in Bournemouth, where delegates were leafleted about the Gay's the Word raid; the first formal meeting of the Group took place in November 1985 (Gay Librarians Group, 1985: 2).

The Group continued for a while as part of the groundswell of opposition to 'Clause 28' (Gay Librarians Group, 1988), but then faded away until re-formed in 1994 as the Burning Issues Group (BIG; see chapter 5).

Museums and archives

In a similar way to the previous periods, we know that there would have been activity in the museums and archives sectors, but no records appear to survive, and I have not been able to find anyone who can recall any specific LGBT activities or events until after 1988 (see chapter 5).

---

12   As noted above: '"Operation Tiger" went into effect on April 10, 1984. Gay's the Word bookshop was raided, its imported titles seized, and thousands of books that were on their way from the United States were denied clearance. An antiquated law that was part of the Customs Consolidation Act of 1876 was used to charge Gay's the Word with conspiracy to import indecent books' (Bryant, 2009).

Chapter 5
1988-2003: Backlash – and the end of the backlash?

The social and political background

Chapter 4 noted the large increases in social division and social exclusion which had taken place by the mid-1990s. As Alwyn Turner described it: 'the 1980s were characterized by increasing divisions, between rich and poor, between north and south, between those in work and those without, divisions that were manifest in civil disorder, rising crime and rioting' (Turner, 2010: xv).

This came to a head in 1990 with the introduction of the 'poll tax'[1] – and the fierce opposition to it (culminating in the mass demonstration and subsequent rioting in central London on 31 March).

During the 1990s, it became clear that, whilst there were pockets of wealth throughout Britain, there were also significant levels of poverty and social exclusion, which were both widespread (Aberdeen University, 1994), but also more concentrated in particular areas, more in 'northern than in southern Britain and greater in large cities than in small towns and rural areas' (Green, 1994: 1), often leading to polarisation between better-off and poorer communities (Noble and Smith, 1994).

So, by the general election of 1997, there was a head of steam building around tackling social exclusion and promoting social justice. Following the Labour Party's victory in the election, they were quick to establish the Social Exclusion Unit (SEU) which was set up by the Prime Minister later the same year, with a brief to report on: 'how to develop integrated and sustainable approaches to the problems of the worst housing estates, including crime, drugs, unemployment, community breakdown and bad schools etc' (Social Exclusion Unit, 2001a: 6).

The SEU began to work at both a broad policy level (e.g. pursuing policies around Neighbourhood Renewal) and also by investigating and reporting on the needs of some high priority socially excluded groups (for example truants and young people excluded from school; rough sleepers; young people who were not in education, employment or training; and teenage pregnancy). In terms of

---

1   'The Community Charge, popularly known as the poll tax, was a system of taxation introduced in replacement of the rates to part fund local government in Scotland from 1989, and England and Wales from 1990. It provided for a single, flat-rate per-capita tax on every adult, at a rate set by the local authority. The tax was replaced by Council Tax in 1993, two years after its abolition was announced' (Wikipedia, 2012h).

Neighbourhood Renewal, the SEU published an important National Strategy report in 1998 (Social Exclusion Unit, 1998), one of the proposals of which was to establish 18 Policy Action Teams (PATs) to take forward this work around specific themes. None of these included LGBT issues specifically.

The PATs drew on the Government's earliest definition of social exclusion: 'a shorthand term for what can happen when people or areas suffer from a combination of linked problems such as unemployment, poor skills, low incomes, poor housing, high crime, bad health and family breakdown' (see Social Exclusion Unit, 2001b).

The importance of this definition is the flagging-up of social exclusion as 'a combination of linked problems'. As time went on, there was a growing recognition that the definition needed to be widened, so that, for example, people who suffer direct or indirect discrimination (e.g. BME groups; LGBT people; disabled people; people with mental health problems), those who may suffer from multiple disadvantage (e.g. children and young people, older people) and those who are frequently denied access to power (e.g. working class people) needed to be considered.

Towards the end of this period, there was a growing emphasis on policy responses to tackling social exclusion (for example: Scottish Executive, 1999; Social Exclusion Unit, 2001b) and on exploring urgently ways of building community cohesion (Home Office, 2001a, 2001b); however, these responses barely mentioned LGBT issues, and this was particularly significant in relation to a report on the 'drivers' of social exclusion (Bradshaw *et al.*, 2004) which appeared to ignore work that showed the effects on young people of homophobic bullying, the links between being LGBT and some health risks, and so on.

LGBT background

Colin Spencer has argued that 'British society grew more homophobic' (Spencer, 1996: 381) throughout the 1980s, partly as a reaction to AIDS, and partly as a reaction to moves towards LGBT equality – although he does describe this belief that LGBTs were equal as 'ideal or fantasy' (Spencer, 1996: 382)!

I assessed the position in 1999 and highlighted 'what seems to be a widening gap between the acceptance of cultural images and the reality of discrimination' (Vincent, 1999: 63) – for example:

> [LGBT] images are everywhere: Hayley, the transgendered character in Granada Television's long-running 'soap', *Coronation Street*; the adventures of Stuart, Vince and Nathan in Channel 4's ground-breaking series, *Queer as Folk* (1999); lesbian poet U (Ursula) A Fanthorpe in the running to be Poet Laureate; Ian McKellen's well-reviewed performance as the gay film director, James Whale, in *Gods and Monsters* (1999); Lily Savage not only has her own show but is also starring in the musical, *Annie*, on the London stage ... Waheed Alli ennobled;

Dana International winning the Eurovision Song Contest in 1998. (Vincent, 1999: 63)

Yet, at the same time, discrimination was widespread; some examples include:

- Murder of LGBT people, the poor clear-up rate by the police (Powell and Richardson, 1997, 1999) and the passing of lighter sentences when the 'homosexual panic' defence was used (Richardson, 1995);
- Attacks, harassment, bullying and verbal abuse (see for example: Mason and Palmer, 1996);
- Discrimination at work (Trades Union Congress, 1994);
- Discrimination by Health Authorities, for example on the level of spending on HIV-prevention on gay men (National AIDS Trust, 1999);
- Discrimination against specific LGBT groups, for example Black lesbians[2];
- Age of consent – in 1999, for men, it was 18;
- Public displays of same-sex affection: 'two men or two women can be fined simply for kissing in the street' (Wintemute, 1995: 501);
- Discrimination against LGBT publications: the most famous example was the successful prosecution of *Gay News* and the raid on Gay's the Word (as noted in the chapter 4), but it also included the seizure of books by the then Customs and Excise; the raid on the LGBT shop, Clone Zone, in London and the seizure of magazines and videos (Hamilton, 1995); and the seizure by the police of the book *Mapplethorpe*[3] belonging to the Library of the University of Central England (Dyer, 1998; Nicolson, 1998; Powell, 1998);
- Discrimination by omission – LGBTs were (and still are) often omitted from history.

The effects of this period have been summarised in recent research as follows:

Local Authority responses to LGBT social exclusion have varied over the past twenty-five years. The 1980s saw many Local Authority anti-discrimination initiatives for Gay men and Lesbians (public awareness campaigns, same sex tenancies, adopting and fostering initiatives etc.). However, without legislative underpinning, these remained short-term. Successive Local Government Bills severely limited Local Authority responses to LGBT need. Notably the 1985 act abolished the Greater London Council (a major driver for increasing

---

2   'There have been Black people in Britain for at least 500 years and for all that time there have been Black lesbians too. But isolation, racism and homophobia have made us invisible … We were required to break our identities into acceptable fragments: we were Black in Black groups, women in the women's movement and lesbians on the lesbian scene' (Mason-John and Khambatta, 1993: 11).

3   This was a collection of artworks by the photographer Robert Mapplethorpe (Mapplethorpe and Danto, ca. 1992).

social justice in London) and the 1988 act contained the controversial anti-gay amendment known as Section 28 (which precluded Local Authorities from the 'promotion' of homosexuality). Such legislative attacks fostered an atmosphere of hostility in which many Local Authorities were pilloried by the right wing and populist press as 'loony left'. By the late 1980s, LGBT need and concerns had been excised from social care and anti-discrimination policy and practice. The government response to LGBT population need focussed increasingly on HIV prevention and treatment for Gay men and, with few exceptions, the LGBT rights agenda stalled. (Keogh *et al.*, 2006: 2)

One of the major areas of work that caused controversy was that on positive images and 'political correctness' (described briefly in chapter 4), linked to a growing number of local authorities adopting equal opportunity policies which included LGBT people, and also the giving of grant-aid and other support to LGBT centres (for example, the London Lesbian and Gay Centre, LLGC).[4]

As columnist Yasmin Alibhai-Brown wrote: 'Having created the Ultimate Threat, commentators and public figures felt free to let rip with the most rabid and cataclysmic language which they used to describe anything that questioned existing orthodoxies or iniquities' (Alibhai-Brown, 1994).[5]

In an emotive speech, which criticised all sorts of issues around the education of young people and linked teaching about positive images with 'extremist teachers', Conservative Prime Minister Margaret Thatcher said:

> But it's the plight of individual boys and girls which worries me most. Too often, our children don't get the education they need – the education they deserve.
>
> And in the inner cities – where youngsters must have a decent education if they are to have a better future – that opportunity is all too often snatched from them by hard left education authorities and extremist teachers.
>
> And children who need to be able to count and multiply are learning anti-racist mathematics – whatever that may be.

---

4   The LLGC was set up in 1985 by the Greater London Council which donated three-quarters of a million pounds to its establishment (Wikipedia, 2011g).

5   Just as an example, one parallel 'political correctness' myth was that of Winterval – the *Daily Mail* reported in 1998 that Christmas had been renamed Winterval in some local authorities, and this myth was picked up and embroidered by a range of newspapers: 'The myth was not just repeated, either. It was also gradually distorted to become ever more removed from the original misconception. What started as a myth that one council had rebranded or renamed Christmas became a pluralised, open-ended narrative that "councils" and "authorities" were rebranding or renaming Christmas as "Winterval"' (Arscott, 2011). However, the *Daily Mail* has now (2011) admitted that: 'Winterval was the collective name for a season of public events, both religious and secular, which took place in Birmingham in 1997 and 1998. We are happy to make clear that Winterval did not rename or replace Christmas' (Daily Mail, 2011).

Children who need to be able to express themselves in clear English are being taught political slogans.

Children who need to be taught to respect traditional moral values are being taught that they have an inalienable right to be gay.

And children who need encouragement – and children do so much need encouragement – so many children – they are being taught that our society offers them no future.

All of those children are being cheated of a sound start in life – yes cheated. (Thatcher, 1987)

Looking back, it is clear that this signalled publicly the start of a further attack on liberal values – and LGBT rights in particular.

LGBT background: 'Clause 28'

In 1986, Lord Halsbury[6] tabled a Private Member's Bill in the House of Lords (House of Lords, 1986), described by him as 'a Bill to restrain local authorities from promoting homosexuality' (Hansard, 1986) – this Bill passed through the House of Lords, and was adopted by then-MP, Jill Knight;[7] but, overshadowed by the forthcoming general election, the Bill ultimately failed.

However, in December 1987, David Wilshire MP[8] introduced an amendment – Clause 28 – along the same lines into the 1988 Local Government Bill; this amendment was also championed by Jill Knight (and by Michael Howard, then Minister for Local Government). Jeffrey Weeks suggested that the key to the whole issue of Clause 28 is summed up by David Wilshire in a letter to the press: 'Homosexuality is being promoted at the ratepayers' expense, and the traditional family as we know it is under attack' (Letter to the *Guardian*, 12 December 1987, cited in Weeks, 1991: 138).

Many of the fallacies on which the pro-Clause-28 lobby built their case have been clearly identified by Anna Marie Smith – and this also indicates the 'mood' of the times:

> Early speakers in the debates make several fallacious charges. It is claimed that lesbian and gay books were displayed in two Lambeth play centres, that the book *Young, Gay and Proud* [(Alyson 1985)] was recommended for children by the Inner London Authority and stocked by a Haringey library, and that the text *Jenny Lives with Eric and Martin* was stocked at an ILEA teacher centre and its publisher grant-aided by the GLC. (Smith, A.M., 1990: 44)

---

6   John Giffard, 3rd Earl of Halsbury, 1908-2000 (Wikipedia, 2012l).

7   Joan Christabel (Jill) Knight, 1927-, Baroness of Collingtree (Debrett's, 2012).

8   David Wilshire, 1943- (Wikipedia, 2012j).

These may, of course, be fallacies, but it is essential to emphasise that there is nothing intrinsically wrong with any of the three issues: Lambeth Library Service certainly did lend a range of stock to play centres for young people, and it may well have included LGBT material; and *Young, Gay and Proud* and *Jenny Lives with Eric and Martin* were certainly, rightly, available in public libraries, if not Haringey and the Inner London Education Authority (ILEA) as suggested.

Smith continued:

> These fallacies then become self-perpetuating: later speakers cite the same 'evidence' as if its legitimacy and significance were already well known. In the final debates, simply citing the names of five local authorities, Camden, Haringey, Lambeth, Brent, and Ealing, is deemed sufficient to evoke the figure of the 'promoter' of homosexuality. Local councils' support for lesbian and gay youth groups and discos is presented as if the local councils invented these activities to brainwash teenagers, though of course they actually originated in the gay community, rather than in any local authority plot. Furthermore, although the speakers claim to be concerned with the welfare of children, they also cite publications and policies aimed at adults. (Smith, A.M., 1990: 44)

The Bill passed through the House of Lords, with Lord Caithness[9] singling out for particular criticism some areas of work that were very close to the cultural sector:

> What we are seeing in some places is an attempt to sell homosexuality, to ensure that people see it in a favourable light. For this purpose we see all the techniques of modern public relations deployed—entertainments, exhibitions, campaigns, posters. Every local authority service that can possibly be used in some way to put over the message is twisted to serve the same purpose. We see gay library collections, gay consciousness courses for local authority officers and homosexual material produced for children's playgroups. We have homosexual and lesbian units which comment on every report that is going to the council. Everything then is done to glamourise [sic] homosexuality, to make all aspects of homosexuality seem attractive. (HL Deb, 1988)

Despite considerable opposition, the Act became law in May 1988 (Great Britain, 1988).

Speaking in the House of Lords some 10 years later, Jill Knight explained why she was so committed to the Clause (and, looking back, it is fascinating to see the importance that was placed on books):

> Why did I bother to go on with it and run such a dangerous gauntlet? I was then Chairman of the Child and Family Protection Group. I was contacted by parents who strongly objected to their children at school being encouraged

---

9   Malcolm Sinclair, 20th Earl of Caithness, 1948- (Wikipedia, 2012n).

into homosexuality and being taught that a normal family with mummy and daddy was outdated. To add insult to their injury, they were infuriated that it was their money, paid over as council tax, which was being used for this. This all happened after pressure from the Gay Liberation Front. At that time I took the trouble to refer to their manifesto, which clearly stated:

> 'We fight for something more than reform. We must aim for the abolition of the family'.

That was the motivation for what was going on, and was precisely what Section 28 stopped …

Parents certainly came to me and told me what was going on. They gave me some of the books with which little children as young as five and six were being taught. There was The Playbook for Kids about Sex in which brightly coloured pictures of little stick men showed all about homosexuality and how it was done. That book was for children as young as five. I should be surprised if anybody supports that.

Another book called The Milkman's on his Way explicitly described homosexual intercourse and, indeed, glorified it, encouraging youngsters to believe that it was better than any other sexual way of life. (House of Lords, 1999)

Interestingly, these two books (Blank, 1982; Rees, 1982), plus *Jenny lives with Eric and Martin* (Bösche, 1983), were still being used in 2009 as examples to show that it is 'wrong for councils to spend their residents' money promoting homosexuality' (Phibbs, 2009).

The 1988 Act included the following wording:

> 28 (1) The following section shall be inserted after section 2 of the Local Government Act 1986 (prohibition of political publicity) –
>
> 2A - (1) A local authority shall not –
> (a) intentionally promote homosexuality or publish material with the intention of promoting homosexuality;
> (b) promote the teaching in any maintained school of the acceptability of homosexuality as a pretended family relationship. (Great Britain, 1988)

The immediate impact was one of fear of crossing this legal barrier, creating an atmosphere of uncertainty for school and local authority staff, for example. Certainly, for the cultural sector, the impact was strong, even if no one was actually prosecuted. One effect of this was:

> within schools there has undoubtedly been an enormous amount of self censorship. Some teachers believe that Section 28 does apply directly to their work and are, therefore, afraid of tackling issues of sexuality. Others have used

it as a way of avoiding issues which they find uncomfortable and difficult to deal with. Yet others have, no doubt, welcomed it because it legitimated their own homophobia. (Epstein, 1994: 7)

Similar self-censorship also seems to have taken place in libraries[10] and museums, with some local authorities not waiting for a prosecution, but using Section 28 to justify self-censorship (Hasted, 2012); there is evidence that it also led to a self-imposed ban on collecting by museums and the use of anything but LGBT keywords to classify items – which means that they are difficult, if not impossible, to track down later (Shopland, 2012).

According to the *Guardian*:

> While no one was ever prosecuted under the section, it had a wide effect, with libraries refusing to stock gay papers, gay websites blocked on school and college computers, and Glyndebourne Touring Opera being forced to abandon a staging of Death in Venice. (Gillan, 2003)

There was a number of instances of refusal to display LGBT-related material, for example:

Lesbian Line Hit by Section 28

> Three items have been removed from the Lesbian Line part of a display in York public library because it was claimed that they might contravene Section 28 of the UK Local Government Act.
>
> The display was part of an exhibition staged as part of International Women's Week and items removed were a copy of the Lesbian Custody Charter, a *Pink Paper* article about coming out and a *New Internationalist* feature on homosexuality.
>
> Lesbian Line is not letting the matter rest and hopes to gather more information about similar displays to convince the local authority in York that such material can be legally displayed. (Gay and Lesbian Humanist Association, 1990)

In 2000, *Impact* (the journal of the then Chartered Institute of Library & Information Professionals Career Development Group) approached Stonewall to ask for their interpretation of the law, and the results – challenging terms in 'Clause 28' and linking intolerance and homophobia – were an important opinion-former. In

---

10   At a major Arts Council Conference held in April 1998 ('Reading for Life' 22-23 April 1998), one of the seminars, 'Bigger issues – promoting literature with lesbians and gay men', led by Michael Clarke, then Head of Libraries and Information Services, Leicester City Council, focused on the queer contribution to literature, the effects of 'Clause 28' (the most insidious of which he identified as self-censorship) and strategies for inclusion (Arts Council of England, 1998).

addition, their article showed some of the variations in the way that the Clause had been applied, with projects such as Corby Lesbian Line, Cardiff Lesbian and Gay Mardi Gras and a proposed Birmingham City Council young people's guide all denied; whilst the Stockport Young Gay Men's Project and Lesbian/Bisexual project, and London Lesbian Line, for example, were supported (Stonewall, 2000a). The same issue of *Impact* also included a short selection of testimonies showing the impact that 'Clause 28' was having on people's lives (Stonewall, 2000b).

In reality:

> There is only one case of Section 28 being used to bring a case to the courts against a council. In May, 2000 – the first and last case of its kind – the Christian Institute unsuccessfully took Glasgow City Council to court for funding an AIDS support charity which the Institute alleged promoted homosexuality. (Wikipedia, 2011f)

It is also worth emphasising that, despite 'Clause 28', there was still strong and positive support for provision by local authorities, for example by the LGA (Local Government Association, 2001).

Recently, journalists have argued that the spirit of Clause 28 lingers on, for example in the furore over Opera North's request for a change of wording in Lee Hall's opera 'Beached', and, in his article about this case, Chris Ashford recalled some of the effects:

> Even before the Act came into force, the Director of Leeds College of Music banned the students' Lesbian and Gay Society from meeting on College premises.
>
> In May 1988, the same month that the legislation came into effect, East Sussex County Council withdrew a National Youth Bureau directory from its schools. The directory listed numerous organisations that offered voluntary work opportunities for young people. One organisation listed was an organisation that sought volunteers over the age of 14 with 'a positive attitude to their sexuality'.
>
> Whether this constituted 'promotion' is clearly dubious, but such was the fear that the Act instilled into local councillors that they didn't dare take chances. Later, in September 1988, a production of the play *Trapped in Time* was due to be performed by the Avon Touring Theatre in a secondary school. The School Head, unsure of the legislation, banned the play on account of one scene within the play entitled 'Queen Victoria's Coming Out' in which one character informs his friends of his homosexuality.
>
> These instances of effective censorship continued under Blair's government. In 1999, a North Bristol performing arts college was forced to consider re-writing the end of a play to be performed by students. The play featured a lesbian couple who closed the play with a positive romantic ending. However, the course tutor, wary of Section 28 decided to end the play with the couple splitting up so as not to 'promote homosexuality as a pretended family relationship'. (Ashford, ca. 2011)

The effect on schools, young people and their parents/carers included increased bullying (Carvel and White, 2000) and more young people having to try to 'pass' (Wallace, 2000):

> In 1991, a Health Education Authority survey of more than four thousand 16- to 19-year-olds found that over 80% had been told nothing about homosexuality in their sex education lessons and 45% regretted that they had not received more information at school about gay and lesbian relationships. Why should there be this serious deficiency? (Stafford, 1993)

Here is just one example of the effect on a young person:

> For me, Section 28 was the 'silent enemy' at school, I knew I was different from about 12 or 13 years old. I knew I was gay without really knowing what 'gay' was. I knew I needed to discuss it, and seek help, but feared the consequences. I didn't know why, but now I do!
>
> Thanks to Section 28 I had a very lonely childhood, had very few friends. I was a loner because I was different and picked on for being a loner … Section 28 and other 'anti-gay' legislation made my childhood hell. Don't let this happen to others. (Letter from James in Hertfordshire to Stonewall, December 1998, quoted in: Fairbrother, 2000)

In her research for the ESRC, Davina Cooper concluded that:

> S. 28 of the Local Government Act 1988 impacted heavily on work in the field of lesbian, gay and bisexual equalities. Actively opposed by some authorities, and ineffictive [sic] in legislative terms, s. 28 nonetheless led to widespread (if patchy) self-censorship. Less proactive authorities used it as an excuse to avoid work concerning lesbian and gay equality; others sought legal advice whilst continuing to do some work. Overall, s. 28 created a climate of fear, whilst existing at odds with both burgeoning legislation in other areas of equalities work (race and disability) and a increasingly inclusive social climate. (Cooper, 2005: 5)

Finally, a House of Commons Research Paper concluded:

> It is arguable that Section 28 has done what its supporters wished, by limiting the discussion of homosexuality in schools, but that this is more to do with misconceptions about its scope and meaning rather than its effectiveness as legislation. Many on both sides of the debate agree that schools should not promote homosexuality, but that the provision is nonetheless badly drafted: even supporters of Section 28 have suggested that its language seems almost deliberately provocative. (Thorp and Allen, 2000: 13)

Opposition to 'Clause 28' continued to grow (although there was also continuing support); from 2000 onwards, attempts were made to repeal the legislation in England and Wales, but these were defeated in the House of Lords. However, despite these successive defeats in the House of Lords, the Labour government passed legislation to repeal this Section as part of the Local Government Act 2003 (Great Britain, 2003) by a vote of MPs, and it was abolished in England and Wales in November 2003 (Gillan, 2003). The Scottish Parliament abolished 'Clause 28' in 2000 (BBC News, 2000).

The repeal was carried out moderately quietly, so, although it meant, of course, that the cultural sector could now develop their work with LGBT people, many people had not realised that the Section had been repealed (and, when asked today, a considerable number of people working in the cultural sector are either unsure or believe that it is still in force). As noted above, the effects are very much still with us.

Since 2003, whilst there are still some people in favour of having such legislation available, the general political 'mood' has changed: for example, the then Conservative Party Chairman Francis Maude told *Pink News* in 2006 that the Party's stance on 'Clause 28' was wrong (BBC Home 2006); and, in 2009, Prime Minister David Cameron issued an apology for his Party's having introduced the law (despite his having supported it) (Chapman, J., 2009).

The cultural sector

As noted above, early in the period 1988-2003 there was a surge of interest in tackling social exclusion, and, whilst much of this work did not automatically include LGBT issues, nevertheless it did set the scene for a radical reassessment of the role of libraries, museums, archives and the cultural sector more widely.

Key documents include:

- public libraries: Government policy guidance (DCMS, 1999) and research into 'Public Library Policy and Social Exclusion' (Muddiman *et al.*, 2000a, 2000b, 2000c);
- museums: report from the Group on Larger Local Authority Museums (Group for Larger Local Authority Museums, 2000);
- archives: an audit report from the National Council on Archives (National Council on Archives, 2001b);
- libraries, museums and archives: a 'way forward' report from the Department for Culture, Media and Sport (DCMS), following the earlier consultations (DCMS, 2001).

Tackling social exclusion also began to be picked up in the professional press (for example: Museums Journal, 1999; Vincent, 2000b). At the same time, the Museums, Libraries and Archives Council (MLA) and its regions also began to draw up policies and strategies for tackling social exclusion (MacKeith and Osborne, 2003; National Council on Archives, 2001a; SEMLAC, 2005), and these began to have a noticeable local influence.

Libraries

So, what was happening in public libraries?

Survey of public library provision in London, 1992

A ground-breaking, small-scale piece of research was carried out by Phil Brett (1992) which focused on library provision for lesbians and gay men in three London boroughs. Using a mix of questionnaires (for library staff, Councillors, publishers, bookshops and LGBT groups) and public surveys, together with stock checks, Phil Brett drew up a picture of library provision as he explored the proposition that: 'the level of provision and service varies according to the politics and governance of the library authority' (Brett, 1992: 198).

In the course of the study, Phil Brett also highlighted a range of other interesting – and key – issues, such as the lack of stock policies and censorship versus selection (see Vincent, 1986b); whether positive action was appropriate; the arrangement, display and promotion of stock and services; and issues surrounding the provision of material for children and young people.

In particular, the study focused on the debate about the role of public libraries:

> People clearly felt that homosexuals were discriminated against in society and that libraries should not support such prejudice. This included the sample of the public which might have been perceived to have the opposite view. This opinion did, however, have limitations. For example, whilst the public survey indicated a desire that libraries should be non-homophobic there was opposition to libraries being anti-homophobic. The public were against libraries being used to fight discrimination as this was seen as political interference in the neutrality of the library. The library staff and other professionals were in favour of an interventionist role, and the library should have an active role within the community which included the library taking a 'progressive' role.
>
> The results of the survey suggest that in certain areas libraries might follow policies of which the public disapprove. Such as in the issue of gay titles in junior collections and the implementation of a 'positive images' policy. In both cases library staff were in favour, whilst the public were against (although in each case there was an important minority taking the opposite view). The acceptance of this indicates that those connected with libraries feel that whilst libraries should respond to the wishes of the general public there should be care taken to take into account the wishes of minorities. The balance between the two is not an easy one. There did however appear to be a consensus view that

the library role is not just one of mirroring the lowest common denominator but educational. One could ask what the librarian's response should be if the majority were against black authors being stocked. (Brett, 1992: 207-208)

Interestingly:

> How far minorities are catered for again raises the question of whether a library should be merely non-discriminatory or be anti-discriminatory. The majority of answers from the broad based questionnaire were in favour of the latter, however, in practice this did not appear to be the case ...
>
> It would appear logical that for a library to be truly non-homophobic it cannot avoid taking a more active stance. There was perceived to be a lack of support and information for/by/on gays in society. The survey suggests that libraries can fill this gap. Stocking material which is available is a good first step, but what if that which is made available by publishers is minimal, as is the case with children's books, reference material and large print? The material available is not balanced, the respondents agreed that, so to merely replicate the publishers['] decisions is to replicate the bias. Therefore, a balanced stock is impossible. To achieve a balance libraries need to influence publishers to publish a wider choice. (Brett, 1992: 208)

Finally, Phil Brett concluded:

> The findings would seem to suggest that the majority of those questioned believed that a public library should attempt to provide a balanced stock. In attempting to do so it is necessary to acknowledge that it is not a balanced world. Libraries can not cure society's failings but they can play a subjective role in attempting to provide material by or for people who either question society or are themselves questioned by society. In doing so a public library can make a contribution to humanity. (Brett, 1992: 210)

Public libraries suffer the backlash

Sadly, public libraries were an easy target for backlash, partly because they had become high profile (particularly with some of the stories circulating about 'political correctness' in some London boroughs and the ILEA) and partly because they were becoming centre-stage for possible contracting-out and/or severe reductions in resources. As a result, there was a spate of stories – true or otherwise – about 'book-banning', and, to cope with this unwelcome focus, many libraries simply stopped their positive stock selection and equalities work.

As Rosemary Stones, one of the founder members of the Children's Rights Workshop and the 'Other Award', succinctly put it, there was: 'a new social climate of ridicule and alienation around equalities issues which it has become socially acceptable to dismiss as "political correctness"' (Stones, 1994).

This theme had already been identified by then *Gay Times* columnist Terry Sanderson:

> Now that the loony left is no more, right-wing propagandists have had to find another vehicle with which to launch attacks on their 'progressive' enemies. The new bogey is 'political correctness' which is, of course, a close cousin of the loony left. It began last year with a spate of stories about barmy 'left-wing' activities – like the revising of Enid Blyton's books in order to expunge all traces of racism, classism, homophobia and sexism ... As a result of the emphasising of these extremes, it is now taken for granted that 'political correctness' is undesirable. (Sanderson, 1993)

At the same time, in her survey of the attitudes of library directors in Canada and the UK, Ann Curry (1997) uncovered some strong, and ultimately horrifying, attitudes: 'It is a dangerous political situation to say that the library promotes social change. If you say that with a hung council ... the library will get short shrift and funding reductions down the road' [UK director] (Curry, 1997: 42):

> [A] factor noted only by the British directors involves a different kind of 'high' demand: that of special interest groups and council politicians for 'politically correct literature on politically correct themes'. Material dealing with women's and gay/lesbian issues was mentioned specifically in this context. Four directors felt that their libraries were being exploited in a power struggle when they purchased widely and deeply in these areas, only to discover that the people who had demanded specific items were not reading them. (Curry, 1997: 51)

> Most directors, while agreeing or strongly agreeing that 'positive' homosexual literature should be included in public library collections, feel that positive images should be provided for *all* groups in society and that negative images of homosexuals should also be provided. (Curry, 1997: 69, my emphasis)

Curry concludes, worryingly, that 'Overall, the British appear to be reluctantly compromising services to gays/lesbians to avoid Section 28 prosecution', although she is also clear that personal views may have an effect: 'Sex, politics and religion are things which one keeps to oneself. I have no objection to homosexuality, provided it is kept quiet and out of sight as that sort of thing should be. I object to it being paraded' [UK director] (Curry, 1997: 224).

Regaining some ground

There was a clear backlash against the role of libraries in providing positive images and materials reflecting LGBT lives (the effects of which can still be felt today), but, at the same time, there were also some major new developments (despite Clause 28).

For example:

> I was involved in The Hackney Council LGBT celebration in 1988. This
> certainly was one of the first times that every department in the council was
> required to have a stall to show what they did for LGBT people. At that time
> there were booklists & pamphlets with support & entertainment information.
> This was quite a controversial conference with a huge backlash in the local
> paper. The reaction and also the passing of Clause 28 sent a lot of this activity
> into the background. (Logan, 2013)

In 1989 (as noted in chapter 4), the Association of Assistant Librarians (AAL)
published a major booklist of lesbian material (Allen *et al.*, 1989) aimed at library
staff and users – as the compilers emphasised, it is important to portray 'lesbians as
well-rounded, three-dimensional productive human beings, and not as miserable
perverts whose lives are full of unhappiness' (Allen *et al.*, 1989: 2).

They pointed up too the importance of this in the light of 'Clause 28':

> We must not allow 'promotion' to be interpreted as presenting positive images,
> because positive material can help to challenge homophobia ... Books do help
> people make sense of their world and put their experience into a recognisable
> context: they help validate the experiences of lesbians and lesbian viewpoints,
> and help women to form a positive view of themselves and their lesbianism.
> Librarians have a duty to provide material which expresses the experience
> and reality of the lives of a sizeable proportion of the population. (Allen *et al.*,
> 1989: 2)

Some speakers also kept the issue of 'Clause 28' alive on conference agendas, for
example at the 1988 Public Libraries Group Weekend School (Carter *et al.*, 1988).

Burning Issues Group/Sexuality Issues in Libraries Group

A new focus on LGBT provision was provided by the work of the Burning Issues
Group (BIG) from 1994 onwards. In October 1995, the Community Services
Group of the Library Association had put on a well-attended course, 'Less equal
than others', a course on library services for LGBT people: what was remarkable
about this was, firstly, that it was the first time that a Library Association Group
had organised a course on this topic – although the AAL, South-East Division,
had organised sexuality awareness training for their committee (Montgomery and
Behr, 1988), and Alison Behr had also organised a course for the AAL, South-
East Division in 1990 on 'Section 28: 2 years on' (Behr, 1990); and, secondly,
that, even in 1995, some attendees were nervous of being there, for fear that their
employers might find out.

This course was followed by a highly successful course organised by the
London Borough of Southwark, 'Burning Issues – a conference on library services

to lesbians and gay men', 27 June 1996. Participants from these courses were invited to attend a follow-up meeting in September 1996, and, in November 1996, the Burning Issues Group was formed as a network for library workers interested or involved in service delivery to LGBT people.[11]

In 1997, BIG carried out a survey of public libraries in London (plus Brighton & Hove). The results (which were never published) show just how patchy services were; only nine organised any events, for example to tie in with Gay Pride (and one authority responded specifically that they did not have any events because there was a lack of political support). Asked about performance indicators or other ways in which they assessed the need for and take-up of the services, most used only their issue figures. Library authorities were making an effort to develop service provision, despite lack of resources, yet, at the same time, there were clear indications of authorities treating their library users as all being the same or invisible: as so little surveying of the needs of LGBT users had been carried out, it is hardly surprising that these authorities could not say why a service was required[12] (Burning Issues Group, ca. 1997).

In June 1999, BIG held a training day which included an examination of some of the areas of discrimination that LGBT people face; a look at the case for LGBT people being included in any work to tackle social exclusion; a report by Mark Norman on his research in Brighton & Hove Libraries (Norman, 1998); and a series of workshops (Burning Issues Group, 1999).

In 2000, BIG and The Network organised a Briefing, 'Clause 28 and its effects', which highlighted areas of concern and recommended more sharing of good practice; more information about library materials and sources of supply being made available; the development of guidance and training for staff in working with LGBT people and in dealing with any 'backlash' against service provision (Vincent and Hardie, 2000). Latterly, the Group changed its name to the Sexuality Issues in Libraries Group, in order to make its remit clearer.

Open to All?

Funded by, successively, the British Library Research and Innovation Centre, the Library and Information Commission, and Resource, *Open to All?* was an

---

11   The minutes of the first meeting were headed 'Librarians interested in services to lesbians and gay men'. In its application to the then Library Association to become an Organisation in Liaison, BIG described itself as: 'an organisation, open to anyone, that is committed to investigating current library provision for lesbians and gay men, publishing the results, sharing best practice and thereby working towards improving services generally' (Murray, ca. 1997).

12   There was also an indication that those authorities which, in the past, had established services specifically targeted towards women, the Black communities, disabled people and LGBT people had largely abandoned these, either for budgetary reasons or for fear of being labelled 'politically correct'.

18-month research project which looked at the public library in the UK and its capacity to tackle social exclusion (Muddiman *et al.*, 2000a, 2000b, 2000c). Part of the research process was the production of 'Working Papers' which explored the issues around social exclusion and public library responses to it, and one of these papers focused on LGBT people (Vincent, 1999); it also included a list of 16 recommendations, many of which are still valid today (and the recommendations are included in Appendix 2).

A growing focus on LGBT issues

There was a flurry of articles in the professional press, which raised key questions about Clause 28 and its effects on library services for LGBT people. Judy Hendry wrote about the importance of making LGBT information available to children and young people, despite Clause 28 (Hendry, 1997); *Community Librarian* for Spring 1998 included two important articles (Fairbrother, 1998; Warburton, 1998), as well as a half-page promotion for the Burning Issues Group; and the Autumn/Winter issue of *Community Librarian* carried a letter from Evelyn Healy, responding to John Warburton's criticisms of Glasgow Libraries and briefly setting out some of their services (Healy, 1998).

There were some public library services which were providing high levels of service to LGBT people; one leading authority was Brighton & Hove which provided not only successful collections of materials but also had a high level of user involvement in the provision. Mark Norman carried out a research study on the service (Norman, 1998) and concluded that:

> This study shows that the [LGBT] Collection is an important information resource in Brighton & Hove for the [LGBT] community ... the Collection appears to be successful because it attempts to fulfil gay men and lesbians' different information needs ... Respondents' reasons for use suggest the [LGBT] Collection has important educational, cultural and economic roles, providing access to resources that may be difficult to find or expensive ... Respondents were aware [that LGBT] services are poor in the UK and praise the Collection for being better than other library authorities. Their comments suggest some have high expectations of the Collection, requiring closer liaison with them to prevent expectations from greatly exceeding library capabilities.

There was also renewed enthusiasm by some library services for the purchase and promotion of stock (despite the threat of 'Clause 28'): for example, Hackney Libraries produced a resources guide (London Borough of Hackney, 1995); Islington Libraries produced a booklist and information guide in 1996 (Islington Council, 1996); Brighton Library produced booklists of lesbian and gay materials (Brighton Central Library, 1996a, 1996b); and Northamptonshire Libraries and Information Service launched 'Out on the Shelves', a 'collection aimed specifically at members of the gay, lesbian and bisexual community', supported by a resources list and staff awareness training, all part of a response to concerns that LGBT people had raised (Northamptonshire Libraries and Information Service 1999).

The reader development programme 'Branching Out' (Opening the Book, ca. 2006a) organised by Opening the Book, ran a successful promotion, 'Loud and Proud' (in conjunction with libraries and with the suppliers, Books for Students) from an early pilot in 1999. They produced a list of library materials, and this (together with lists from Croydon, Trafford and Blackpool Library Services) is still available to see in the archived website (Opening the Book, ca. 2006b).

Museums

Progress in museums' collecting and exhibiting material relating to LGBT people has been very slow. As Anthony Tibbles indicated in the background summary to his article on the 'Hello Sailor!' exhibition, compared with Australia and the US: 'In Britain, progress was much slower and it is only in just over the last decade that museums have tackled any displays with an LGBT content' (Tibbles, 2012: 163).

Part of the reason for this was that the 'difficulty of addressing LGBT issues has been compounded by the lack of any professional support or network within museums to share information or to provide guidance or support in developing appropriate initiatives' (Tibbles, 2012: 163).

In addition: 'the notion that a museum might openly and directly acknowledge to visitors the sexual orientation of, for example, an artist, a prominent local figure or a collector, is unthinkable prior to the legalisation of homosexuality and before the gay rights movement gathered momentum' (Sandell and Frost, 2010: 155).

One of the earliest attempts to discover what lesbian and gay materials were held in British social history museums was the survey by Gabrielle Bourn (Bourn, 1994) which discovered that there was very little in the way of holdings; whilst some museums had small collections (for example, Leicester Museum had Joe Orton's life mask), only Glasgow, Stoke-on-Trent, Hackney, Islington and Enfield museum services were actively collecting (Bourn, 1994: 8; Vanegas, 2002: 98).

Angela Vanegas then took this work a stage further, and contributed a ground-breaking chapter (Vanegas, 2002) to Richard Sandell's important investigation of the social roles and responsibilities of museums (Sandell, 2002).[13] In 2000, she had contacted the same departments:

---

13   In 2000, the School of Museum Studies at the University of Leicester organised an international conference, 'Inclusion', 'in response to increasing calls from museum professionals for opportunities to explore the relevance of social inclusion to the sector' (Sandell, 2001: xviii). This conference provided a 'springboard' for *Museums, Society, Inequality* and also included references to lesbian and gay issues (Sandell, 2002; Vaswani, 2000).

to find that little had changed, except that the Museum of London had taken in about fifty items from their *Pride and Prejudice* exhibition. Only Tyne and Wear Museums appeared to be actively collecting lesbian and gay material, as part of a larger contemporary collecting project called *Making History* ...

And so, at the start of the twenty-first century, most British social history collections contain little or nothing to represent lesbians or gay men and few curators are doing anything to rectify the situation. (Vanegas, 2002: 98)

Gabrielle Bourn had also asked in her survey whether the museums held any temporary exhibitions of lesbian and gay interest over the preceding 10 years: eight replied positively, including Bruce Castle Museum, Tottenham ('Vera the Visible Lesbian' and The Hall Carpenter Archives); Leicester Museum (an exhibition about Joe Orton); the V&A ('Street Style'); Islington Museum ('Love Stories' and 'Fighters and Thinkers'); Glasgow Museums ('Glasgay'); and Bradford ('Positive Lives') (Bourn, 1994: 10-11; Vanegas, 2002: 104).

Angela Vanegas recorded thirteen more: as she said, the majority were exhibitions on broader topics that included some gay material (e.g. 'Dressing the Male' at the V&A); and some included gay men in the context of AIDS, with the danger that, 'if this is the *only* place in such institutions that gay men are represented ... the implied message is that gay men are sick and they are sick because of their sexuality' (Vanegas, 2002: 104, emphasis hers).

Only three temporary exhibitions were specifically about gay and lesbian topics: these included two smaller-scale displays, 'Pride Scotland' in Glasgow and photographs of London pride at the Museum of London, plus the major exhibition 'Pride and Prejudice – Lesbian and Gay London', at the Museum of London in 1999 (Museum of London, ca. 1999), 'the first comprehensive exhibition about lesbian and gay history in Britain' (Vanegas, 2002: 104).

As well as collecting information about holdings and exhibitions, Angela Vanegas asked museums why so little was being done to represent lesbians and gay men: there was a range of reasons given, including:

- 'Some curators were content to borrow material from their local lesbian and gay archives' (Vanegas, 2002: 99), which posed questions about whose responsibility it was to collect LGBT material.
- Some curators knew that there was lesbian- and gay-related material in their collections, but it was not catalogued as such, and so was impossible to retrieve.
- 'Several respondents said that many things in their collections could just as easily have been used in the everyday lives of gays and lesbians as anyone else and this may be true ... The history of objects has to be recorded or their real meaning is lost' (Vanegas, 2002: 99).
- 'A few curators replied that they had material that could possibly be interpreted as lesbian and gay, and then mentioned items such as body-piercing jewellery or AIDS ephemera. The underlying message seemed to

be that, because lesbians and gay men are defined by their sexuality, they can only be represented by objects relating to sex … ' (Vanegas, 2002: 99).

She summed this up by stating that: 'many museum staff appear confused about who should collect gay and lesbian material, how to record it and, indeed, what it might be' (Vanegas, 2002: 99).

In addition, because of Clause 28:

> Some museums have excluded gay and lesbian materials in response to real or imaginary local authority pressure …
>
> However, most museum staff have not even attempted to portray lesbian and gay history; Section 28 has protected curators from having to deal with the issue. Some curators spoke of possibly losing jobs or funding, but many had not even identified it as an issue. Others have said that they could not represent lesbians and gay men because they have nothing in their collections. Needless to say, these were not the ones who were actively collecting. Several were afraid of complaints from their existing audiences and felt that sexuality was not a suitable topic for a family audience …
>
> Some museums prefer to ignore, or even lie about, the sexuality of the people they represent. At Shibden Hall in Halifax, the sexuality of its celebrated Georgian owner, Anne Lister, was ignored until the appointment of a new curator in 1990. A few years ago, I attended a dramatisation of the life of Lord Leighton at his Kensington home, which stated that he had never wed because he was married to his art!' (Vanegas, 2002: 105)[14]

To counterpoint all this, Angela Vanegas also included an outline of how Croydon Museum and Heritage Service went about collecting material for 'Lifetimes', an exhibition about the lives of local people from 1830 to the present, which included life stories of lesbians and gay men;[15] Rachel Hasted, one of the two interviewers who gathered this material, wrote:

> exhibition visitors can be challenged in their assumptions and prejudices … they are confronted with human beings, not with stereotypes, people speaking with strength, humour and pathos, anger about recognisable human situations … Over 300 voices in the gallery offer their accounts of the past with the authority of personal experience … within this context, lesbian and gay experience can be presented not as an anomaly, but as one aspect of complex lives. (Hasted, 1996: 5; Vanegas, 2002: 103)

---

14   Gabrielle Bourn suggested that Clause 28 was 'a convenient tool that can be used by homophobic councillors' (Bourn, 1994: 16; Vanegas, 2002: 105).

15   Croydon were pioneers in seeing the history of sexuality as a necessary topic to cover in any accurate portrayal of the social and cultural history of the borough (Hasted, 2012).

Unfortunately, technical problems meant that the opening of 'Lifetimes' was delayed; in its place, Croydon organised three temporary art exhibitions, which featured lesbian and gay themes, and Angela Vanegas described how, despite some opposition from councillors (and threats that the works involved contravened Clause 28), these went ahead:

> We also demonstrated that terrible things will not happen if lesbians and gay men are represented in exhibitions. We weren't prosecuted under Section 28 and most comments were complimentary. The total public backlash consisted of eight homophobic or racist comments, plus a few suggestions that children should not be allowed in because of some nude photographs. (Vanegas, 2002: 107)

In 2004, Mark Liddiard wrote about the identity and direction of UK museums, including comments on sexuality as a way of 'illustrating the shifting milieu within which museums are currently working' (Liddiard, 2004: 15), and came to very much the same conclusions:

> It is difficult to make general observations about the ways in which museums present sexuality, given that they are so heterogeneous. Nevertheless, it is intriguing that in spite of the wide variety of museum forms, with their highly diverse collecting and exhibiting policies, the theme of sexuality has long been almost uniformly ignored in museum displays and exhibitions, a point which has been noted before. (Liddiard, 2004: 22)

> In many respects, the conventional idea is that the role of museums is to simply react to shifts in mainstream ideas and beliefs, albeit with a time-lag during which ideas about history and historical interpretation first become well established. In other words, the role of the museum is very much a *reactive* one, slowly reacting to shifts in popular thinking. However, in the context of the history of sexuality, it may well be that museums also have the capacity to act in a *proactive* manner, vigorously promoting alternative and innovative interpretations of the past. In other words, it may well be that museums are at the forefront, or at least have the potential for being at the forefront, of new and potentially challenging interpretations of the past. (Liddiard, 2004: 26, his emphases)

Sadly, some expected progress in 2006 fell by the wayside:

> National Museums Liverpool and Proud Heritage were successful in obtaining a grant from the Museums Libraries and Archives Council ... in 2006 to explore the establishment of a subject specialist network for LGBT heritage within museums. This allowed some preliminary work in identifying possible individuals and museums with an interest in the subject to be undertaken and funded a small but enthusiastic meeting of interested people in November 2006. A workshop on LGBT heritage at the Museums Association Conference in the

same year attracted an audience of over 60 participants and was further evidence of interest. An application to MLAC to develop the proposed network was not successful, however, and the momentum for any coordinated activity seems to have been lost for the time being. (Tibbles, 2012: 163-164)

Anthony Tibbles concluded his overview of LGBT work in museums by saying:

> One of the major problems for museums approaching this subject is the almost total absence of objects to assist in telling the story. Traditionally museums have not even considered this as an area of collecting and even if they had attempted to do so, it would have been almost impossible to know where to begin. It is only just over 40 years since homosexuality was decriminalised and for much of the intervening period LGBT people have continued to be stigmatised and to suffer prejudice. Many older people still come from a generation which finds it difficult, if not impossible, to discuss such matters.
>
> Few attempts have been made to engage with the LGBT community and, perhaps surprisingly, there has been little demand from the gay community for representation within museums. This may partly relate to a lack of confidence amongst LGBT populations and the lack of organisations within the community with an interest in their heritage. It may also be that a community which has only had official sanction for a matter of a few decades and which has yet to achieve the full recognition and acceptance that it deserves, has yet to value its own history and experience. (Tibbles, 2012: 164)

Archives

In the USA, members of the Society of American Archivists founded the Lesbian and Gay Archives Roundtable in 1989:

> The group, which welcomes non-members of the Society and people of all sexual orientations, promotes the preservation and research use of records documenting lesbian, gay, bisexual, and transgender history and serves as a liaison between lesbian, gay, bisexual, and transexual [sic] archives and the Society of American Archivists.
>
> We are committed to bringing information about lesbian, gay, bisexual, and transgender archives to the public ... and to helping small community-based archives with information about archival practices. (LAGAR, 2012)

In the UK, progress was much slower, and the focus on identifying LGBT archives issues did not start in earnest until after 2004 (please see chapter 6).

Chapter 6

2004-2013: Are we making progress?
A brief overview of the position of LGBT
people in the UK today

Introduction

This chapter looks at what has been achieved in terms of equality for LGBT people, and also outlines some key issues which LGBT people continue to face – it focuses on the position in the UK.

It is clear that much has been achieved over the last 10 years or so. However, it is also worth noting here that much of the recent progress in the UK (led particularly by Stonewall) has been via what Craig Rimmerman has called the 'assimilationist' approach (which may not be to everyone's liking):

> The assimilationist approach typically embraces a rights-based perspective, works within the broader framework of pluralist democracy … and fights for a seat at the table. In doing so, the assimilationists celebrate the 'work within the system' insider approach to political and social change … Assimilationists are more likely to accept that change will have to be incremental and to understand that slow, gradual progress is built into the very structure of the U.S. framework of government. In this way, they typically embrace an insider approach to political change. (Rimmerman, 2008: 5)

The approaches taken by the Gay Liberation Front (GLF) in its very early days and, more recently, by OutRage! (2012), for example, are clearly different:

> A second approach, the liberationist perspective, favors more radical cultural change, change that is transformational in nature and often arises outside the formal structures of the U.S. political system. Liberationists argue that there is a considerable gap between access and power and that it is simply not enough to have a seat at the table. For many liberationists, what is required is a shift in emphasis from a purely political strategy to one that embraces both structural political and cultural change, often through 'outsider' political strategies. (Rimmerman, 2008: 5)

It is also worth noting that queer theorists and activists have developed the liberationist position even further, so that, rather than trying to define people as lesbian or gay, they suggest that those people 'whose sexuality does not fit into the cultural standard of monogamous heterosexual marriage have adopted the "queer" label' (GLBTQ, 2006).

Overview of achievements

There has been rapid and welcome change in the period since 2004. Some examples follow.

Government, local government, legislation

- The crimes of buggery and gross indecency (used so often for arrests in the 1950s and 1960s) were abolished via the Sexual Offences Act (2004).
- The Civil Partnership Act was passed, giving same-sex couples the same rights and responsibilities as married heterosexual couples (2004).
- The first civil partnerships took place in Northern Ireland on 19 December 2005, followed by Scotland on 20 December and then England and Wales on 21 December.
- The Equality Act 2006 came into force, which established the Commission for Equalities and Human Rights (now the EHRC) and made discrimination against lesbians and gay men in the provision of goods and services illegal.
- Section 28 was repealed in the Isle of Man (2006).
- The Equality Act (Sexual Orientation) Regulations 2007 became law on 30 April, making discrimination against lesbians and gay men in the provision of goods and services illegal.
- Parliament passed provisions in the Criminal Justice and Immigration Act, creating a new offence of incitement to homophobic hatred (2008).
- Provisions from the Human Fertilisation and Embryology Act 2008 came into force to give legal recognition to lesbian parents who conceive a child through fertility treatment.
- The law changed in Scotland to give same-sex couples equality in adoption and fostering (2009).
- The Equality Act 2010 was passed, which included the extension of the single public Equality Duty to cover lesbian, gay and bisexual (LGB) people.
- Stonewall secured an amendment to the Equality Act 2010 to remove the ban on religious groups who wish to do so from holding civil partnerships on their premises.
- The coalition Government published the first ever LGBT policy programme, committing it to working towards greater LGBT equality (taken from: Stonewall, 2011a).

In addition, the process by which LGBT people can adopt has become more straightforward (Hill, N., 2012).

From October 2012, '[a]nyone with a historic conviction, caution, warning or reprimand for consensual gay sex, that meets the conditions laid down in the new Protection of Freedoms Act, will be encouraged to come forward and apply to have these records deleted or disregarded' (Home Office, 2012b).

Finally, in February 2013, MPs in the House of Commons voted by a majority of 225 in favour of the new Marriage (Same Sex Couples) Bill (Great Britain, 2013); the Bill will then go through further stages, including the Commons Committee and the House of Lords.

In 2004, the Employer's Organisation for Local Government and the Local Government Association (in collaboration with the Association of London Government, Stonewall and UNISON) published *Sexuality – the New Agenda* (Creegan and Lee, 2004), a milestone in getting LGBT issues onto the local government agenda and which also highlighted good practice; the report was updated in 2007 (Creegan and Lee, 2007), although it has now been overtaken by events.

The Government Equalities Office has continued to take a lead in supporting areas of LGBT rights – for example:

- publishing, in July 2010, the first ever cross-Government work plan on LGBT rights (Home Office, 2010), followed by the action plan in March 2011 (Home Office, 2011c);
- launching the Sports Charter in March 2011 (Home Office 2011a);
- publishing, in December 2011, the UK Government action plan for transgender equality (Home Office, 2011b);
- commissioning research into the barriers to employers developing LGBT-friendly workplaces (Government Equalities Office, 2011; Metcalf and Rolfe, 2011).

In addition, the Equalities Office has responsibility for the provisions within the Equality Act 2010, which protect LGB people: 'It is illegal to discriminate on the grounds of sexual orientation when providing goods, facilities or services, in education, when selling or letting premises or when exercising public functions' (Home Office, ca. 2012).

The Equality Commission for Northern Ireland has also been ensuring that LGBT issues are kept on the agenda, for example by marking Trans Memorial Day in November 2012 (Equality Commission for Northern Ireland, 2012b), and by promoting a key piece of research into the experiences of disabled LGBT people (McClenahan, 2012).

Work with children and young people

Some schools have made strides in tackling homophobia and bullying in general (Ofsted, 2012a) – for example, the outstanding work at Stoke Newington School and Sixth Form College developed by Elly Barnes (Head of Year 7) (Ofsted, 2012b); the setting up of a Gay-Straight Alliance club at Copland Community School in Wembley (Vasagar, 2012). In addition, Ofsted have produced a briefing for use during inspections of maintained schools and academies, *Exploring the school's actions to prevent homophobic bullying* (Ofsted, 2012a), which gives specific guidance to assist inspectors in their assessment of schools' role in dealing with LGBT issues.

LGBT History Month

In February 2005, Schools OUT (Sanders, 2012b) initiated the UK version[1] of LGBT History Month. It is now organised by a voluntary steering group, with related Scottish events being organised by LGBT Youth Scotland (LGBT Youth Scotland, ca. 2012) and Welsh events by the LGBT Excellence Centre (Heritage Lottery Fund, 2011; LGBT Excellence Centre, 2011).

LGBT History Month 2012 was the most prominent so far. For the first time, an official guide to the month was provided as a free pull-out in a national newspaper. In his foreword to the guide, which appeared in the *Guardian*, David Cameron wrote:

> The LGBT community contributes a huge amount to the UK and I hope this month is a well-deserved celebration of that… There is certainly more work to be done, but together, in 2012, we can show the world what it means to live in a country that is determined to make life free and fair for everyone. (Cameron, D., 2012)

The theme for 2012 was sport; this was reflected in many of the events, and, in addition, LGBT History Month gained a high profile in all four Home Nations:

> many areas organised matches and tournaments. In Norwich, a five-aside tournament termed 'Kick Homophobia out of Football' … was held on February 19th, birthday of the late Norwich City star Justin Fashanu – still the only professional football player to ever come out as gay during his career. In Bristol,

---

1   LGBT History Month originated in the United States and was first celebrated in 1994; it is celebrated in October (which was chosen because National Coming Out Day was already in that month, and it also commemorated the first march on Washington by LGBT people in 1979).

meanwhile, a match was held between two gay-friendly rugby clubs, Bristol Bisons RFC and Manchester Spartans RFC, to celebrate the month.

... in Wales, leading dignitaries declared their support for [LGBT] people at the opening event of LGBT History Month Cymru 2012 on the 1st of February at the Senedd in Cardiff. Welsh government minister Huw Lewis opened proceedings, followed by speeches by Kirsty Williams, Member of the National Assembly for Wales (AM), leader of the Welsh Liberal Democrats, and Lindsay Whittle, AM for Plaid Cymru.

Gillian Clarke, National Poet for Wales, concluded the launch with a poem written specially for the occasion, marking the first time a national poet has ever officially celebrated LGBT people. Entitled 'Sarah at Plas Newydd, July 5th 1788', the poem concerned Eleanor Butler and Sarah Ponsonby, the famous 'Ladies of Llangollen' who lived together in Wales from 1780 to 1829, and who some believe were a lesbian couple ... The National Assembly for Wales also flew the rainbow flag outside the Senedd ...

Meanwhile, in Scotland, an Equal Marriage March was held on February 14th – Valentine's Day – down the Royal Mile to the Scottish Parliament. The event was organised by a number of groups, including the Scottish Youth Parliament and Stonewall Scotland, and followed a public consultation in December on same-sex marriage and civil partnerships, which the Parliament is currently reviewing. Over a thousand people turned out with colourful banners to demonstrate their support for marriage equality. The march culminated in a rally outside the Scottish Parliament, with speakers including Patrick Harvie, co-leader of the Greens and Scottish Youth Parliament chairman Grant Costello ...

Events during the month explored both the history of LGBT people, and their current experiences. Historical guided tours, such as 'Peers and Queers' in Brighton, 'The Queens of Eltham Palace' in Greenwich's royal palace, and other walks throughout Britain – from Bath to Nunhead Cemetery in Southwark – helped the public discover the often unacknowledged LGBT individuals throughout history.

At the same time, contemporary issues were presented and debated by occasions like Queer Question Time on February 1st at Southwark's Glaziers' Hall. This long-running event had the theme of homophobia and transphobia in sport this year, and the panellists included activist Peter Tatchell, sports broadcaster Bob Ballard and Kelly Simmons, Head of National Game for the FA. Other talks and exhibitions also dealt with the modern day lives of LGBT people, including 'Talking Heads' in Cardiff, an evening where people told ten minute stories about their lives, and 'I am a Poem' in Folkestone, a fortnight of poetry, art and performance organised by artist Vince Laws. (Sanders, 2012a)

LGBT media visibility

In addition, LGBT visibility in the media seems at an all-time high – even recognising the limitations identified by Stonewall's recent report (Stonewall, ca. 2010) – with, for example, gay men and lesbians featured in soaps such as

Coronation Street and *EastEnders*; in award-winning comedies such as *Benidorm*; high-profile presenters, such as Clare Balding and Gok Wan; and a rash of new TV and media stars coming out, such as singer and *X Factor* winner Joe McElderry (Watts, L., 2011) – even if he is still the focus of some homophobic abuse (Park, 2012) – Marcus Collins (*X Factor* runner-up) and Nick Grimshaw, new host of BBC Radio One's *Breakfast* show (Out in the City, 2012).

Faith and religion

During 2012, much was being made of 'clashes' between LGBT people and some elements of faith communities. Some of this has arisen from the legal interpretation of the Equality Act (Great Britain, 2010): as the EHRC have described, '[t]he law in relation to equality, human rights and religion or belief is relatively new and far from settled … There has been a considerable amount of litigation, much of which has been controversial' (Donald *et al.*, 2012: vi-vii).

Certainly there is prejudice, as one interviewee has identified:

> In more recent years, an event to celebrate Pride at one of my libraries … attracted a large audience including a Muslim man who came wearing latex gloves and harassed a Muslim member of staff running the event, demanding to know his sexuality and when he told him he was gay, being extremely abusive before being ejected. Religious objectors still surface quite regularly and I had lengthy correspondence with another customer regarding the availability of the *Pink Paper* in one particular library before having to inform her that I wouldn't be continuing the dialogue and that the paper would be staying. (Whittle, A., 2013)

However, recent research by Stonewall (Hunt and Valentine [2011]), based on discussions with six focus groups with people who are Christian, Muslim, Jewish, and Hindu, and lesbian and gay people within those faith communities, showed that this was by no means an universal opinion:

- Participants acknowledged that some parts of their faith community objected to lesbian and gay sexuality.
- However, participants suggested that these objections were often over-emphasised and narrowly reflected by both religious leaders on the one hand and by the media on the other (Hunt and Valentine [2011]: 2).

Attitudes towards LGBT people

Finally, recent research by Stonewall has shown that, although there are still many improvements required, nevertheless attitudes in the UK have changed:

- Three in five people of faith (58 per cent) support Government plans to extend civil marriage to same-sex couples.

- Four in five people (81 per cent) believe it is right to tackle prejudice against LGB people where they say it exists.
- Seven in ten people (71 per cent) support the Government's commitment to extend the legal form and name of civil marriage to same-sex couples (Guasp and Dick, 2012: 3).

And yet ...

However, despite these major developments, there is still some considerable way to go to see full LGBT equality – and to end discrimination against anyone who is identified as 'different'. Commentators in Scotland have questioned whether progress on equality for LGBT people has been quite as thorough and ongoing as is often suggested (Miller, O., 2011). In Northern Ireland too there seems to be much work to do:

> The Commission's recent Equality Awareness Survey showed that a quarter of people responding expressed negative attitudes to the prospect of having a gay, lesbian or bi-sexual person as a neighbour and 40% said they wouldn't want a close relative to be in a relationship with a gay person. (Equality Commission for Northern Ireland, 2012c)

It is also clear that there is still a lot that is not known about LGBT people, particularly in the workplace:

> Traditionally, sexual orientation has been seen as a private matter, not the business of wider society. Of course, the private lives of individuals are not for public consumption, but without clearer evidence – on where LGB people live, where they work, what their experiences and needs of public services are – we are missing a vital piece of the jigsaw when it comes to making public policy. Evidence is the key to making services reflect everyone's experiences and meet their needs. Therefore we consider it vital to start collecting more robust data. (Phillips, 2009: 5)

This 'lack of visibility' means that:

> In many places, there are no obvious lesbian, gay and bisexual 'communities'. This may be because in these areas lesbian, gay and bisexual people are geographically dispersed and do not have contact with others through social networks or commercial venues. However, it may also be that because of social or personal pressures they are not able to openly express their sexuality or fear hostility if they do. While some people may be content with this, for others it can be difficult and isolating. (Creegan and Lee, 2007: 10)

In addition, of course: 'The word 'communities' can also be misleading. LGB people are not a homogenous group and many may feel uncomfortable with the term. Even in towns and cities with gay "villages" or "scenes", such places do not attract everyone' (Creegan and Lee, 2007: 11).

Some of the key issues are explored briefly below – and, in relation to LBT women, are all looked at in more depth in a recent report from the Women's Resource Centre (Gage, 2010).

Hostility, prejudice and homophobia (and related issues)

Research by Stonewall (2003), which was expanded in 2004 (Valentine, G., and McDonald, 2004), identified five different kinds of prejudice against LGBT people, and it is clear that these remain:

- aggressive
- banal (mundane examples that may be intentional or unintentional and which pass unnoticed)
- benevolent (positive views which may still produce negative consequences)
- cathartic – 'a release of views recognised as being less positive about minority groups, and therefore unacceptable, that is justified and therefore rendered acceptable' (Valentine, G., and McDonald, 2004: 16)
- unintentional.

There is currently no legal definition of a homophobic or transphobic incident. However, the Crown Prosecution Service has adopted the following definition: 'Any incident which is perceived to be homophobic or transphobic by the victim or any other person' (Crown Prosecution Service, 2009: 3).

The police and the Crown Prosecution Service have been taking homophobic crimes more seriously – as well they should, given the incidence (Dick, n.d., ca. 2008; Home Office, 2012a) – and there is an increasing focus on justice and the equalities aspects of hate crimes (see, for example: Crown Prosecution Service, 2012; Dick, 2009).

The EU has recently published a major report on discrimination against transgender and intersex people across the EU which, it is hoped, will lead to action at a pan-European and national level (Agius and Tobler, 2011).

The impact of negative reporting by the media was illustrated in 2008 by the immense pressure put on the project, 'No Outsiders':

> No Outsiders was an ambitious project trialled in 15 primaries, which aimed to promote tolerance and introduced children as young as five to the words gay and lesbian.
>
> But it was forced to cancel its launch this month after tabloid claims that it was teaching 'the pleasures of gay sex' to children. (Brettingham, 2008)

This has also been explored in some depth in relation to gay politicians in the UK, where, whilst media coverage is generally improving (for example in terms of the language used to describe LGBT people), nevertheless politicians (and, by extension, possibly anyone focused on by the media) have to steer a complex course if they are to be 'acceptable' to the press. Donna Smith has argued that the media tend to see things in simplistic, binary terms, so a 'positive' media image for a politician would be someone who is private about what they do, but is 'out', is regarded as a 'good' person and is also seen as 'safe' and 'clean'. She shows that politicians who do not conform to all these criteria – such as Peter Tatchell – are cast as 'bad' LGBT people by the press and are treated accordingly (Smith, D., 2012).

The level of intolerance (and homophobia) in business in the UK has recently been criticised by Lord Browne[2] – and picked up by the national media (Bawden, 2012). As he said in a speech to the new LGBT network established by the engineering and design consultants, Arup: *'Being gay* didn't harm my career. But hiding my sexuality *did* make me unhappy and, in the end, it didn't work' (Browne, 2012: 2, his emphases):

> Despite the exemplary diversity policies in many companies, my sense is that the business world remains more intolerant of homosexuality than other worlds such as the legal profession, the media and the visual arts ...
>
> I am one of only a handful of publicly gay people to have run a FTSE 100 company.
>
> In some industries, the situation is particularly bad. Among the many people I know in private equity, where I now work, fewer than 1% are openly gay.
>
> Even today there are many people out there still afraid to reveal who they really are for fear of marginalisation and abuse. (Browne, 2012: 4)

There also still appear to be different standards in relation to media coverage of lesbians and gay men, for example:

> It's strange that lesbianism has enjoyed a public rehabilitation that male homosexuality hasn't ... It's depressing, though, because it has roots in the fact that male sexual impulses must be thought of as dangerous, where female ones are just a bit of a game, comical even, and these perceptions don't help anyone, gay or straight. At a time when attitudes should be evolving to match infinite social variety, we seem to be battening down the hatches and becoming ever more entrenched in handy archetypes that won't challenge the

---

2   John Browne, Baron Browne of Madingley (1948-), 'is President of the Royal Academy of Engineering and was group Chief Executive of BP until his resignation on 1 May 2007. Since 2001, he has been a crossbench member of the House of Lords' (Wikipedia, 2012o).

status quo. We need to understand that sexuality isn't just black and white. (Walker, H., 2012)[3]

Finally, a reminder from one of the interviewees of the day-to-day reality for many LGBT people:

> Personally I have not experienced hostility either in the workplace or on the street, but I do adapt my behavior when in public and do not risk showing affection to my wife on the tube or walking down the street. As I have always done this, I don't know what it would feel like to be able to give a kiss or a cuddle as a natural thing out in the open. I think this eventually does affect the way we are together, because there is always a thought process to go through regarding safety before you can emotionally express yourself.
>
> The only time this has been possible is during a big LGBT festival such as the Gay Games when you are surrounded by thousands of Gay people all being open with affection. That is really something special. (Logan, 2013)

Sport

The general assumption is that homophobia is rife in sport; however, there is some recent evidence that this may be increasingly inaccurate, for example that 'wider cultural and social changes in relation to homophobia are starting to manifest themselves in more relaxed and tolerant attitudes within team sports' (Warwick University. Department of History, 2010).

Whilst this heartening trend may well build into much greater tolerance in sport in the future, the position in 2012 is still far from rosy. For example, young people looking for sporting role models will be hard pressed to find many in some sports (such as football and boxing); and a recent report by the National Union of Students has identified a number of intimidating barriers to LGBT people's participation in sport, for example finding the 'culture around sport alienating or unwelcoming' (NUS, 2012: 5). Sporting bodies and the Government have made a commitment to 'make sport a welcoming environment for lesbian, gay, bisexual and transgender (LGBT) people' (Sport England, 2012).

Coming out

What's the need for anyone to come out? A frequent cry is that there is no need for anyone to come out in the twenty-first century and/or that what someone does in their private life is their own business.

True though these claims may be, people do still come out:

---

3   Harriet Walker was commenting on a bizarre-sounding article in *Tatler*, 'Where are all the lesbians? London's loveliest, liveliest lesbians tell it like it is' (Tatler, 2012).

because, sooner or later, they can't stand hiding who they are anymore. They want their relationships to be stronger, richer, more fulfilling and real. Once we do come out, most of us find that it feels far better to be open and honest than to hide such a basic part of ourselves. We also come to recognize that our personal decision to live openly helps break down barriers and stereotypes that have kept others in the closet. And in doing so, we make it easier for others to follow our example. (Lesbian Advocacy Services Initiative, n.d.)

Yet, in a recent survey:

Only half of lesbians, gay men and bisexual women and a third of bisexual men felt they could be open about their sexual orientation without fear of prejudice or discrimination in schools, colleges or universities. Around half of lesbians and gay men, a third of bisexual women and a fifth of bisexual men believed they could be open in their local police station. Only 28 per cent of gay men and lesbians felt they could be open about their sexual orientation when walking through their local neighbourhood. Fear of prejudice was less acute, although still present, for many people in their workplaces, local health services and their families.

When asked about incidents of prejudice and discrimination that were related to their sexual orientation, the majority of gay men (63 per cent) and lesbians (66 per cent) said they had experienced name calling and other forms of verbal abuse. Around half of lesbians and gay men and a third of bisexual women and men reported that they had suffered stress. Around four in ten lesbians and gay men reported that they had been bullied, or felt frightened, and had suffered from low self-esteem. Around one in five gay men reported they had been physically assaulted and six per cent of lesbians that they had been sexually assaulted. Nine per cent of gay men and fourteen per cent of bisexual men reported a current mental health condition, as did 16 per cent of lesbians and over a quarter (26 per cent) of bisexual women. This contrasts sharply with just three per cent of heterosexual men and eight per cent of heterosexual women. (Ellison and Gunstone, 2009: 11)

In addition, there is still a very real need for a range of role models, especially for young people – and role models of different types, as Charlie Condou, writer, gay rights activist and *Coronation Street* actor, argued: 'I think there are a number of ways of challenging the toxic homophobia that is present in many schools. First, I do think that role models are important; the more gay actors, sports stars and public figures who are living their lives openly and honestly, the better' (Condou, 2011).

Elton John too has emphasised the need for 'different' families to come out (John, 2011), again to make it 'normal' for children to have parents of the same gender.

Sadly, for 2012, there are still huge issues about LGBT actors coming out. As out gay actor Ben Daniels stated:

> There are actors I know who won't come out, and I can see it crippling them as human beings. It's a great shame that people can't be who they are in the twenty-first century, and people won't let them be who they are … Of course, there are gay A-list movie stars in existence. It's just that we, the public, don't know who they are ... Lying about one's sexuality seems to be one of the ridiculous rules of what constitutes being a Hollywood movie star. (Park, 2011)

At the time of writing, Equity (the actors' union) had just launched an initiative to support LGBT actors coming out (Broch, 2012).

Some famous people have come out despite warnings that it could affect their careers, for example Ricky Martin: 'He added that he had kept his sexuality hidden because advisers had told him coming out could hurt his career' (BBC News, 2010).

Yet it does not have to be like this! Some very positive coming-out stories include:

- Orlando Cruz, boxer (Dirs, 2012)
- Frank Ocean, singer (Walker, T., 2012)
- Laura Jane Grace, punk musician (coming out as trans) (Walker, T., 2012)
- Anton Hysén, at the time of writing the only out gay professional footballer in the world (The Justin Campaign, 2011)
- Mary Portas, businesswoman and retail expert (Cochrane, 2010)
- Gareth Thomas, rugby player (BBC Sport, 2009)
- Donal Óg Cusack, Irish hurler (Moynihan, 2009)
- John Amaechi, former basketball star (Younge, 2007).

At a less celebrity level – but still rare as an example – Bristol City Council have produced a positive record of LGB people's experiences of working in the public sector (Bristol City Council, 2012), perhaps best summed up by a Youth Justice Social Worker: 'To make my life easier, I decided to be out and I have no intention of not being out as I am a role model to the young people around me. I think it's important that LGB staff are seen in a positive light' (Smart, 2012).

In addition, there is a small, but growing, trend for 'straight' men to support LGBT rights, for example retired rugby-player, Ben Cohen, setting up his Foundation to tackle bullying and homophobia (The Ben Cohen StandUp Foundation, 2012); and a wide range of 'celebrities' featuring on the cover of *Attitude*, for example: footballers David Beckham and Matt Jarvis; boxer Luke Campbell; actor Daniel Radcliffe; musicians Harry Judd and McFly, JLS (although, in some cases, this may well also have been a handy career move!).

Of course, the day when people do not feel the need to come out at all would be very welcome; commenting on the coming out of Frank Ocean (and contrasting this with the outing of Anderson Cooper, the Cable News Network anchor), Owen Jones wrote:

> But the very fact that coming out – whether you're a TV anchor, pop star, teacher or train driver – remains such an event shows how far the struggle for equality has to go … We will have achieved total equality when 'coming out' is completely abolished as a process. Being gay will not be seen as a separate, defining identity. The frequent social segregation of LGBT and straight people will be ended. (Jones, O., 2012)

Young people

Despite all the improvements that have taken place, life for young people can be tough: 'There is no doubt that, in many ways, things have got better for us queer folk and yet, despite all the progress, we still live in a country where two-thirds of gay teenagers are bullied at school. Why are things so slow to change?' (Condou, 2011).

Recent research by Stonewall has shown that 'Levels of homophobic bullying have fallen by 10 per cent since 2007 and the number of schools saying that homophobic bullying is wrong has more than doubled, to 50 per cent' (Summerskill, B., 2012b), but that schools can still be damaging places (Guasp, 2012, n.d.).

The facts are grim:

- Almost two-thirds (65 per cent) of young LGB people experience homophobic bullying in Britain's schools.
- Ninety-seven per cent of gay pupils hear derogatory phrases such as 'dyke' or 'poof' used in school.
- Ninety-eight per cent of gay pupils hear 'that's so gay' or 'you're so gay' at school.
- Seventy-five per cent of young gay people in faith schools experience homophobic bullying and are less likely than pupils in other schools to report it.
- Only a quarter of schools say that homophobic bullying is wrong in their school. In schools that have said homophobic bullying is wrong, gay young people are 60 per cent more likely not to have been bullied.
- Thirty per cent of lesbian and gay pupils report that adults are responsible for homophobic incidents in their schools.
- Of those who have been bullied, 92 per cent have experienced verbal homophobic bullying, 41 per cent physical bullying and 17 per cent death threats. (Hunt and Jensen, ca. 2007: 3)

This picture has been reinforced by more recent research in Greater Manchester, which found, for example, that 85 per cent of teachers reported observing or overhearing pupils being subjected to homophobic abuse, discrimination and/or bullying (Greater Manchester NUT, 2012); in Scotland, where '69% of all LGBT respondents had experienced homophobic or biphobic bullying in school with the number still high at 25% in college and 14% at university' (LGBT Youth Scotland, 2012); and in South Yorkshire, where recent research into discrimination against young people found:

> Young people identified the existence of homophobic bullying in relation to young people identifying as (or rumoured to be) LGB, those with parents in same-sex relationships, and those that were perceived to be "different" in some way, thereby marking them out as potentially gay. This included much experience of verbal abuse, though was not restricted to this. (Formby, 2011: 6)

This was echoed in the Stonewall report *Different Families*, which identified some of the issues faced by young people whose parents were lesbian or gay (Guasp, 2010).

Research has also shown that homophobic bullying has a major impact on young people's lives; for example:

- leading to a greater risk of suicide
- absenteeism from school, truancy
- can lead to underachievement. (Warwick *et al.*, 2004: 23)

In a Northern Ireland study:

- Twenty-nine per cent of young people taking part in the research had attempted suicide.
- Forty-four per cent of young people were bullied at school because of their sexuality.
- Of the 63 per cent of young people who experienced negative attitudes in school around sexual orientation, only 13 per cent of these sought support.
- Sixty-nine per cent of young people who left school earlier than they would have preferred were also bullied.
- Young LGBT people are five times more likely to be medicated for depression.
- Fifty per cent of young people who identified as transgendered had self harmed.
- Fifty per cent of young people experienced a negative attitude towards sexual orientation whilst being a member of a youth organisation. (YouthNet, 2003: 3)

This situation has been recognised in prioritising sexual orientation as one of the areas of Key Inequality (Equality Commission for Northern Ireland, 2008, 2012a), and in the work being undertaken to produce guidance for school and college staff in Northern Ireland (Cowley, 2011).

Reinforcing this, a European study of young LGBT people (Takács, 2006) identified the key areas of social exclusion as being:

- invisibility (including invisibility in research)
- mental health
- school environment.

And an earlier NYA study (Valentine, G., *et al.*, 2003) of why some young people are particularly 'vulnerable' to social exclusion found that they were being marginalised in three important areas:

- home
- educational institutions
- the workplace.

Schools are frequently poor at responding:

- Almost three in five (58 per cent) lesbian and gay pupils who experience bullying never report it. If they tell a teacher, 62 per cent of the time nothing is done.
- Half of teachers fail to respond to homophobic language when they hear it.
- Just 7 per cent of teachers are reported to respond every time they hear homophobic language. (Hunt and Jensen, ca. 2007: 3)

They may also be providing almost no information for young LGBT people (from a survey carried out in Birmingham in 2011): 'When asked if they were aware of any information and resources available at their schools about sexual orientation, just 1.1% (5/469) gave an unqualified "Yes"' (Wood, 2011: 45).

'Only five people out of 458 indicated that there was a little information available at school on gender identity. This equates to 1.1%. These five people were all from the Under 35s group. For the older cohort, there was a unanimous "No"' (Wood, 2011: 46).

The impact on young people can be devastating:

- Seven out of ten gay pupils who experience homophobic bullying state that this has had an impact on their school work.
- Half of those who have experienced homophobic bullying have skipped school at some point because of it and one in five has skipped school more than six times.
- Seven in ten gay pupils have never been taught about lesbian and gay people or issues in class.
- Over 60 per cent of young lesbian and gay people feel that there is neither an adult at home nor at school who they can talk to about being gay.

- Four in five young gay people have no access in school to resources that can help them (Hunt and Jensen, ca. 2007: 3).

A recent study in the USA on teenage suicide (Hatzenbuehler, 2011) found that 'Lesbian, gay and bisexual teens are five times more likely to attempt suicide than their heterosexual peers – but those living in a supportive community might be a little better off' (Pittman, 2011). In addition, the myth that young people need 'protecting' from knowing about LGBT issues is perpetuated:[4] for example, a recent survey by Stonewall (ca. 2010) of television programmes watched by young people found not only very low levels of LGBT issues presented, but also that they were often portrayed as negative images and stereotypes:

> Groundbreaking research ... found that ordinary gay people are almost invisible on the 20 TV programmes most watched by Britain's young people. Just 46 minutes out of 126 hours of output showed gay people positively and realistically. Three quarters of portrayal was confined to just four C4 and ITV1 programmes: *I'm a Celebrity...*, *Hollyoaks*, *Emmerdale* and *How to Look Good Naked*. BBC1 transmitted 44 seconds of positive and realistic portrayal of gay people in more than 39 hours of output. (Stonewall, 2011c)

However, it is also important to note that, from his recent research, Mark McCormack (McCormack, 2012) has suggested that this is not the full picture and that, whilst there are still areas where young people experience hostility, in many homophobia – and homohysteria – are on the decline.[5]

---

4   This view had been reinforced by the effects of Clause 28 – for example: 'post Thatcher's Clause 28 hysteria, one of the Councillors went mad when he discovered I'd made a list of "How to deal with homosexuality" [books] for youth leaders. When I talked to the Diocesan Youth Organiser, his comment was "it is always some adult who thinks there's a problem and in his/her ignorance creates a fuss"' (Hartley, 2012).

5   Mark McCormack also takes a critical side-swipe at Stonewall: 'Although some research published in nonacademic sources continues to argue that schools are highly homophobic, most of these studies lack both the methodological and the analytical rigor required to contribute to academic discussion of homophobia in schools ...' (McCormack, 2012: 61), citing two Stonewall reports (Guasp, no date; Hunt and Jensen, 2007) as examples.

> He goes on to suggest that: 'It is also worth noting that those who report the most homophobia are often tied to organizations designed to prevent it. For example, Stonewall ... still argues that there is an "epidemic" of homophobia in schools. However, in doing so, it damages both its own credibility and potentially the experiences of closeted students who are attempting to assess the homophobia of their school environment' (McCormack, 2012: 61).

Racism and other issues facing BME LGBT people

Despite many people having ambitions for a 'rainbow' coalition of people united against discrimination and inequality, nevertheless there are strong elements of racism within LGBT communities (and homophobia amongst BME communities):

> As black LGBT people, we face the dual challenges of racial prejudice and of homophobia, within society at large but particularly from within those communities we belong to, both sexually and ethnically. Few other groups of individuals will have to endure such prejudices simultaneously and to such a debilitating degree. (Sylla, 2011)

'Any social or cultural history on the black experience and the wider gay community which does not include us is misleading' (Ajamu, 2011a).

Based on his research into the lives of Black British gay men (following the 2007 Reunion of participants in the UK's first and only Black Gay Men's Conference),[6] Antoine Rogers has argued that there is a need to look at 'the complex intersection of race and sexuality in a British context' (Rogers, A., 2012: 43); that much of the investigation into the needs of Black gay men is too simplistic and assumes that their situation is the same as that of white gay men; and he concluded that: 'Traditional discourse related to sexuality, "coming out" and engagement with the wider LGBT social and cultural context do not always account for differences in the negotiation of sexual identity (and the factors that impact on that negotiation of that identity) that clearly exist within this community' (Rogers, A., 2012: 56).

Antoine Rogers quoted from an interview with a young Black man, Steven, who explains clearly some of the complexities:

> Coming out or being gay is different for me and a lot of Black gay men I know. They (white gay men) come out and tell everyone; friends, parents, the postman. When I talk with them (white gay men) and they realize my parents and a lot of people in my life don't know, they assume I'm in some kinda denial or closeted ... I'm happy with myself, who I am but I wasn't gonna throw this in my family's face ... I don't agree with my family's views obviously but I know how much their faith and values helps them survive the shit they go through. God – their God – seems to get them through so who am I to blatantly contradict their values ... What good would it serve? (Rogers, A., 2012: 51)

---

6   The original Conference, 'In This Our Lives', was held in October 1987; the Reunion took place in October 2007. There is further discussion about the role of the Conference and Reunion, and the importance of collecting Black British LGBT people's archives in *Archivaria* (Ajamu, X., *et al.*, 2009).

A recent report from Stonewall and the Runnymede Trust has emphasised how many services are failing to recognise that people from BME communities may also be LGBT – which 'assumption can then lead to poor service delivery and inappropriate service responses' (Guasp and Kibirige, 2012: 2). A major cause is the lack of awareness and training for service staff in understanding the needs of people with multiples identities.

One way of working progressively may be to create shared spaces for Black LGBT people, such as happens at UK Black Pride (Oyekanmi, 2011; UK Black Pride, 2011).

New arrivals – refugees, asylum-seekers, migrant workers

Refugees who have fled their country of origin because of their sexuality[7] are not always made welcome on their arrival in the UK; for example, a blog-post by Angela Hsu for the Migrants' Rights Network suggested: 'Not only are refugee and asylum bureaucracies gender-blind and often discriminatory towards women, but the UK asylum system turns a blind eye to the realities of gay and lesbian asylum-seekers' (Hsu, 2011).

The Runnymede Trust has shown that, despite:

> [a] landmark judgement by the British Supreme Court in July 2010 [which] ruled that the Home Office could not send gay and lesbian asylum seekers back to their home country where there was a culture of homophobia and persecution of gay and lesbian people, even if they could live 'discreetly' ...
>
> ... the Home Office is increasingly dismissive of evidence that an asylum seeker is gay. This leads not only to the asylum seeker being at extreme risk when they are sent back to their home country, but also to a level of injustice that is hard to stomach. (Gibbs, 2011)

This is despite the fact that 'if a person does have a well founded fear of persecution because they are gay or lesbian then they can qualify for asylum' (UK Lesbian & Gay Immigration Group, n.d.).

---

7   'State-sponsored homophobia and transphobia remain prevalent in many parts of the globe. At least 80 countries around the world criminalise sexual contact between consenting adults of the same sex, and in some of them, for example Iran, Mauritania, Saudi Arabia, Sudan and Yemen, as well as parts of Nigeria and Somalia – homosexual conduct is punishable with the death penalty' (Cowen *et al.*, 2011).

In addition, at the time of writing, there was particular concern about LGBT people from Uganda (Changing Attitude, 2011; Day 2011); and Jamaica (BBC News Stoke & Staffordshire, 2011). Stonewall maintain webpages devoted to immigration and asylum (Stonewall, 2013).

Getting older

Older LGBT people are often 'invisible' (Traies, 2012) – regarded by medical and care practitioners more in terms of their age than their specific requirements – and, where they are identified, trans people in particular face high levels of discrimination and, often, harassment (Bailey, 2012; Learner, 2012; Whittle, S. *et al.*, 2007).

The specific needs of older LGBT people are, finally, being recognised, for example across Europe, by Stonewall and by the Joseph Rowntree Foundation (JRF).

In Europe, AGE Platform Europe and ILGA-Europe have published a policy paper, calling for action to be taken both at European and national levels:

> [They] advocate for a comprehensive and coherent approach to tackling multiple discrimination on the grounds of age, sex, sexual orientation, gender identity and gender expression and call for the development of adequate policy responses to support ageing LGBTI communities. (ILGA Europe and AGE Platform Europe, 2012)

Stonewall have published a report on older LGB people:

> Getting older can be much more complex for lesbian, gay and bisexual people than heterosexual people as they are more likely to face the prospect either alone or without as much personal support as their heterosexual counterparts …
> Lesbian, gay and bisexual people are nearly twice as likely as their heterosexual peers to expect to rely on a range of external services, including GPs, health and social care services and paid help.
> However, at the same time lesbian, gay and bisexual people feel that providers of services won't be able to understand and meet their needs … As a result nearly half would be uncomfortable being out to care home staff, a third would be uncomfortable being out to a housing provider, hospital staff or a paid carer, and approximately one in five wouldn't feel comfortable disclosing their sexual orientation to their GP.
> Significant numbers of disabled lesbian, gay and bisexual people also report that they have not accessed the health, mental health and social care services in the last year that they felt they needed. (Stonewall, 2011b: 3)

In early 2012, JRF published a new Web resource (Joseph Rowntree Foundation, 2012), supported by papers identifying needs of different groups of older people – the one on LGB people (Knocker, 2012) highlights some key areas of concern.

Health

A lesbian and bisexual women's health-check, published in 2008, found that:

- half have had negative experiences in the health sector in the last year, despite the fact that it is now unlawful to discriminate against lesbian and bisexual women;
- half of lesbian and bisexual women are not out to their GP;
- one in ten say that a healthcare worker ignored them when they did come out;
- just three in ten lesbian and bisexual women say that healthcare workers did not make inappropriate comments when they came out;
- just one in ten felt that their partner was welcome during a consultation (Hunt and Fish, 2008: 4).

In 2012, Stonewall published a survey of gay and bisexual men's health, and found a similar picture:

> With 6,861 respondents from across Britain, this is the largest survey ever conducted of gay and bisexual men's health needs in the world. However, it demonstrates that many of those needs are not being met and that there are areas of significant concern – most particularly in mental health and drug use – that have been overlooked by health services which too often focus solely on gay men's sexual health.
>
> This report also provides hard evidence that gay and bisexual men nationwide are more likely to attempt suicide, self-harm and have depression than their straight peers. They are also more likely to smoke, drink and take illegal drugs. It ill-serves our gay and bisexual communities when these uncomfortable truths are ignored.
>
> Patients accessing healthcare should be confident that they'll be treated compassionately, confidentially and with complete openness. But this pioneering research reveals that for many gay and bisexual men in Britain this is simply not the case. (Summerskill, B., 2012a)

The Department of Health published a series of briefings in 2007 (Fish, 2007) which set out barriers and ways of overcoming these, but these have not yet percolated through to all areas of health provision.

Conclusions

It is undoubtedly true to say that the position for some LGBT people in the UK has improved – and some enormous hurdles have been overcome – yet, at the same time, as this chapter indicates, there is still a long way to go before everyone achieves social justice and is treated fairly and equally.

How have these changes been reflected by the cultural sector? This will be explored in chapter 7.

And are we making progress in the cultural sector?

Introduction

After the repeal of Clause 28 across the UK (and lastly in England in 2003), there was a mood of some optimism, both broadly, but also more specifically in the cultural sector, and this chapter looks at the pace of development of services and initiatives (and whether these have reflected general societal changes). What is particularly noteworthy is the sudden development of practice in museums and archives, and possible reasons for this – and what can be drawn from them – are considered further in chapter 9.

LGBT History Month

One of the major developments has been the growing involvement of the cultural sector in LGBT History Month – examples are cited in Appendix 2.

Libraries

There have been immense developments in the library sector since 2004 – but there is still considerable progress to be made: in the words of David Murray, 'provision is a patchwork made up of rich and impressive threads and the very threadbare' (Murray, 2012).

This view is very much echoed by Elizabeth L. Chapman:

> I have been working in the library sector for a relatively short period of time (starting in 2003) but, based on articles I have read about the situation in the 1970s, 80s and 90s, I sadly don't think things have changed very much over this period. Then, as now, there seemed to be a few enthusiastic voices urging for greater attention to LGBT library users (as well as other diverse user groups), but these pockets of activism were surrounded by a great deal of inactivity in the rest of the sector. In many cases, I think that the problem is more to do with lack of awareness than overt prejudice; in my own research on provision of LGBT-related fiction to children and young people, I found that librarians freely admitted that they just hadn't thought about this area. However, within

the LGBT spectrum I feel that there are certain groups of people, such as trans and genderqueer people, who suffer disproportionately from other people's prejudice and lack of understanding. (Chapman, E.L., 2012b)

This section looks at the following key areas: service provision; engaging with LGBT communities; LGBT events and activities; and staff awareness and attitudes; and then it explores a number of outstanding issues.

Service provision

Examples of services that have been developed include:

- allocating a proportion of the stock fund for purchasing LGBT-related material;
- putting together LGBT collections, for example at the five largest libraries in Tameside (Tameside Metropolitan Borough, 2012), and often including magazines as well as books and other materials;
- producing promotional booklists, for example: Barnsley; Devon (Devon County Council, n.d.); East Sussex (East Sussex County Council, n.d.); Hampshire (Hampshire County Council, 2012b); Hertfordshire; Highland Council (The Highland Council/Comhairle na Gàidhealtachd, 2012); Medway (Medway Council, 2012); and West Sussex;
- provision of information;
- celebrating events, such as LGBT History Month, and ensuring that there is a LGBT visibility in all other celebrations, such as Black History Month.

Engaging with LGBT communities

With the increasing recognition of the importance of consulting and engaging LGBT communities, this area of work has developed to include, for example in one authority, a simple consultation process (Brighton & Hove City Library Service, n.d.), as well as more complex community engagement work elsewhere. An action research project in Bournemouth, Poole and Dorset, which ran between June 2003 and September 2006, and which explored the needs, experiences and aspirations of older lesbians and gay men, led to positive links between Bournemouth Libraries and local older LGBT people (Gay and Grey in Dorset, 2006).

As with engaging with any actual or potential library users, one of the important elements is continuity – of contact, of service, of commitment – and, unfortunately, it has not always been possible to maintain this, so there is a pattern of good initiatives being developed, which then disappear if a key member of staff leaves or the service faces budget reductions.

LGBT events and activities

The following were cited by the Local Government Authority (LGA) in 2007 as examples of good practice (Creegan and Lee, 2007: 47, their emphases):

> *Birmingham City Council* has taken a number of actions in relation to its library services. These include treating lesbian, gay and bisexual people as a priority group within the Annual Library Plan and, depending on local needs and circumstances, either having designated areas in local libraries or integrating lesbian, gay and bisexual books into different sections. They also include: publicising 'Proud to Read' book lists; providing information on lesbian, gay and bisexual health, legal and support services; publicising local and national lesbian, gay and bisexual links on the council's website; and having a Libraries Department stall at the City's LGB Pride event.
>
> *Westminster City Council's* website refers to a list of contemporary lesbian and gay writing currently available in the borough's libraries. Several libraries have separate lesbian and gay sections, including material not available elsewhere.
>
> The library service at *North Yorkshire County Council* has been strengthened by participation nationally in the 'Branching Out' reader development programme. Amongst specific achievements highlighted by the council is a 'radical approach' to the widening of fiction stock into areas such as lesbian and gay novels.
>
> In 2003 *York City Council* sponsored the Libertas Lesbian Arts Festival which included a lesbian film festival, lesbian theatre, creative writing workshops, concerts, lesbian opera, poetry and lesbian book festival. The council provided assistance with venues, administration, equipment and advice.
>
> In 2003 *Lewisham Council* awarded Short and Girlie productions, a theatre group for lesbian, bisexual and transgendered women, a one-off grant to develop workshops for children with gay, bisexual or transgendered parents.

More recently, a number of library authorities has started a LGBT reading group, for example: Croydon 'organised by Croydon Area Gay Society ... in conjunction with Croydon Library' (Rainbow Reading Group, 2012); Glasgow (Glasgow Libraries 2010); Portsmouth (Portsmouth City Council, 2012); Wolverhampton (Wolverhampton City Council, 2011).

Staff awareness and attitudes

There has been an increasing number of staff development activities, courses and conferences.

In March 2005, The Network organised a half-day workshop for SINTO,[1] 'Cultural awareness: lesbians, gay men, bisexual and transgendered people'; and this was followed in September 2006 by a one-day course, 'Library Services for LGBT Communities'. This included sessions on engaging local LGBT people, supporting young people, stock selection and stock promotion.

The then Chartered Institute of Library & Information Professionals (CILIP) Diversity Group held its second conference in February 2006, and broke new ground by taking as its theme '"Pride or Prejudice?" How well are libraries serving lesbian, gay, bi- and trans- communities?' I gave the keynote presentation, opening the conference by asking 'How well do we do?' There was considerable positive work going on in libraries across the UK, but I also identified the following issues:

- 'Clause 28', although repealed, has left its legacy: many people think it's still in force; people think that we still cannot put on LGBT displays or produce booklists in libraries.
- Many library authorities are buying stock for LGBT people, but some face enormous prejudice from staff who don't want to see it in their libraries.
- When they hear about LGBT issues, some library staff treat the issue with polite dismissal.
- I met a transgendered person on one training course I ran, but she was nervous about saying anything in the group, because her colleagues were not supportive.
- Some people seem unable to judge appropriate ways of behaving towards LGBTs.
- People say things such as 'John's course was fine, but he didn't have to tell us he was gay ...'
- Because I work quite a lot with teenage boys (and I don't think this is my being over-sensitive), a few people behave as though this is completely wrong (Vincent, 2006: 2).

The conference also included presentations on Brighton & Hove's consultations with their local LGBT communities (Harvey, 2006) and on transgender issues (Chambers and Cole, 2006); as well as two workshops on the 'Impact of fiction on the knowledge, self esteem and well-being of women, in particular those who identify as lesbian or bisexual' (Goldthorp, 2006).

In June 2009, LibrariesWest and the Bristol Area Social Inclusion Network (with The Network) organised a seminar, 'Out in the library – supporting lesbian, gay, bisexual and transgendered library users and staff' (LibrariesWest, 2010: 9-10), which included sessions on stock selection; investigating the role that libraries should play in supporting LGBT users and staff; understanding some

---

1 'SINTO is a partnership of library and information services in ... Yorkshire and north Derbyshire with the goal of improving services to users through co-operation, training and planning' (SINTO, 2011).

of the issues facing LGBT people, which may well have an impact on their library use; consulting LGBT communities; working with LGBT young people; and exploring the new Equalities Framework and how to cover LGBT issues in an Equality Impact Assessment. It was also a timely reminder – as one of the co-organisers commented:

> I found it very interesting that my pre-conception of a seminar aimed more at enlightening and educating hetero library staff should have been responded to by so many lesbian and gay staff. I heard comments about how wonderful they found it, that it was morale boosting and life enhancing. (BASIN course co-organiser, 2009)

At the 2011 CILIP Umbrella Conference, I took part in a panel session on 'Equalities issues in libraries: the emerging tensions'. My session looked at 'Am I really a sinner? Where do LGBT issues fit into the equalities framework?' (Diversity Group, 2011).

Finally, a growing number of library authorities also organises in-house training, for example: Hertfordshire and Kent (The Network) and Devon Library Service (Intercom Trust).

Outstanding issues – 'personal and institutional anxieties'

Despite all the positive advances, it is clear that LGBT people may still receive a poor-quality service. For example, in her MA dissertation, Laura Armstrong examined 'the attitudes and anxieties of a sample of library staff in [two major UK libraries] regarding the promotion of minority genres, British Black/Asian and gay and lesbian literature' (Armstrong, 2006: ii).

As she noted in her conclusions:

> It was quite evident early on in this study that the pairing of Black British/ Asian and gay and lesbian fiction was not as straight forward as might first have been thought. There is a spread of questionnaire responses regarding front line staff confidence promoting Black British/Asian literature and gay and lesbian with some respondents strongly disagreeing about their ability to promote either genre. However library managers appear far more at ease with Black British/ Asian fictions generally than they are with gay and lesbian fiction. (Armstrong, 2006: 61)

In addition:

> The researcher felt that there was much more anxiety generated by both libraries in their approach to gay and lesbian literature. This anxiety was spread across all aspects of promoting this genre, from the knotty problem of segregation or interfiling, discretion, offending patrons, the balance between the amount of gay

literature to that of lesbian literature and the general content of gay and lesbian literature. (Armstrong, 2006: 62)

Probably the greatest anxiety was around how lesbian and gay material should be displayed in the library, a point we shall come back to.

Amongst Laura Armstrong's recommendations was that:

> Each library would benefit from [multicultural and gay & lesbian] champion librarians. They would be able to be proactive in the promotion of minority genres and support staff. Champion librarians would have informed views about stock selection, focus groups and offer in-house minority genre training to all staff. (Armstrong, 2006: 67)

Outstanding issues – library materials for children and young people

Until relatively recently, there were few titles for children and young people which reflected being LGBT in a positive way:

> What do the books tell young people about being homosexual? In novels or short stories for teenagers, being gay or lesbian and young is almost universally shown to be hard. Sometimes the difficulty lies in the young gay or lesbian not wanting to accept his or her own sexuality. For example, Marco in William Taylor's *Jerome* [(1999)] only confronts his own homosexuality when his friend Jerome commits suicide—apparently because of his unrequited love for Marco ... More often, it is the real or imagined reactions of friends or family that fill the young gay or lesbian with apprehension. (Clyde and Lobban, 2001: 22)[2]

The position in the UK has improved considerably. Elizabeth L. Chapman has been researching the provision of LGBT-related fiction to children and young people in public libraries (Chapman, E.L., 2007) and has produced a recommended list of fiction available (Chapman, E.L., 2012c), as well as a fuller spreadsheet of titles (Chapman, E.L., 2012a).

She has added:

> Provision for children and young people is my own particular area of interest, and I think it is still frequently neglected. Increasing numbers of library services are making some effort at adult LGBT provision, but haven't thought about the need for materials for children and young people. There is still quite a lot of anxiety about this area – unfortunately, some people still seem to believe that anything 'LGBT' is unsuitable for younger children, and that discussion of

---

2   This article was a follow-up to the authors' long-term research project, 'Out of the closet and into the classroom' (Lobban and Clyde, 1996).

the subject will require parents to explain 'complex' issues.[3] In fact, a large (and probably increasing) number of children have parents who are LGBT, and discussion of the topic fits easily into National Curriculum schoolwork on different family structures. In the event of any complaint from other patrons, libraries should be able to justify their inclusion of LGBT materials for children and young people with reference to a robust stock policy that specifically states the need for provision of materials for all sections of the community, including LGBT people. (Chapman, E.L., 2012b)

Outstanding issues – is lesbian fiction still inaccessible?

In her research paper, Jacqueline Goldthorp looked at:

how Scottish public library services have responded to providing a service to a virtually invisible minority group, i.e. lesbians who enjoy reading lesbian fiction ... The research found there to be an inequity of service provision for lesbians in terms of recreational reading and, in the light of this, recommends a reassessment of certain library practices. In particular, there is a need to raise awareness of LGBT people among library workers by encouraging contact with LGBT people and their support networks and providing diversity training linked with training in how to develop collections of lesbian and gay fiction and how to promote those collections to their main audience. (Goldthorp, 2007: 234)

However, as she said:

It would be unjust to state that there has been no work done by Scottish local authorities in conjunction with library service managers to provide recreational reading services for lesbians, but examples of this are very rare. Glasgow City Council provides funding and accommodation for the Glasgow Women's Library (membership is by subscription) who own a private collection of lesbian fiction, and house the lesbian archive. However, this example is one of taking an 'exclusive' approach. Therefore, however worthy an endeavour this is, it still does not address the issues raised in this research within the public library arena in Scotland.

What is not in doubt is that, with few exceptions, Scottish public library services have failed, even at the most basic level, to promote lesbian fiction to the group of users who are most interested in it and would benefit most from having access to it. The attempts that have been made to engage with LGBT people and their support networks are extraordinarily limited and those that have been attempted have not been evaluated to gain an understanding of their success or otherwise. (Goldthorp, 2007: 241)

---

3   And one issue that young people may face is that they feel they 'Can't get books about being gay out of library because librarian knows Mum' (Cowley, 2011: 57).

This research demonstrated too that improvements are taking a long time – the issues that Jacqueline Goldthorp identified echoed those found by Heike Seidel in 1998 (Seidel, 1998).

More recently, Jacqueline Goldthorp has argued that the issue is even more widespread, not just lesbian fiction, but the provision of LGBT material in public libraries altogether:

> across the board improvements and strategic developments are patchy and often the long term impact and viability of those projects are diminished when key library staff who promoted those projects move on or leave the service. Funding is inconsistent and even in the face of successes is often not sustained to carry those improvements forward. (Goldthorp, 2012: 38)

Outstanding issues – "The right 'man' for the job?"

The Centre for the Public Library and Information in Society, Department of Information Studies at Sheffield University carried out this important piece of research which was published in 2008. It was:

> designed to investigate public library staff attitudes towards social inclusion policy and disadvantaged groups in society, and to test the relationships between the ethnic, social, cultural and professional background of staff and their capacity to make an effective, empathic contribution to social inclusion objectives. (Wilson and Birdi, 2008: 4)

The research included a literature review, a national survey, focus groups and interviews, job vacancy profiling, compiling case studies and a research workshop. In the East of England focus group, someone commented:

> I have had problems with LGBT issues from staff and users... if the gay collection is very in your face the users get a bit uptight... I was aware of one member of staff who would carefully move the pink paper... I once worked in a library that put Gay Times in a brown envelope, that was three or four years ago, I don't know if they do it now... but there are still pockets of resistance on occasion. (Wilson and Birdi, 2008: 97)

A rather dismissive view came from a participant in a West Midlands focus group:

> I think it's when councils or libraries have these mad cap, well not mad cap because we're not allowed to say that, but you know these short term funding projects that it goes astray... if they stopped looking at these short term little pockets of activity... and silly political correctness... we had gay and lesbian fiction, now it's gay, lesbian, bisexual, transvestite... could they add any more

initials? You know does it matter? A good book is a good book, does it matter if
it's written by or aimed at a gay person or lesbian? (Wilson and Birdi, 2008: 59)

Concerns were also voiced in one of the group discussions:

Identify groups and engage with them – but how do you identify e.g. LGBT
users? You can't quantify – yet figures are what the SMT [Senior Management
Team] wants.

Why should people declare disability, sexuality, ethnic origin? So how can
you be expected to have numbers (i.e. to please SMT etc.)? (Wilson and Birdi,
2008: 171)

Outstanding issues – need for more staff development around LGBT issues

There are repeated calls for training for and greater awareness by library staff, for
example:

the Government must take its equality message beyond the boundaries of
parliamentary buildings into local communities, encouraging equality of
provision by motivating senior library managers and providers of library
education to raise awareness of diversity issues and to provide effective training
in the techniques and tools that are available to enable good service provision for
LGBT people; and by challenging those who work in public libraries to engage
with this minority group and to be innovative in the use of the resources they
have to meet the needs of their local LGBT community. (Goldthorp, 2007: 242)

Finally, just in case we think that libraries' work is highly developed and highly
visible, here is a reality check from John Pateman: 'It's good to hear that there's
lots of LGBT activity in UK public libraries, but it all seems to be below the radar
as I don't hear people talking about it and there is nothing in the professional press.
Perhaps it's a taboo subject (like social class) or even a legacy of Section 28?'
(Pateman, 2012).

Museums

The period since 2004 has seen an increased focus on LGBT people by museums:
'The last two decades have seen concerns for equality, diversity, social justice and
human rights move from the margins of museum thinking and practice, to the core'
(Nightingale and Sandell, 2012: 1).

The purpose of museums has also been the subject of regular reassessment,
and as Fiona Cameron suggested: 'The emancipatory museum also offers a home
to feminism, ecology, anti-imperialism, localism, gay/lesbian perspectives as well

as the perspectives of other liberationist and social justice movements' (Cameron, F., 2010: 24).

However, progress has been slow, primarily because of a mix of institutional conservatism and 'individual practitioners' reluctance to work on LGBTQ-themed projects in their employing museums' (Sandell and Frost 2010: 159). In addition, as Stephen Welsh has suggested, there may also still be museums that have been unable to move beyond Victorian curatorial orthodoxies and consider it inappropriate to engage with sexuality issues or to go back and reassess their historic holdings (Welsh, 2012).

Finally, progress may also have been affected by attitudes of museums staff (particularly senior staff) towards external 'drivers' and the dilution of the powerful role of the curator (Davies and Paine, 2004).

Writing (damningly) in 2007, Darryl McIntyre said:

> I suspect that, if you were to visit your local museum, it is highly unlikely that you would see any items on display that are explicitly lesbian, gay, bisexual and transgender (LGBT) related and captioned or identified accordingly. It is possible that some might have an LGBT association – perhaps through previous ownership, design or even use – but this provenance or object history is probably unknown to museum staff. This situation is not unusual and indeed possibly applies to most museums worldwide.
>
> Museums, unlike libraries and archives, appear to rarely actively collect LGBT-related material. This is party explained by the nature of the material. Collections of personal papers, media cuttings, oral histories and the like seem to naturally gravitate to libraries and archives, and some institutions have been proactive in this direction. Records held by the National Archives and agencies such as the London Metropolitan Archives hold an extraordinary range of material relating to LGBT issues and personal histories, and the creation and enhancement of online guides to these records provide improved and more immediate access to this material. Regrettably, museums have been a wasteland to date when it comes to collecting LGBT-related materials. (McIntyre, 2007: 49)

Similarly, Jack Gilbert also wrote in 2007 of the results of the 'Proud Nation' survey:

> Very few museums or galleries have really addressed the enormity of their failure to properly collect, frame and interpret the lives and experience of LGBT people. Decades of homophobia still pervade – not necessarily because individual staff are homophobic but because of an institutional failure.
>
> There are those that have conducted very successful, praiseworthy short-term projects, but which nonetheless felt obliged to allow staff to excuse themselves from working on the project or placed the exhibit away from the main thoroughfare. Some heterosexual museum staff have reported experiencing homophobia and a begrudged attitude from colleagues that shocked them.

> The number of institutions that have integrated adequate or any LGBT material into their permanent exhibitions still remains extremely low. Some respondents to our survey, readers of this magazine, were even overtly homophobic. (Gilbert, 2007)

So, what has been developed since 2004? In 2004, the Heritage Lottery Fund (HLF) gave a £100,000 grant to a joint venture between Edinburgh Museums and the Living Memory Association,[4] which created the community-led 'Remember When' project:

> Over 150 people from Edinburgh's LGBT communities – ranging in age from 18 to 80 – came together to share their experiences and create the archive of oral history interviews, photographs and memorabilia recording over half a century of LGBT life in Scotland's capital. This resulted in the exhibition, 'Rainbow City, Stories from Lesbian, Gay, Bisexual and Transgender Edinburgh', at the City Art Centre, which ran from May to July 2006.
>
> The collection consists of 350 objects, 200 photographs and 100 fully transcribed oral history interviews. The objects include items relating to identity, activism, the scene and individual histories.
>
> They include badges, tee shirts and banners for various Pride Marches, Section 28 and other campaigns; archives including minutes and promotional material for different groups and organisations. (Edinburgh Museums & Galleries, n.d.)

In recent years, there has been an increasing number of temporary exhibitions in the UK with same-sex relationships as a main focus, perhaps most significantly 'Hidden Histories' at the New Art Gallery, Walsall, which was also staged in 2004; it was: 'the first show of its kind to focus solely upon the work of artists who had male same-sex relationships' (Sandell and Frost, 2010: 150).

Writing at the time, David Prudames described it in the following terms:

> Hidden Histories is aimed at re-claiming a history by appreciating the full extent of the contribution of gay artists and the ways in which their sexual identity has affected both their work and responses to it.
>
> According to the curator, mainstream art history has in many ways glossed over issues around sexual difference, absorbing gay artists into a history viewed through a heterosexual filter. (Prudames, 2004)

As well as writing a book to accompany the exhibition (Petry, 2004), the curator, Michael Petry, has written about the experience of putting on an exhibition of

---

4   'The Living Memory Association was established in 1984. It is an Edinburgh based group that aims to bring people together through reminiscence and oral history work' (Living Memory Association, ca. 2010).

work by artists who were same-sex lovers, particularly the interference by the local authority (Petry, 2007).

In 2005, the Museum of London carried out a major reassessment of its collections, 'Re-assessing what we collect' (Museum of London, 2005b); this led to the creation of an online resource, in which the Museum of London included essays (Kaur, 2005; Young, L., 2005), and also a webpage with objects of relevance to 'The LGBT community in London' (Museum of London, 2005a). The essay by Raminder Kaur (2005) summarised key issues facing the Museum, particularly how to build on some of its earlier work and how to maintain the LGBT profile of the Museum through its collections and activities.

The Museum of London also began hosting 'Untold London', a listings service celebrating London's diverse population, and which includes events and activities in the cultural sector, including LGBT events – previous examples include an 'LGBT Tour of the British Museum'; 'Writing Joe Orton' at Islington Museum; and 'Other Ways of Seeing' (a writing workshop for young people at London Metropolitan Archives) (Untold London, 2012).

It also promotes 'Write Queer London'; the 2012 programme was announced as:

> The recipe goes like this:
> - take five or six London museums, with interesting LGBT collections or stories;
> - add a knowledgeable curator to explain and answer questions;
> - bring in excellent published writers and poets to lead creative writing workshops.
>
>   Mix all the ingredients together and simmer gently until, amidst the cooking steam, you begin to see visions of the gay past – which might mean a trip to ancient Babylon – or 1960s Islington. (Untold London, 2011)

The year 2006 seemed to be the breakthrough year! The British Museum held a short, temporary special exhibition on sex and society, in which the Warren Cup[5] took centre-stage; this was the beginning of a growing number of exhibitions and activities at the British Museum which acknowledged LGBT history, including the celebration of the relationship between Roman Emperor Hadrian and Antinous in 'Hadrian: Empire and Conflict' (2008); the creation of LGBT history trails (British Museum, n.d.-a); holding the launch of LGBT History Month at the Museum in 2009; and taking part in the annual 'Write Queer London' festival (Parkinson, 2012). In addition, in 2011-2012, the Museum staged the successful exhibition

---

   5 'A silver cup with relief decoration of homoerotic scenes, this object takes its name from its first owner in modern times, the art-lover and collector Edward Perry Warren (1860-1928) ... After Warren's death the cup remained in private hands, largely because of the nature of the subject matter. Only with changing attitudes in the 1980s was the cup exhibited to the public, and in 1999 the British Museum was able to give this important piece a permanent home in the public domain' (British Museum, n.d.-b).

curated by Grayson Perry, 'The Tomb of the Unknown Craftsman' (British Museum, 2012).

Also in 2006, the Museum of London held its 'Queer is Here' exhibition which: 'uncovers a glimpse of the Museum's collection and the hidden histories of the LGBT communities in London. It focuses on some of the issues that affected these communities today and looks at the last 30 years through a gay history time line' (Museum of London, 2006).

The Discovery Museum, Tyne & Wear staged 'Private Lives, Public Battles' (which was shortlisted in the 'Temporary Exhibition Award' category of the 2007 Museums & Heritage Awards for Excellence).

The Victoria and Albert Museum (V&A) established a cross-museum Lesbian, Gay, Bi, Trans & Queer Network; their core areas of activity were around staffing, public programming and 'longer term research into collections for the development of expertise' (Winchester, 2012b: 144):

> The V&A is seeking to unearth previously hidden LGBTQ histories in its collections, researching objects and the histories that surround them. Equally, these investigations look at the ways in which visitors themselves understand and make sense of these objects on the basis of their own identities and lived experience. (V&A, 2012)

In December 2006, the Social History Curators Group and Proud Heritage held a one-day seminar about LGBT history for museums staff (Frost, 2007).

The major exhibition, 'Hello Sailor!', was originally staged in the Merseyside Maritime Museum in 2006-2007, before going on a national (and international) tour; from December 2009, it has formed part of the Museum's permanent displays. Based on research carried out for the book *Hello Sailor!* (Baker and Stanley, 2003), the displays revealed a little-known aspect of the history of the merchant navy (Merseyside Maritime Museum, 2012; Tibbles, 2012).

In February-March 2007, the Museum in Docklands hosted the 'Out in Time' exhibition (funded by Tower Hamlets Council and the Primary Care Trust, along with investment banking companies in Canary Wharf) which highlighted 'the hard-won battles fought by the LGBT community in Tower Hamlets against ignorance and prejudice' (Saini, 2008).

In 2008, Imperial War Museum (North) staged a temporary exhibition, 'Military Pride', which explored the experiences of LGBT people within the context of conflict, war and military service; in addition, as part of their 'Hidden Histories' project, they also recorded four testimonies of LGBT military personnel, which are still available (Imperial War Museums, n.d.).

Also in 2008, the Museum of London put on 'Outside Edge: a journey through black British lesbian and gay history' (Jeater, 2008).

In 2009, the National Portrait Gallery staged the high-profile exhibition, 'Gay Icons', (partly to mark the 40th anniversary of the Stonewall riots):

Gay Icons explores gay social and cultural history through the unique personal insights of ten high profile gay figures, who have selected their historical and modern icons.

The chosen icons, who may or may not be gay themselves, have all been important to each selector, having influenced their gay sensibilities or contributed to making them who they are today. They include artists Francis Bacon and David Hockney; writers Daphne du Maurier and Quentin Crisp; composers Pyotr Tchaikovsky and Benjamin Britten; musicians k.d. lang, the Village People and Will Young; entertainers Ellen DeGeneres, Lily Savage and Kenneth Williams; sports stars Martina Navratilova and Ian Roberts and political activists Harvey Milk and Angela Mason. (National Portrait Gallery, n.d. (2007)-a)

As the chair of the selectors, Sandi Toksvig, is quoted as saying:

How I wish this selection had been available to me when I was young and trying to make sense of my reactions to the world. How inspirational to have had portraits of the great and the good staring out at me telling me that I was not by any measure on my own. (National Portrait Gallery, n.d. (2007)-b)

In 2010, the V&A and the Department of Museum Studies, University of Leicester co-organised a major international conference, 'From the Margins to the Core?' (see: Breward, 2010; V&A, 2010); this included a wide range of papers and sessions on aspects of diversity, including LGBT issues – one of the breakout sessions was on 'Transgender Equality & Culture'. The themes and papers from the conference were developed into a book, *Museums, Equality and Social Justice*, all of which is highly relevant – of particular interest are chapters by Oliver Winchester (2012b), Amy K. Levin (2012) and Richard Sandell (2012).

In 2010-2011, Birmingham Museum and Art Gallery, working with artist Matt Smith, put on the 'Queering the Museum' exhibition,[6] which asked:

[W]hat happens when we stop thinking the world is straight? Through omission and careful arrangement of facts it is easy to assume that the objects held in museums have nothing to do with the lesbian, gay, bisexual and transgender community. Turning the traditional on its head, a queer eye has been cast over the museum.

Objects have been rearranged and brought out of store and new artworks have been specifically commissioned to uncover, draw out – and on occasion wilfully invent – the hidden stories in the Museum's collections. (Birmingham Museum and Art Gallery, 2010; Birmingham Museums and Art Gallery, 2010)

---

6 Running from 4 November 2010 until the end of February 2011, 'Queering the Museum' was an Arts Council-funded exhibition, in conjunction with ShOUT! Festival and Birmingham Museum and Art Gallery.

In his brief assessment, 'Are museums doing enough to address LGBT history?', Stuart Frost wrote positively about the impact that this work was having:

> Some of the displays are humorous; others are more serious, raising issues such as homophobia. Collectively, they highlight the diversity and complexities of LGBT experience rather than offering a simple linear narrative or progressive history. Queering the Museum will close just as LGBT history month is about to begin.
>
> By working with an artist, Birmingham Museum and Art Gallery has been able to look at its collections with fresh eyes.
>
> Although it is a temporary exhibition, it underlines the potential that exists for museums to reinterpret their existing collections in thought-provoking ways, and to integrate LGBT experience and history into permanent galleries. (Frost, 2010)

February 2012 saw the event, 'Queering the Handling Collection at the Geffrye Museum', in which Alison Oram looked at queer households from the 1950s as discussed in the papers of the period; and Cherry Smyth led a poetry workshop based on items from the 1950s in the Geffrye Museum's handling collection (Smith, K., 2012).

In May 2012, Tate Modern organised a major conference, 'Civil Partnerships? Queer and Feminist Curating', which looked at the relationship between the institutional art world and feminist and queer projects (Tate, 2012).

The Science Museum has been involved in two significant events in 2012. Firstly, in June, they launched a major exhibition, 'Codebreaker – Alan Turing's life and legacy', which ran until July 2013 (Science Museum, 2012) – a good example of a major exhibition that also breaks away from being tied to a celebratory week or month. They also worked with Gendered Intelligence on a three-month project, 'I:Trans', during which a group of young people visited different science and technology-themed exhibitions and used them, along with their own experiences as young trans people, as inspiration to produce a range of artwork around the themes of science, technology and gender (Gendered Intelligence, 2012b).

In 2012 also, MOSI (the Museum of Science & Industry) staged 'Behind the Scene: Stories from Manchester's LGBT Communities' which ran until March 2013 (Museum of Science & Industry, 2012).

In July 2012, it was announced that the arts festival Homotopia[7] was launching a two-year heritage project:

> to research, explore and document the experiences of transgender people in Britain over the past 70 years, focussing on the life of trans model and actress April Ashley MBE.

---

7 Homotopia is an international LGBT festival held annually in Liverpool and across various parts of Europe (Homotopia, 2012).

Supported by the Heritage Lottery Fund, there will be a number of 'reminiscence' workshops and opportunities for members of the transgender community to share their own experiences.

One of the outcomes of the project activities will be a 12 month exhibition in collaboration with the Museum of Liverpool. (Pink News, 2012)

To sum up: there have been some important, high-profile exhibitions and other pieces of work in museums and galleries since 2004, but, as Richard Sandell and Stuart Frost argue: 'It is, however, worth remembering that the inclusion of sexual minorities in permanent displays is still relatively rare and the majority of institutions still present exclusively heteronormative narratives in which sexual and gendered difference are denied' (Sandell and Frost, 2010: 170).

Archives

Background

Polly Thistlethwaite (Head of Public Services, City University of New York Graduate Centre Library and long-time volunteer and chronicler of the Lesbian Herstory Archives) has argued that: 'gay and lesbian history is tangible today because lesbians and gays had the will and determination to constitute and reclaim histories by writing books and building presses, and by establishing community-based archives and history projects' (Thistlethwaite, 1995: 10, 24).

Brenda J. Marston – in whose chapter this article was cited (Marston, 1998: 146-147) – extended the argument by adding that: 'Libraries have indeed lagged behind lesbian and gay activists in understanding lesbian and gay issues' (Marston, 1998: 147).

As US-based 'artist activist and free-range librarian' (Bly and Wooten, 2012: contributors' biographies) Angela DiVeglia suggests: 'Members of the LGBT community often take one of two approaches to dealing with the uneven power dynamics inherent in the structure of archives: either they subvert the power structures in order to re-build or reclaim them, or they build their own, more democratic or non-hierarchical alternatives' (DiVeglia, 2012: 72).

Similarly, recently in the UK, there have been three key developments in relation to archives:

- the growth of a small number of LGBT community archives;
- greater recognition of LGBT material by mainstream archives;
- growing collaborations between community and mainstream archives.

Community archives

The UK Community Archives and Heritage Group has started a discussion about the definition of a 'community archive':

> The definition of 'community archive' is the cause of some debate. Broadly speaking, people think of projects as community archives either because:
>
> 1. The subject-matter of the collection is a community of people. The classic example is a group of people who live in the same location, but there are 'communities of interest' as well, such as people who worked in a certain profession.
> 2. The process of creating the collection has involved the community. Typically, this means that volunteers have played a key role, sometimes alongside professional archivists. (Latimer, 2006)

Primarily because of the vast difference in size, the UK does not have the same range of LGBT community archives as there is in the USA and Canada,[8] for example. However, there is a growing number of larger and more local LGBT community archives.

Broader LGBT community archives

Examples of UK LGBT community archives include:

- OurStory Scotland – see below;
- Lesbian and Gay Newsmedia Archive (Vaknin, 2009);
- LGBT archives at Manchester Archives and Local Studies, which 'holds a wide range of archive and printed material relating to the history of Manchester's Lesbian, Gay, Bisexual and Transgender Community' (Community Archives and Heritage Group, 2007c);

---

8   The range of collections in the USA and Canada has been well outlined by Bill Lukenbill (Lukenbill, 2002), Aimee Brown (2011) and Gerard Koskovich (2008); important and interesting examples are ONE National Gay & Lesbian Archives in Los Angeles 'the world's largest research library on Gay, Lesbian, Bisexual, and Transgendered heritage and concerns' (ONE National Gay & Lesbian Archives, 2011); the Canadian Lesbian & Gay Archives which was founded in 1973 and has grown to be the second-largest LGBT archive in the world and which undertakes outreach work with young people (Barriault, 2009; Canadian Lesbian & Gay Archive, 2011; Zieman, 2009); the Lesbian Herstory Archives 'the world's largest collection of materials by and about lesbians and their communities' (Lesbian Herstory Archives, 2012; Thistlethwaite 1990); and the Black Gay and Lesbian Archive in the Schomburg Centre (Fullwood, 2009). In addition, the University of Victoria, British Columbia, Canada has recently received a major gift of papers, plaques, photographs, newsletters, certificates, posters and tapes from Rikki Swin's transgender research institute (Dedyna, 2012).

- Women's Archive of Wales/Archif Menywod Cymru (Community Archives and Heritage Group 2006b);
- Feministwebs archive of women and girls' youth work, 'a collection of materials and oral histories focussing on current feminist youth work with young women and girls, from the North West of England and beyond' (Community Archives and Heritage Group, 2009);
- London LGBT Archive: rukus! (Ajamu, X., *et al.*, 2009; Community Archives and Heritage Group, 2007b);
- 'From History to Her Story' (Community Archives and Heritage Group, 2006a);
- Voluntary Action History Society (Howes, R., 2012).

OurStory Scotland started in 2001 (OurStory Scotland, n.d.-b), and, since then, has been involved in some major exhibitions, including:

- 'sh[OUT]' at the Gallery of Modern Art, Glasgow in 2009 (see below);
- 'OurSpace' at the Kelvingrove Art Gallery and Museum, Glasgow in 2008;
- 'Becoming Visible: Exhibition of Gay, Lesbian, Bisexual and Transgender history in Scotland', which ran at the Glasgow LGBT Centre in 2002-2003 and which is now an online exhibition (OurStory Scotland, n.d.-a).

Their most recent work (at the time of writing) has been 'Love Out of Bounds', an exhibition of images and stories of 'loves ignored or rejected by family, community, culture or faith', which was held at St Mungo Museum, Glasgow in 2012, with follow-up storytelling workshops (OurStory Scotland, 2012).

Local LGBT community archives

Brighton Ourstory had its roots back in the late 1980s, collecting and exhibiting LGBT histories, but re-launched its website and stepped up its activities from 2001 onwards (Brighton Ourstory, 2012a; Community Archives and Heritage Group, 2007a) – recent work includes the exhibitions, 'Gay Girls and Bachelor Boys – The Liberation Years' (Brighton Ourstory, 2012c) and 'The Third Sex in the Third Reich', an exhibition for Holocaust Memorial Day (Brighton Ourstory, 2012b).

Plymouth Pride Forum have developed 'Pride in Our Past – Setting the Record Straight in Plymouth':

'Pride in our Past' was made possible by an award from the Heritage Lottery Fund (HLF) of £35,000 which enabled the Plymouth Pride Forum and other LGBT groups and individuals, from within the city of Plymouth, to work in collaboration with the Plymouth and West Devon Record Office, and create an archive to access, frame and interpret this often unconsidered aspect of Plymouth's history. Much of the specific history of the LGBT community was stored only in the memories of its older members and was therefore likely to be lost if not captured. (Pride in our Past, 2012a)

The project team have carried out oral history interviews and collected memorabilia and artefacts, and the material is being made available via the Plymouth LGBT Archive (Pride in our Past, 2012b). The project was awarded the Community Archives and Heritage Group's 'Most Inspirational Community Archive' in 2012.

In Birmingham:

> Birmingham LGBT has undertaken two Heritage Lottery funded research and oral history projects under the 'Gay Birmingham Remembered' banner.
>
> 'Gay Birmingham Remembered' and its sister project 'Gay Birmingham Back to Back' undertook research into LGBT Birmingham as far back as the 1800s and interviewed around 80 individuals about their experiences in the city. The project materials, along with other LGBT materials, are held in Birmingham City Archives, Central Library and can be accessed by the general public. (Birmingham LGBT, 2013)

Gender Matters[9] has been working with Birmingham Archives on a HLF-funded project, 'Mapping My Journey', which aims to 'identify and record living histories of the transitioning journey of 20 members of the Trans community dating from 1930s/1940s to the present day' (Heritage Lottery Fund, 2012: 2).

West Yorkshire Archive Service set up a digital community archive, via Nowthen – 'a community site that makes local heritage accessible and open' (West Yorkshire Archive Service, n.d.-a):

> This project has created an LGBT online community archives to ensure the experiences and memories of lesbian, gay and bisexual people of West Yorkshire are recorded and preserved for the benefit, heritage and empowerment of West Yorkshire's LGB communities, and as a tool of education and engagement for the wider community. (West Yorkshire Archive Service, n.d.-b)

Greater recognition of LGBT material by mainstream archives

Work has intensified over the last eight years to track down information about and records of LGBT people in existing archives. Archives may hold documents relating to specific events (such as court cases) that have involved LGBT people, but, unless they hold papers belonging to someone who is known or believed to be LGBT, these are not likely to be indexed, so many archives are currently

---

9　'Gender Matters provides a comprehensive programme of practical support, counselling, advice and information for anyone with any questions or problems concerning their gender identity, or whose loved ones are struggling with gender identity issues' (Gender Matters, 2013).

reassessing and indexing their holdings to track down LGBT-related material. A good example of this is The National Archives, where:

> Archus, the voluntary LGBT staff group at The National Archives (TNA), has been putting together a research project to identify and discover the resources TNA hold in relation to LGBT history. This area of research has previous only been at a very high and summary level, giving indicators to document series in which documents would most likely be found, and few actual documents had been highlighted. Members of Archus, together with members from the Ministry of Justice Rainbow Network, have put together list [sic] of document references and details of the contents of those files. Our primary aims are to help foster new research and enquiry into LGBT history and to unlock and share the value of archival resources in this area. (The National Archives, 2011)

In addition, archives can highlight information as it is 'unearthed' and can use this to help promote interest in discovering the LGBT history of a particular place – and of the otherwise hidden role that LGBT people have had. The webpage quoted above continues:

> The National Archives is one of the biggest and most unique resources in the country – and LGBT history emerges throughout a diverse range of records and themes reflecting the political and social movements and attitudes towards sexual orientation and gender identity. TNA holds over 10 million records here and many valuable resources in the collection still need to be identified and surfaced [sic]. We need to look at when and how LGBT people and themes occur in these documents, and when we find them, make sure people record them in cataloguing projects, with accurate terminology that doesn't change the meaning of the document, but that doesn't reiterate homophobias found within them. (The National Archives, 2011)

The National Archives has produced a research guide on 'Gay and Lesbian history', available on The National Archives website (The National Archives, 2013), which explains that searching the catalogue of their holdings becomes fruitful with an understanding of the language and terminology used in earlier times, and how keywords will allow the researcher to identify potentially relevant files. The Research guide includes a list of suggested search terms.

In addition, for example, Old Bailey Proceedings Online have included a section on 'Homosexuality' in their digitised court records (Old Bailey Proceedings Online, 2012).

There is a growing number of collections within mainstream archives, including Manchester Archives and Local Studies (Manchester City Council. Libraries. Archives and Local Studies, 2011) which include documents from the Greater Manchester County Record Office (with Manchester Archives) and the queerupnorth archives. Their work featured on a Community Archives and Local Studies Training Day in April 2007, where 'archivists and local studies librarians [had] the chance to learn from the experiences of a variety of established projects, and to gain an insight into the work and resources of the Ahmed Iqbal Ullah Race Relations Resource Centre at the University of Manchester' (Govier, 2007). The day included a session by Kevin Bolton, Manchester Archives and Local Studies, on 'Queer Archives Up North' which covered initial aims; engaging with Manchester's LGBT community; forming partnerships; increasing access to existing LGBT collections and encouraging new deposits; and the overall benefits gained through this work.

Lancashire Archives has also ensured that work with LGBT people is embedded into the mainstream:

> I worked at Lancashire Archives for two-and-a-half years, and certainly within that short time frame I saw a lot of changes. LGBT History Month was our way in to working more specifically for and with LGBT people, but prior to February 2011 we had not celebrated or considered the month. Inspired by Jeff Evans, by February 2013 we had hosted three public events ('Outing the Past' 1-3); a Cultural Services Training Day for sharing best practice; launched an HLF-funded LGBT 'Hidden Histories' research project based in East Lancashire; brought in a number of archive collections from LGBT groups; and have been involved in numerous, smaller scale partnership events with Lancashire County Council's library and museum service. (Rooke, 2013)

A final example was that of the Gloucestershire Gay & Lesbian Community who, in February 2012, 'made the first LGBT deposit of historical information at Gloucestershire Archives. This is part of an ongoing collection and all donations are welcome' (Gloucestershire Gay & Lesbian Community, 2012).

Growing collaborations between community and mainstream archives

In some areas, the relationship between community and mainstream archives has been difficult, with, for example, wariness on the part of community archives as to the motives of mainstream archives, as well as concerns that ownership of 'their' material might be compromised, perhaps borne out by the experience of the Irish Queer Archive at the National Library of Ireland (Madden, 2012). However, bridges have begun to be built successfully; four major examples are:

- the Hall-Carpenter Archives at the London School of Economics – 'Britain's major resource for the study of lesbian and gay activism in the UK since the publication of the Wolfenden Report in 1957' (London School of Economics and Political Science, 2011);
- the Lesbian and Gay Newsmedia Archive at the Library and Archives of Bishopsgate Institute (Bookey, 2012);

- the rukus![10] Black, Lesbian, Gay, Bisexual and Trans cultural archive at the London Metropolitan Archives (deposited in October 2010) (Ajamu, 2011b);
- the Isle of Man National Archives: Manx National Heritage is currently working with the LGBT community on the Isle of Man. They have recently taken in records for the Isle of Man National Archives, and staff are working with the community to create an oral history record of LGBT experience on the Isle of Man since the 1950s (Weatherall, 2012).

As a result of all this work, a range of activities has developed, discussed in the following sections.

Organising LGBT exhibitions and events

A major development has been that, since 2003, London Metropolitan Archives have organised an annual LGBT conference (Phillpott, 2012; Pimblett, 2012). These have covered a wide range of topics of interest, including:

- 'Why Here? Why Now?', 2003, which was inspired by the work of Alan Bray[11] and his use of the collections at London Metropolitan Archives;
- 'What Are You Looking At?', 2004, which explored ideas of lesbian and gay culture, including a look at the media;
- 'Changing the World', 2005:

> 1985 was a significant year in London LGBT history. In that year the Greater London Council (GLC) published *'Changing the World'*, a charter of gay rights, the *London Lesbian and Gay Centre* opened at 69, Cowcross Street in Farringdon and the *Black Lesbian and Gay Centre* was founded.
>
> Twenty years on, the third annual LGBT Archives and History Conference at London Metropolitan Archives is picking up the theme of 'Changing the World' in response to suggestions and ideas put forward by delegates at the 2004 Conference.
>
> There will be explorations of the history of the actions of individuals and groups who have resisted discrimination and brought about change in many different ways, from club culture to politics. There will also be an examination of current work taking place nationally and internationally to literally, change the world. (London Metropolitan Archives, 2005)

---

10   'rukus! Federation is known for its long-standing and successful programme of community-based work with Black Lesbian, Gay, and Bisexual, Trans artists, activists and cultural producers nationally and internationally' (rukus! Federation, 2011).

11   Alan Bray (1948-2001), historian and gay rights activist (Bray, 1982).

- 'In Olden Days a Glimpse of Stocking ...', 2006, which focused 'on identity, including issues relating to transgendered people, cross dressing and cultural identity' (All in London 2006);
- 'Let's Pretend', 2007:

Back in 1988, Section 28 of the Local Government Act stated that a local authority was not permitted to 'promote the teaching ... of the acceptability of homosexuality as a pretended family relationship'. The London Metropolitan Archives' Fifth Annual LGBT History and Archives Conference, this year, sets out to explore the experience of LGBT families and family life and how these important histories might be recorded for future generations. (LGBT History Month 2007).

- 'Curiouser and Curiouser ...' 2008, which looked at 'the challenges around collecting, conserving and communicating the history of LBGT [sic] people and who and what is that history for?' (London Metropolitan Archives, 2008);
- 'Flights of Fancy' 2009, which looked at the role of the arts in being 'disturbing, dangerous and real instruments of change' (London Metropolitan Archives, 2009); in addition, it included sessions on the issues that arose from the sh[OUT] exhibition in Glasgow (Fenwick, ca. 2009) (see below);
- 'Young Hearts Run Free', 2010, which looked at young people's projects and activities (London Metropolitan Archives, 2010). This event was hard hit by poor weather, so an additional event was run in October 2011, 'Young Hearts Run Free 2', which 'revisits youth projects and the exciting work around collecting, recording and using LGBT history by young people. There will be contributions and workshops to support those wanting to start new projects, particularly in libraries' (City of London 2011);
- 'Resist ... Action ... Change', 2011, which looked at 'the different ways in which people are meeting today's challenges ... The workshops include exploring archive material and using it as a springboard into new and innovative ideas that can be put into action by individuals and groups' (London Metropolitan Archives, 2011a);
- 'Our History – Ourselves', 2012, 'a day of workshops and talks around researching, collecting, conserving, writing and communicating Lesbian and Gay personal, local and community histories' (City of London 2012);
- 'Brave New World?' – the tenth anniversary Conference was held in February 2013 and provided:

the opportunity to look at LGBT history / stories and culture in a variety of ways, identifying genuine progress made and considering retrograde steps. There is room for looking to the future and how heritage and cultural activity generated by formal institutions, community groups and individuals might continue to influence and bring about change. (Curran, 2012b)

LMA have also organised other regular events, such as LGBT Creative Writing Workshops (London Metropolitan Archives 2012).

In February 2006, Tyne and Wear Museums (TWM) hosted its first exhibition to mark LGBT History Month. The exhibition, 'Private Lives Public Battles', was a collaboration with local LGBT group, Our Place in History. The exhibition consisted of three main topics: personal experiences, politics and the LBGT community, and the Scene, and much of what was exhibited was oral history and reminiscences about growing up and coming out as LGBT in the area.

What grew out of this work, however, was the recognition that a single exhibition was not enough and that there were still voices that were not being heard – there was an urgent need to house and develop the material (this piece of work threw up a number of major, important challenges, so the report is quoted at some length):

> But much of the material uncovered was strictly archival: different members had in their homes correspondence and minutes of meetings of various campaigning and support groups such as Lesbian Line, and a complete run of CHE newsletters were amassed. Other people had important personal collections of flyers and posters for one-off nightclubs and Pride events. A substantial archive of correspondence relating to the Campaign for Homosexual Equality was also found to be held in the Centre for Gender and Women's Studies, at Newcastle University. It was recognised that an important task to be done was to bring all these collections together in one place. However, TWM normally recommends that material of this nature should be housed by the separately run Tyne and Wear Archives (TWAS), as the organisation is better equipped to enable researchers to access archival material through its search room facilities. Tyne and Wear Archives also has a staffed conservation laboratory, with expertise in archives preservation. Other parts of the collection brought together important material culture: numerous gay and lesbian badges, Pride T-shirts and personal memorabilia. This material could be better cared for by TWM, which has extensive costume and textile, social history, and science and technology collections with high grade storage facilities and dedicated curators. Oral history is collected by a number of organisations in Tyne and Wear, but TWM is also highly active in this field with a dedicated Keeper of Contemporary Collecting to care for it. The conundrum therefore presented itself of whether to split the collection to ensure its proper preservation, or keep it in the community and risk its potential loss in the future. (Baveystock *et al.* ca. 2006)

In addition, the project lost two of its key workers and also the premises it was using as an office:

> The project therefore illustrates some of the key issues of sustainability in community archive projects. Whilst museums are working with community groups more than ever before, providing them with skills and equipment to

collect their own history, the future of the histories collected are by no means straightforward. TWM would like to continue to make its collections and exhibitions as representative of the local population as possible, and working with communities is essential in doing this. Transferring skills in the process means that more history can be uncovered, however as we have seen this can create a sense of ownership within the community group and a set of priorities (mainly immediate access to material) that museums often cannot guarantee.

For a museum to insist on taking material for its collection can lead to conflict and a breakdown of trust with community groups. However, for the members of a community group to create their own archive means the museum has not added to the publicly held collection, and has not been able to make that collection more representative as an outcome of the project. The knowledge that material is out there, combined with an awareness that community archives often have a fragile existence, may create a frustrating situation for curators trying to promote inclusivity in museums. (Baveystock *et al.*, ca. 2006)

Surrey Heritage[12] has developed a range of approaches, including:

- Working with the charity Gay Surrey, since 2008: Gay Surrey deposited their archives with Surrey History Centre (Surrey Heritage, n.d.); and Surrey Heritage have been holding LGBT History Month displays in their foyer and attending Gay Surrey's International Day Against Homophobia and Transphobia (IDAHO) events – 'The [2010] evening was especially important for Surrey Heritage as Di Stiff, Collections Development Archivist, was presented with the Gay Surrey Heart of Equalities Award for her work to secure Gay Surrey's archive for the History Centre and the 2010 LGBT History Month campaign' (Stiff, 2010: 1).
- Displaying information about 'Surrey's gay icons' (including Dirk Bogarde and Dame Ethel Smyth) prominently on their 'Exploring Surrey's past' website (Surrey Heritage, ca. 2011).
- Producing for LGBT History Month 2011 a brief LGBT booklist (Surrey Heritage, 2011b).

---

12 Surrey Heritage brings together the following 'arms' of the County Council: The Stewardship & Preservation and Public Services Teams, which work to collect, preserve and make accessible historic documents and books relating to Surrey from the twelfth to the twenty-first centuries; the Heritage Conservation Team (HCT), which provides impartial advice on all aspects of managing, preserving and understanding archaeological remains and historic buildings; Heritage Enterprise (including the Surrey County Archaeological Unit), which provides high-quality archaeological services to commercial and public sector clients, including consultancy services; the Learning, Museums & Partnership Team, which provides a vital link with colleges, schools and museums and a wide range of other partners to help discover Surrey's history and ensure that the experiences of Surrey's diverse communities are recorded for all time (Reynolds, 2011).

- Supporting Out, Loud and Proud, a LGBTQ youth group, who not only gave a presentation at Surrey's IDAHO event in 2011, but also won an Heart of Equality Award from charity Gay Surrey for their contribution to promoting equality and inclusion in Surrey (Surrey Heritage, 2011a).

Taking part in LGBT exhibitions and events

[Sheffield] Archives and Local Studies were invited to participate in 'Spring Out' again in 2009 where staff led a workshop called 'Hidden Histories' using original records dating back to the early 1800s. Sheffield Archives and Local Studies were presented with a 'Spring Out 2009' award by the Centre for HIV and Sexual Health/Shout! for their positive contribution to LGB communities.

'Spring Out' brought Sheffield's LGBT history to a much wider audience. As a result, the 'Hidden Histories' workshop was presented at a number of venues across the city including at the Centre for Sexual Health and HIV as part of the national LGBT history month in February 2010.

Links continue to strengthen with LGBT communities and in June 2010 staff from Sheffield Libraries and Archives ran the Sheffield City Council's stall at Sheffield Pride. This included a display on the life of radical 19th century gay campaigner Edward Carpenter which drew considerable interest. (Sheffield Archives and Local Studies, 2010).

sh[OUT]

From 2001, the Gallery of Modern Art in Glasgow developed a social justice programme which 'sought to … directly and explicitly engage visitors in debates pertaining to different human rights issues' (Sandell, 2012: 199). The fourth such programme, 'sh[OUT]', explored rights issues relating to lesbian, gay, bisexual, trans and intersex (LGBTI) communities.

The issues that arose have been well covered elsewhere (for example: Sandell, 2012; Sandell *et al.*, 2010); what it demonstrated was the power of sexual images (and maybe LGBT images particularly) still to cause controversy; the offence taken by some people over religious issues: 'The artwork which invited visitors to write themselves "back into the Bible" seemed to attract the most controversy from the media and from visitors – including a protest by campaigners held outside GoMA' (Sandell *et al.*, 2010: 38); the potentially negative role of the media; and yet also the very strong role that a museum can play:

Despite the controversy that surrounded the sh[OUT] exhibition in the media, the analysis of the response cards reveals that – in contrast – visitor reactions were very positive, although there are tensions between the different viewpoints adopted by visitors. The majority of visitors expressed their support for the exhibition, supporting the choice of artworks, the message conveyed that celebrated (for most) the importance of equal rights for everyone in society and the need to extend those rights to the LGBTI community. Visitors found it challenging and provocative but in a positive way, informing their views and, for some, impacting upon their identity or informing them about an issue they previously knew very little about. (Sandell *et al.*, 2010: 39-40)

Perhaps also of critical importance, given one of the themes that runs through this book, was an unresolved issue:

the fact that LGBTI rights are an especially contested and timely topic. This means that some within the LGBTI community, for example those with a more radical identity politics, are keen to present one set of ideas – based around emphasising difference and demanding respect for those differences – whilst others wish to emphasise sameness and a mainstreaming of LGBTI culture. (Sandell *et al.*, 2010: 15)

Cultural and heritage organisations

This book has concentrated primarily on libraries, museums and archives, but, in this final section, it is worth highlighting briefly the work that has been developing in cultural and heritage organisations.

There is heightened visibility of LGBT owners of 'country houses', such as Anne Lister at Shibden Hall: 'Anne was 34 years old when she inherited Shibden from her Uncle James. She was a remarkable woman; an intrepid traveller, an astute business woman and, as her diaries disclose, a lesbian' (Calderdale Council, 2012).

Historian Alison Oram has also been exploring 'queerness, gender and the family in historic houses' (Oram, 2012a, 2012b), looking, for example, at Plas Newydd, home of the Ladies of Llangollen; and Sissinghurst, the garden created by writer Vita Sackville-West and her husband Harold Nicolson (Oram, 2011).

The National Trust has been working with the arts organisation Unravelled to reinterpret some of its properties; of particular significance is the work that they have been undertaking at Nymans (Unravelled, 2012), where, for the duration of the exhibition, they not only highlighted the theatrical setting and the lifestyle of Oliver Messel and his sister, Anne, but also, following the exhibition, the National Trust decided to recognise formally Oliver Messel's relationship with Vagn Riis Hansen and have added him to the family tree.

The National Trust also worked with partners on the 'Gay Birmingham, Back to Back' project, which researched the period from the 1850s up until the 1970s:

After a period of research, project partners Women & Theatre developed a series of site specific performances at the National Trust Back to Back Housing on Hurst Street, Birmingham. We uncovered and characterised the lives of real life gay men Charles Record and Fred 'Jester' Barnes and through a series of reminiscences and interviews created characters representing the lives of lesbian and bi women during World War 2 and the experiences of Black lesbians during the 1970s. (Birmingham LGBT, 2012)

As noted in Appendix 2, English Heritage organised in 2012 the first public event specifically for LGBT History Month offered at one of their sites, 'The Queens of Eltham Palace'.

Finally, in December 2011, the British Museum co-organised and hosted a major conference, 'Cultural Equalities Now', in collaboration with the Institute for the Public Understanding of the Past (IPUP) and the Diversity in Heritage Group (DHG) (Institute for the Public Understanding of the Past, 2012), which included lunchtime 'Talking Table' discussions around themes including 'LGBT programming and audiences' (Diversity in Heritage Group, 2011).

Chapter 8

Good practice – ideas and innovation

Having assessed the work by the cultural sector to meet the demands and needs of LGBT people since the 1950s, what have we learned? And what can we draw out as good practice by the cultural sector? This chapter aims to set out practical examples and lessons learned.

Before you start ...

- Develop your (and your colleagues') awareness of the national context;
- Explore what other similar organisations have been doing in this area of work;[1]
- Are there local and/or regional issues that you need to consider; for example, are you working in an area where there is rural isolation and few large urban centres where LGBT people may meet?

Ensuring your values are transparent

For example:

- Integrity, honesty, transparency: make it clear why you want to build the relationship with local LGBT people.
- Being realistic: be prepared for scepticism:

  There may be those who have experienced discrimination in the past and are sceptical about collaboration; those who are suffering from 'consultation fatigue' and are unconvinced that their input will be taken seriously or those who are unaware that authorities are now obliged because of ... community strategies to consult with marginalised groups. (Creegan and Lee, 2007: 16)

- Being open and responsive, both to the local community and to your colleagues, for example: 'In response to a staff attitudes survey, housing management organisation, Your Homes Newcastle, took action to address

---

1 For example, The Network coordinates a JISCMAIL list for people interested in developing and sharing their LGBT work (The Network, 2013).

concerns of lesbian, bay and bisexual (LGB) staff, including reviewing all its policies, introducing LGB mentors and ensuring all new policies include LGB aspects where appropriate' (Foster, 2011: 8).
- Respecting confidentiality and providing a safe environment.
- Being welcoming.
- Being inclusive. As Elizabeth L Chapman suggests:

> Within the LGBT community, some groups are less well-served than others. Bisexual, trans and genderqueer people tend to get overlooked, so collections or events that are billed as 'LGBT' may not in fact include any content specifically targeted at these communities. Other groups, such as asexual and intersex people, are even omitted from the acronym. (Chapman, E.L., 2012b)

Getting to know our communities

How do we find out about LGBT people in our area?

- You may be lucky enough to have had a survey of some sort carried out in your area, such as those in Birmingham (Wood 2011); Lambeth (Keogh *et al.*, 2006); Norfolk (NHS Norfolk, 2010); Stoke-on-Trent (LGBT Network Stoke-on-Trent & North Staffordshire, ca. 2011); West Dunbartonshire (Equality Network, 2012).
- Work with an existing local or regional forum, such as the Intercom Trust in south west England, who coordinate the community consultation CEDAR Project (Intercom Trust, 2007).
- Make contact with and visit local LGBT community groups, meeting-places, pubs/bars/clubs: use magazine listings, Internet searches to find groups and venues in your area.
- Talk to and/or gather information from your own colleagues and from other local authority contacts, e.g. in Adult or Children's Services, Health, Planning. Can the local authority produce statistics such as how many of their children in care identify as lesbian or gay?
- Carry out your own research and/or monitoring: NHS Northwest has produced a good introduction (Grant and Williams, 2011; NHS Northwest Health Equality Library Portal, 2009).
- Draw on sources of broader information, for example the Gender Identity Research and Education Society (GIRES) (GIRES, 2012).

Consulting

Having got a broad idea of who might be in our area, how can we find out what their demands and needs are? Common methods are:

- meetings
- visits
- focus groups
- reaching out to non-users (e.g. via outreach, the Internet and social media).

Good practice in consulting with LGBT people also includes:

- building joint ownership of the consultation process;
- avoiding being victim focused;
- using appropriate language: 'At the outset of consultation meetings, ask lesbian, gay and bisexual people how they would like to be addressed' (Creegan and Lee, 2007: 17);
- checking comments received using a touchstone (Are you being directed by one person and their hobby-horse? What are other people's experiences of this issue?);
- remembering: 'No one speaks for all LGBT people or any one group within that' (Hasted, 2012);
- not being misleading (e.g. in terms of what services you could offer);
- remembering that 'it can be challenging to reach groups who may have felt in the past that the service had little to offer them' (Chapman, E.L., 2012b).

Engaging – where to start?

From your consultations, you should be getting a picture of local needs. Where do you start in terms of actually doing something?

- Assess what your service can contribute on existing resources.
- Maybe start with an event that you can focus on and/or organise around, e.g. LGBT History Month, local LGBT Pride activities, specific temporary exhibitions and/or events that will raise your profile; 'hold a library conference and have LGBT issues as a workshop' (Logan, 2013).

Seeking good-practice ideas

Some good examples are:

- The *Community Engagement Toolkit* produced by Manchester City Council has a wealth of practical ideas (Manchester City Council. Communities and Neighbourhoods, 2005).
- Working with BME LGBT people: the recommendations in the Stonewall/ Runnymede Trust report include:
  - Don't create a hierarchy between identities;
  - Get your monitoring right;
  - Improve staff training;
  - Talk to BME LGB people;
  - Don't let sexual orientation dominate the discussion – but signal that people can be open about their orientation;
  - Provide practical support, 'such as resources, information and opportunities which are targeted at them';
  - Make openly gay BME people visible (taken from: Guasp and Kibirige, 2012: 26-29).
- Stonewall's guide for youth workers, *Everyone is Included* (Stonewall, ca. 2012a), has some good practical advice about working with young people, and how to make your organisation 'gay friendly'.
- Stonewall's good practice guide, *How to Engage Gay People in Your Work*, offers 'practical advice on how to engage lesbian, gay and bisexual people in decision-making about local services in cost-effective and appropriate ways' (Miles, 2011).
- 'Becoming a trans positive organisation': GALOP's (Lesbian, Gay and Bisexual Anti-Violence and Policing Group) guide includes the following:
  - Integrate fully at every level;
  - Reach and engage a broad range of trans people;
  - Create a welcoming environment;
  - Challenge prejudice;
  - Challenge prejudice: spotlight on harassment, abuse and sexual violence;
  - Acknowledge past mistakes;
  - Plan full trans-inclusion in projects, services and lobbying work;
  - Understand trans experiences;
  - Be an effective ally;
  - Have fair employment practices (taken from: Gooch, 2011).

How can this translate into an ongoing, sustainable activity?

One of the dangers identified throughout this book is that of running one-off projects (or pieces of work that rely on one individual and their expertise). To develop something ongoing, we need to look at:

- Management commitment: there need to be 'champions' who will help promote this work within and across the organisation (and who will lend support were anyone to object to the development of LGBT provision).
- Staff commitment: whilst an individual often has the passion to get a service and/or activity started, they will burn out unless other staff are also involved (and, as an 'official' service, there should be no excuse for the non-involvement of others).
- A broad, cross-organisation approach (together with the local community):

    My main experience has been in the borough where I live and now work. In 2000, the council organised a UK Gay sports festival, and libraries were involved with that project. It was huge and really pulled local LGBT people together, and since then there has been an LGBT forum which meets with the council. This year there is an extensive programme for LGBT History Month with 4 film nights, an author event and an advice session. The libraries have been running a lesbian reading group for 4 years now and it is advertised along with everything else quite openly. (Logan, 2013)

- Volunteers and community involvement, for example in running or co-running a LGBT reading group.
- Resources: for example to develop the service; promotion and/or advertising; running events.
- Policies: for example on stock selection, buying, collecting; cataloguing and describing; on ensuring that LGBT issues run through all the organisation's policies and practices; a critical part of equality and diversity policies.
- Co-production and sharing information: for example, in Barnsley, the library service has 'been working with the local LGBT forum to get a library presence on their website with links to themed booklists of our LGBT bookstock & DVDs. We are also trying to get a reciprocal link to their own website and for them to provide us with a list of their recommended LGBT website links' (Mann, 2012).
- Ensuring that library suppliers (e.g. via consortium purchasing) include LGBT material in their offer – and also using specialist suppliers and/or lists to inform and add to this (Valentine, S. *et al.*, 2002).
- Museums can use the Accreditation Scheme to help raise standards and to ensure that they are being responsive to user needs and expectations (Arts Council England, ca. 2012).

Into the mainstream

It is vital that the cultural sector not only celebrates events such as LGBT History Month and LGBT Pride, but also engages in programming LGBT-related activities throughout the year – and also weaves them into other activities (such as mainstream exhibitions or displays) and events (such as Black History Month); for example:

- London Metropolitan Archives hosted a presentation in October 2012 by Ajamu about his work recording Black LGBT people and his forthcoming exhibition, *Fierce*, at Guildhall Art Gallery (LGBT History Month, 2012).
- In 'Family Album' (National Portrait Gallery, 2012), 'a National Portrait Gallery partnership exhibition that travelled to Sunderland, Plymouth and Sheffield, the inclusion of one portrait meant that same-sex relationships and civil partnerships were part of the changing concepts of family explored in the show' (Frost 2010); this portrait was of Peter Pears and Benjamin Britten[2] (Tseliou, 2011: 5).
- In 2012, the Science Museum launched a major exhibition, 'Codebreaker – Alan Turing's life and legacy', which ran until July 2013 (Science Museum, 2012).
- The exhibition, 'Hitched: Wedding Clothes and Customs", shown at Sudley House in 2010-2011, included civil partnership suits and pictures (National Museums Liverpool, 2012; Tseliou, 2011: 5).

It is also vital that we ensure that our events become 'inclusive and meaningful to people who don't see themselves as belonging to that community. There still seems to be a feeling that a 'Gay History' is outside of and irrelevant to social history more generally and that you would only go to an LGBT History Month event if you yourself were out as LGBT' (Rooke, 2013).

Reassessment of what you hold

- Archives may have important collections of material (e.g. court records or literary papers) which have not been reassessed recently, and, when they were listed, the LGBT elements may not have been highlighted (Hall, 2012).
- You may find references to LGBT people in other records that are in the archives, such as criminal records, e.g. Quarter Sessions; hospital or asylum records; other institutional records; local government and political records (e.g. of suffragettes) (Rooke, 2012).

---

2   Sir Peter Neville Luard Pears; (Edward) Benjamin Britten, Baron Britten.

- The National Archives have produced a valuable guide to finding records relating to gay and lesbian history, which also includes a glossary and list of suggested search terms (The National Archives, 2013).
- Material may include cryptic notes, written at the time to hide the true nature of the information, and these need to be revisited (see Liddington, n.d.).
- 'A lot of LGBT materials come from small presses or US publishing houses, so will not appear on suppliers' lists or in supplier selections; you will need to seek them out. Most supplier contracts include a clause which allows you to buy elsewhere in the event that the supplier doesn't provide an adequate range in a particular area' (Chapman, E.L., 2012b).
- 'Mention LGBT materials in your collection development policy and your supplier specifications. Currently, many services use a general formulation such as "all groups in the community", but mentioning specific groups can help to ensure that they are not overlooked' (Chapman, E.L., 2012b).

Promoting the service and its resources

- The London Metropolitan Archives publishes a series of Information Leaflet guides to their holdings – this includes one on the LGBT-related archives they hold (and which also helpfully signposts enquirers to other sources too) (London Metropolitan Archives, 2011b).
- The Wellcome Library has produced a list of archive sources about sex, which includes material of LGBT interest (Wellcome Library, 2012).
- The LGBT Excellence Centre Wales[3] 'has launched a unique project funded by the Heritage Lottery Fund that focuses on the cultural heritage of lesbian, gay, bisexual, and transgender people in Wales: *Welsh Pride.* Working in partnership with the National Museum Wales and others, the project will research stories, experiences, anecdotes, ideas, artefacts, photographs and collections of Welsh people or people who lived in Wales in the last century. The project aims to create the greatest archive of Welsh LGBT Culture and History to be used as a base for leaning, raising awareness, fighting discrimination and promoting equality' (LGBT Excellence Centre, 2012c). They have also developed 'a listing of Welsh libraries and the number of books they hold when using the key word searches of homosexual, lesbian, bisexual and transgender in CatCymru. The word gay was not included as it will return thousands of hits which are not necessarily related to gay people' (LGBT Excellence Centre, 2012a).
- Providing tailored lists of holdings, booklists etc. For example, Sheffield Local Studies and Sheffield Archives have published a guide

---

3 'The LGBT Excellence Centre Wales is a social enterprise and a charity that supports people, organisations and businesses with issues concerning sexual orientation and gender identity' (LGBT Excellence Centre, 2012b).

to sources for studying LGBT history (Sheffield Libraries Archives and Information, 2009).

- Cataloguing and indexing – there needs to be:

> a taxonomy for cataloguing and indexing LGBT history within museum collections. Without this kind of serious and fundamental professional work, finding anything after the local research project or temporary exhibition remains a challenge. This has been tackled with partial success for women's history, BAME history and many other topics, but we still need to get national, digitally searchable access to assets in collections across the sector. When this happens, I will know LGBT has been mainstreamed. (Hasted, 2012)

The image that we present

> I think ALL the imagery in libraries should challenge the White, Male, Heterosexual, Able-bodied, Middle-Class, Cis-gendered, British narrative that is omnipresent in our society in advertising, media and television etc. If a library was an oasis of different messages, perhaps more people and more minorities in general would feel comfortable and welcomed into them as spaces of encouragement and inclusion? (Lorne, 2012)

Stock arrangement and promotion

One issue that is often seen as daunting is that of how to arrange the stock in a library. Should it be in a separate section? Or interfiled with other stock?

Public libraries have experimented with both,[4] and there are pluses and minuses for each.

- Separate sections mean that the stock is visible, and library users do not need to ask staff to find it. However, anyone who is nervous of approaching shelves labelled as LGBT in some way may not pluck up enough courage

---

4   As with many initiatives, different methods of arranging stock come in and out of fashion: 'It's fascinating how, perhaps a couple of decades or so ago, having, for example, a separate LGBT section was a really powerful statement. Rows of [Gay Men's Press] books with their pink triangles on the spine, complemented by the pink triangles of the Council's categorisation scheme, was a very clear statement of intent - this is your library as much as anyone else's. All of this supported by outreach work into the community … Then gradually a shift, as fiction and other materials were integrated into the mainstream shelves, reflecting a sense, perhaps, that the "liberation" was complete (which of course it wasn't, and isn't)' (Murray, 2012).

to use the collection; also, there is less chance of anyone happening across a book by chance; and, finally, unless someone takes full responsibility for keeping the separate collection up-to-date and interesting, there is a danger that it ends up tired and unused.
- Interfiling the stock means that people can find titles with LGBT interest alongside other stock, but only if they know the author – or by chance.

What many libraries do successfully is to:

- interfile their stock for most of the year, but pull out LGBT material to display for LGBT History Month and/or Pride;
- highlight LGBT material with an identifiable spine-label (e.g. a rainbow flag);
- identify material of LGBT interest in the catalogue;
- produce booklists that promote the stock.

Interviewee Lorne suggests:

> perhaps on the 'this week's recommended titles' shelves that a lot of libraries have, the librarians could ensure a good mix of options, if LGBTQQAIP[5] books are mixed in across genres and on mixed shelves *as well as* in their own sections, it would go some way to 'usualising' the existence of LGBTQQAIP issues in society, as well as help that young TQIP person to find a title without 'outing' themselves by lingering in the 'Lesbian and Gay' aisle!
>
> Also, change the name of these aisles to include other identities beyond just LG people. Perhaps the aisle could be signposted as 'Sexuality, sexual orientation studies' and there could be Trans, Gender-variant issue books in an aisle with, 'Gender, women's studies, and gender identity' being together? (Lorne 2012, his emphasis)

Staffing

- Staff need to be 100 per cent confident in dealing with LGBT visitors, staff, content – and any issues that may arise.
- Ensure that your organisation's policies are positive and clear about welcoming LGBT staff and service users (and also about how any issues of homophobia or harassment will be dealt with).
- Ensure that senior managers speak out about the importance of an inclusive workplace – and that their actions mirror this (Anderson, M.J. and Gilmour, 2012).
- Recruitment: for example, does your organisation target any of its recruiting specifically towards LGBT people? Are your recruitment practices positive (for example, towards someone who is transitioning)?

---

5 Lesbian, Gay, Bisexual, Transgender, Queer, Questioning, Allied, Intersex & Pansexual.

- Monitoring: 'Encourage the council to put a LGBT question in its staff satisfaction survey to get local activists to come forward' (Logan, 2013).
- Training and awareness-raising are vital.
- Mentoring: for example in four local authorities in West Yorkshire: 'In a collaboration between four local councils, a viable mentoring scheme was set up, with the aims of improving motivation and leadership development of lesbian, gay, bisexual and trans employees' (Somerset, 2011: 13).
- Working with and/or supporting workplace and Trade Union LGBT groups:
  - Amgueddfa Cymru/National Museum Wales – 'As part of our own diversity programme, we are also working towards internal aims such as setting up an LGBT staff network, amongst other things' (Jones, 2012).
  - Barnsley – 'An LGBT staff page has been set up on the intranet & an LGBT staff group formed' (Mann, 2012).
- Professions' approaches: does your professional body have a current set of policies about supporting LGBT people? Does it have up-to-date information about the make-up of its members? What is its stance on supporting members over homophobia?

Benchmarking

- Participate in the Stonewall Diversity Champions programme,[6] 'Britain's good practice employers' forum on sexual orientation' (Stonewall, 2012):
  - Amgueddfa Cymru/National Museum Wales – 'On the non-public side, we joined Stonewall's Diversity Champions scheme, the first Museum to do so (and possibly still the only one) ...' (Jones, 2012)
  - Barnsley – 'The Council has taken part in the Stonewall Workplace Equality Index & from that an action plan for the Council has been created in which libraries are involved. This includes all staff having to complete an Equality & Diversity workbook on induction. Several awareness raising sessions on LGBT issues have taken place (Mann, 2012).

---

6 'Britain's good practice forum for LGB workplace issues, Diversity Champions brings together top employers from across the UK to promote diversity in the workplace. The programme has been helping businesses and public services to develop inclusive workplace cultures for a decade, ensuring that all of their staff can perform to their full potential' (Stonewall, ca. 2012b: 2).

Wider community involvement

Examples of wider community involvement include: 'Barnsley Council has a zero tolerance policy on hate crime and the Central Library is now a reporting centre' (Mann, 2012). And:

> One of my proudest moments of recent times, when I was a very senior manager indeed, was the fact that the central library was overwhelmingly the obvious choice to host so many LGBT events for the city – Pride drop in, LGBT History Ball, community awards … a sign we were doing something right … As communities everywhere face serious challenges, now is exactly the moment for libraries to cement themselves as key to communities, and all of the diverse groups that make living together what it is. (Murray, 2012)

Monitoring and evaluation

It is vital to evaluate this work, for example:

- to check if what we are doing is worthwhile and is working;
- gathering learning which can lead to change – What lessons have we learned from this? What goes well? And less well?
- benchmarking;
- evidence gathering;
- testing hypotheses;
- gathering information to report to funders;
- giving participants a voice;
- gathering information and learning in order to develop advocacy;
- gathering information which will feed into the political and economic contexts in which we work;
- to build up a demonstrable model of practice;
- to share good practice;
- to demonstrate impact.

Some helpful guides include:

- *Everything you wanted to know about sexual orientation monitoring … but were afraid to ask* (Grant and Williams, 2011; NHS Northwest Health Equality Library Portal, 2009);
- Stonewall's *Monitoring: how to monitor sexual orientation in the workplace* (Cowan, 2006);
- UNISON's *Workforce monitoring for sexual orientation and gender identity* (UNISON, 2007).

'Politics'

Finally, despite all your preparation and hard work, there are bound to be some people who complain! These complaints may be politically motivated, for example, or to do with views of faith and/or religious groups.

One of the key reasons for getting management commitment is so that there will be support for this work in the face of criticism and complaints; be prepared too for controversy, sometimes involving local media.

Don't become 'frozen'

There will be complex areas to explore and understand, but one of the greatest barriers is becoming 'frozen' – so worried that we do not do anything (or ignore what we have found). A key area where this may happen links to the previous point – that of competing equality claims, 'instances where the "equalities" claimed by one group or individual threaten, or are perceived to threaten, the equality of others' (Afridi and Warmington, 2010: 3).

This is where the background you have built up, locally and more widely, comes to the fore, in terms of consulting and exploring practice as widely as possible.

After all this, there will still be occasions when we make mistakes – but surely this is preferable (and, if you have the community on your side, forgivable) than doing nothing at all.

Chapter 9

Conclusions

Background

As indicated in the Preface, this book has aimed to explore the role that the cultural sector can play in working with and supporting LGBT people:

> Whilst I recognise that young (and not-so-young) people may well find it easier to come out today – and, indeed, the necessity to have life framed by coming-out stories may be fading – nevertheless we know that many people still struggle and still have to face hostility, threats, even violence. One of the motivators for much of my work (writing, running courses, talking to people about being gay and the issues we still face) is to try to improve the situation for those who 'come after' me, to try to prevent more young people being bullied and feeling so overwhelmed that they self-harm or take their own lives.
>
> I think that the cultural sector can play a huge part in this by providing safe, informed (and informative) spaces where people can explore who they are – and be who they are too. However, not all the cultural sector understands this – or wants to play this role – so this books is intended to make visible the needs and demands of LGBT people, and to demonstrate the good practice that parts of the cultural sector have developed, as well as identifying gaps where this is not happening.

The intention in this concluding chapter is to assess what we have learned, to point up areas where there are considerable gaps and to highlight what still needs to happen. First, however, we need to consider money.

Resources

Given how critical funding is to much of our work, this book could not finish without some mention of money. The period from 1950 to date has been one of repeated 'boom or bust',[1] which has led to regular expansions and contractions of the resources available, especially for the cultural sector. To take just one example, the early 1970s was a period of relative 'boom', especially in inner-city local authorities, where there was additional central government funding available; by the late 1970s, the economy was contracting again and services started to be cut back.

---

1   'Rapid economic growth and inflation (a boom), followed by ... [a] period of economic contraction/recession (falling GDP, rising unemployment)' (Pettinger, 2012).

We know that, to have any real impact (particularly on groups that are socially excluded), provision needs to be targeted, tailored and mainstreamed (see: DCMS, 1999), and this approach has been emphasised in the good-practice examples in chapter 8.

In addition, resources are also required for innovation to flourish – although, that said, creating the attitudinal climate for good practice to flourish may actually cost very little.

Therefore, in an ideal world, what would be required is, firstly, project funding to test ideas, experiment and investigate different methods of provision to different communities. Once such work has been fully evaluated, and provided it has demonstrated that it has had the right sort of impact, then, ideally, mainstream funding should be available to implement and embed the work in mainstream practice.

That is the ideal … What happens in reality is that, all too often, the project stage happens, but, once the work has been evaluated, it is then not mainstreamed. In addition, because 'core' funding is under pressure, cultural sector organisations either refuse to take on work with 'new' communities until the resources are found or expect such work to be funded by an external funder.

Some of the issues around project funding have been highlighted in a recent Paul Hamlyn Foundation report (Lynch, 2012) which shows that it can lead to 'disillusionment and disengagement, and an overall lack of direction to the work. Many of the staff members talked about feeling "stuck" … unable to escape the merry-go-round of projects that were not having the long-term local impact desired' (Lynch, 2012: 6).

Project funding may also end up limiting what can be achieved longer term: 'A more profound systemic transformation is needed than what a project can achieve alone, but that transformation needs to draw on learning from innovative project and partnership work. Catalysts and leaders are needed to nurture new ways of working' (Carpenter, 2010: 18).

So – whilst project funding is highly beneficial at some stages, it can also divert from embedding good practice into the organisation's mainstream.

In the current climate, it frankly seems very unlikely that external funders are going to support a cultural sector organisation to build links with local LGBT communities or to develop work that, by rights, should already be being provided; it is critical, therefore, that cultural sector organisations move beyond this over-reliance on external funding and find different ways of delivering services as part of their 'core'.

What have we learned?

There has been a lot of excellent work being developed in the cultural sector, particularly in the period since 2004. Firstly, what might have caused this development?

We can identify the following as significant reasons for this – and also note them as pointers to future growth and consolidation of work with LGBT people:

- There was a number of notable, strong individuals championing this work.
- Some managers also started to champion work with LGBT people and to support the increased engagement of LGBT staff.
- Organisations, both inside and outside the public sector, made strong equality commitments (and local authorities, for example, developed equality targets).
- DCMS required more of the nationals and other museums (especially via Public Service Agreements and National Indicators).
- There was also a growing global interest in rights and equality.
- Finally, there was a strong recognition that a generation of people were getting older and, if their oral histories and personal collections and stories were to be added to the record of historical material, then action needed to be taken to encourage deposits, encourage community collecting activity, supporting strategies for sharing and so on.

However, this development is still patchy, and the differences between different parts of the sector are quite marked. The following comments are generalisations, but broadly sum up the position:

- Some public libraries led the way in the 1970s and 1980s, with active stock purchase and promotion, and the start of building links with their local LGBT communities, but this was by no means universal. After the 1980s, this work went through a period of being very low-key (perhaps a response to Clause 28), but, since 2004, it has been rising up the agenda, especially in relation to LGBT History Month. However, it is very much event-led and not necessarily infiltrating the mainstream service.
- Some museums have led the way recently, with major developments having taken place since 2006. However, again, this is by no means universal and, possibly because of Clause 28 or because of issues around reinterpreting the past, has been very slow to develop. It is salutary to think that it is only within the last three years that LGBT issues have featured at the annual Museums Association conference.
- Archives and local studies departments – spurred on by the lead from The National Archives – have begun to make significant developments recently, but, again, this is by no means universal.
- The cultural heritage sector more widely has also just begun to recognise the need to reflect LGBT histories in their activities and properties.

Although this is less common than it used to be, nevertheless provision for LGBT people is still seen by some in the cultural sector as a peripheral activity which is not a central part of what they do.

In earlier chapters, we identified examples of innovative practice and also looked at how the cultural sector has developed since 2004 – we now need to build on this foundation to take the work forward.

Where are there considerable gaps? And what still needs to happen?

Briefly, the gaps in development and what should happen next can be summarised as follows:

- There has been a real growth recently in recognition of the importance of LGBT History Month – however, this is by no means universal, so it is important that all cultural sector organisations get involved in this.
- At the same time, it is also important to ensure that activities are not just restricted to February, but are programmed throughout the year and as part of all the organisations' other work.
- Staff attitudes are absolutely critical, and there needs to be a real effort across the sector to increase staff development opportunities and to tackle prejudice as it arises. Professional elitism has also been identified as a key issue, and, again, there has to be a real move to ensure that all staff are engaged with and supporting their organisations' social justice work.
- There is very little recorded LGBT history within the cultural sector before the 1970s-1980s. Urgent work is required to capture the history of LGBT library, museum, archive and heritage work and reminiscences of staff from the 1950s and 1960s.

And the outlook?

At the time of writing, the position in the UK for LGBT people seems positive; just as one example, despite considerable opposition, the 'gay marriage' Bill (Great Britain, 2013) was passed through the House of Commons (see: Sparrow, 2013) – though still not enacted as yet.

However, at the same time, wider political coalitions are being formed and re-formed, for example in Europe, with dubious consequences (Traynor, 2009) and the danger of links being formed with states with homophobic policies: 'Macedonia's state controlled media has been whipping up homophobia and outing allegedly gay members of the opposition ahead of the country's local elections in little over than two months' (Littauer, 2013b). 'Belarus's ministry of justice rejects gay rights group registration, while its members are subject to harassment from the authorities' (Littauer, 2013a).

Also, not far beneath the surface may lay all sorts of reactionary views:

> A poll in Germany found that while the majority did not mind the idea, a quarter
> of voters said they would not support a gay person as the nation's leader ... The
> poll also questioned whether voters would support an ethnic non-German in the
> role, producing similar figures: 29% opposed the idea while 11% supported it.
> (Pinfold, 2013)

As the world faces struggles for resources, there is a real danger that this could
herald a new period of hatred and oppression of minorities, including LGBT people
(see: Forced Migration Online, 2011; Werz and Conley, 2012). We therefore need
to ensure that the cultural sector plays its part in keeping LGBT issues to the fore.

Rachel Hasted gives this sense of progress being fragile and not necessarily
permanent – certainly, as we have seen, developments have been and are very
patchy:

> I have seen a lot of changes from the 1970s to the present but they have been
> uneven across the sector. Ideas that are now taken for granted in some museums
> remain novel and threatening to other parts of the cultural heritage sector. I have
> seen the prevailing political wind locally, or nationally, make a great impact on
> what museums felt able to do at any point. The equality laws covering rights for
> LGBT people, backed by the EU, have been a wake up call for some managing
> bodies since 2000, while the 'business case' for attracting an LGBT audience or
> customers has influenced others. I do not yet feel that any of this is irreversible.
> (Hasted, 2012)

Therefore, there needs to be a real commitment to ensuring that LGBT rights
remain high on the agenda; that we remain vigilant to make sure that current gains
are not eroded; and, nearer to home, to embedding the best practice into work
across our sector to ensure that LGBT people are not left out or given second best.

Appendix 1
Some current debates around LGBT terminology and definitions

Who are LGBT people? Some definitions

Background – and the dangers of labels

Sexuality is often presented in over-simplistic terms. This is not a very recent phenomenon – in fact there have been doubts for some considerable time over trying to define people narrowly by their sexuality – for example, are we describing their sexual activity? Or their sexual attraction? Is this something that is fluid or fixed? As long ago as 1970, the US writer Laud Humphreys introduced his famous research (*Tearoom Trade*) by describing it 'not a study of "homosexuals" but of participants in homosexual acts' (Humphreys, L., 1970: 18; cited in: Savin-Williams, 2009: 5).

Today, increasing numbers of young people are choosing not to define themselves with a label:

> This has become increasingly acute during the past few years because current cohorts of same-sex oriented teenagers are resisting identifying themselves with sexual terms, for personal, political, and philosophical reasons. Some identify as gay and have no same-sex attraction or behavior, while others have only same-sex attraction and behavior and do not identify as gay because the concept does not fit their experience. (Savin-Williams, 2009: 34)

These themes will be explored a little more below.

Lesbian

To take the broadest possible definition: a lesbian is 'a woman who is attracted to other women' (NHS Northwest Health Equality Library Portal, 2009: 14). This can include romantically and/or sexually.

Gay

Similarly: 'Gay men are men who are affectionally [sic], romantically, and/or sexually attracted to other men' (Greenblatt, 2011b: 5).

Bisexual

Bisexuality:

> is a broad umbrella term which may include the following groups and more:

- people who see themselves as attracted to 'both men and women';
- people who are mostly attracted to one gender but recognise that this is not exclusive;
- people who experience their sexual identities as fluid and changeable over time;
- people who see their attraction as 'regardless of gender' (other aspects of people are more important in determining who they are attracted to);
- people who dispute the idea that there are only two genders and that people are attracted to one, the other, or both. (Barker *et al.*, 2012: 11)

Trans

This book has drawn particularly on the work of the Gender Identity Research and Education Society (GIRES) (GIRES, 2012), Gendered Intelligence (Gendered Intelligence, 2012a) and the Women's Resource Centre (Women's Resource Centre, 2012).

The terminology around transgender is constantly shifting and will continue to evolve (as, indeed, it is with sexuality and gender generally). Some recent definitions include:

> Transgender is an all-encompassing term for people that cross gender boundaries, permanently or otherwise. Many prefer trans as the umbrella term. Trans includes, but is not limited to: people who live in the opposite gender to that registered at their birth, whether or not they have undertaken gender reassignment surgery, transvestites who cross-dress, intersex people who are born with anatomy or physiology which differs from norms associated with male and female anatomy, and others who do not identify with traditional female and male norms. Some people may not identify with being male or female and may prefer 'third gender'. (Women's Resource Centre, 2010: 1)

The Scottish Transgender Alliance helpfully represents the range of gender definitions using a 'Transgender or Trans Umbrella' – this includes:

- transsexual women (male to female)
- transsexual men (female to male)
- intersex people [see below]
- androgyne and polygender people
- cross-dressing and transvestite people (Scottish Transgender Alliance, n.d.-c).

Androgyne people:

> Some people find they do not feel comfortable thinking of themselves as simply either male or female. Instead they feel that their gender identity is more complicated to describe. Some may identify their gender as right in the middle between male and female, while others may feel mainly male but not 100% male (or vice-versa not feel 100% female). Alternatively, they may entirely reject defining their gender in terms of male and female in any way. As their gender does not conform to traditional ideas of gender as binary, they have created new words to describe themselves, the most common are *androgyne*, *polygender*, *genderqueer* or *third-gender*, although other terms are also occasionally used. However, some people will prefer not to define themselves using anything more specific than just transgender or trans. (Scottish Transgender Alliance, n.d.-b: their emphases)

Cross-dressing people:

> People (usually males) who call themselves *cross-dressing* or *transvestite people*, dress as the opposite gender for emotional satisfaction, erotic pleasure, or just because they feel more comfortable doing so. They feel a strong recurring desire to cross-dress but are generally happy with their birth gender and have no wish to permanently alter the physical characteristics of their bodies. (Scottish Transgender Alliance, n.d.-a: their emphases)

Queer

Queer was originally a synonym for 'odd' or 'weird', but became a derogatory term for gay men and lesbians in the twentieth century:

> Although many people still use 'queer' as an anti-gay slur, there emerged a movement in the 1980s that sought to reclaim the term and rob it of its negative meaning. In this usage, 'queer' is an inclusive umbrella term that designates all those who are sexually dissident, even if they are not strictly homosexual, and all 'transgressive' forms of sexuality. Many lesbians and gay men, transsexuals, bisexuals, and even heterosexuals whose sexuality does not fit into the cultural standard of monogamous heterosexual marriage have adopted the 'queer' label. Some gay men and lesbians, however, remembering the hurt caused by its pejorative meaning, dislike the term, even in its 'reclaimed' usage. (GLBTQ, 2006)

Queer theory

> Queer theory is a set of ideas based around the idea that identities are not fixed and do not determine who we are. It suggests that it is meaningless to talk in

general about 'women' or any other group, as identities consist of so many elements that to assume that people can be seen collectively on the basis of one shared characteristic is wrong. Indeed, it proposes that we deliberately challenge all notions of fixed identity, in varied and non-predictable ways. (Gauntlett, ca. 2008)

'What makes queer studies "queer" therefore, is not that it concerns homosexuality or that its practitioners are lesbians or gay men, but that it questions assumptions that are steeped, often subtly, in heterosexist biases' (Kaczorowski, 2008).

Questioning

'Questioning' refers to people who are questioning their gender, sexual identity, sexual orientation, or all three.

Intersex

'Intersexed people are individuals born with anatomy or physiology which differs from contemporary ideals of what constitutes "normal" male and female' (UK Intersex Association, n.d.).

'For example, a person might be born appearing to be female on the outside, but having mostly male-typical anatomy on the inside. Or a person may be born with genitals that seem to be in-between the usual male and female types' (Intersex Society of North America, 2008).

Heteronormativity

The term 'heteronormativity' is used to describe: 'the marginalisation of non-heterosexual lifestyles and the view that heterosexuality is the normal sexual orientation' (NHS Northwest Health Equality Library Portal, 2009: 14).

Heterosexism

The term 'heterosexism' is shorthand for: 'attitudes, bias and discrimination solely in favour of heterosexual orientation and opposite-sex relationships' (NHS Northwest Health Equality Library Portal, 2009: 14).

Homophobia

'Homophobia is the hatred or fear of people who are gay or lesbian' (NHS Northwest Health Equality Library Portal, 2009: 14). Similarly, biphobia is the hatred or fear of bisexuals, and transphobia is the hatred or fear of trans people.

Numbers

Given all of the above, it is easy to understand why trying to come to a numerical grip on just how many LGBT people there are is almost impossible. The Equality Act 2010 (Great Britain, 2010) has established nine 'protected characteristics' (people's characteristics which cannot be used as a reason to treat them unfairly). These are: age; disability; gender reassignment; marriage and civil partnership; pregnancy and maternity; race; religion and belief; sex; and sexual orientation (Equality and Human Rights Commission, n.d.).

In order to monitor progress and to assess whether there has been discrimination, there is a strong requirement to collect data (Botcherby and Creegan, 2009).

However, there is a current problem with numbers, especially the often-quoted figure from the then DTI (Department of Trade and Industry, 2003), prepared as part of its final regulatory impact assessment for the Civil Partnership Act 2004, of 5-7 per cent of the population being lesbian, gay or bisexual: 'Whilst no specific data is available, a wide range of research suggests that LGB people constitute 5–7 per cent of the total adult population' (Aspinall 2009: 50).

This 'estimate is, itself, of questionable validity, comprising data for different dimensions and from highly disparate surveys' (Aspinall, 2009: 59). Recent research by the Office for National Statistics suggested that just one in 100 people are lesbian or gay, and one in 200 identify as bisexual (Rouse, 2010). These figures appear quite low: this is likely to be as a result of this being the first time that this survey was carried out, and data-collection took place on doorsteps or by telephone, which may deter people from giving accurate responses – particularly if they are not 'out' at home.

Further discussion of labelling

New research by Eric Anderson and Mark McCormack has argued that the previous rigid delineation of sexuality is blurring. In his book, *Inclusive Masculinity* (Anderson, 2009), Eric Anderson coined the term 'homohysteria' – 'the cultural fear of being homosexualized' (McCormack, 2012: 44) – which is immensely important as a way of gauging the level of fear of LGBT people; and suggested that, at times when homohysteria declines, then the rigidly-demarcated masculine role becomes less powerful. Via his theory of inclusive masculinity, Eric Anderson also argued that 'when a culture is no longer homohysteric, there will be a marked expansion in the range of permissible behaviors for boys and men' (McCormack, 2012: 45). Mark McCormack draws on this research to support the findings in his own research, especially 'in a culture of decreased homohysteria, physical affection and emotional intimacy between heterosexual male students are both common and esteemed' (McCormack, 2012: 137).

Mark McCormack also argues that Eric Anderson (Anderson, 2009), Ritch Savin-Williams (Savin-Williams, 2005, 2009) and his own work 'address the same social phenomenon – decreasing homophobia among youth' (McCormack, 2012: 127).

Indeed, since the development of 'queer studies'/'queer theory' – and subsequent thinking about sex, sexuality and gender, such as what has been termed 'new sexuality studies' (Seidman *et al.*, 2011) – there has been a growing argument that it may be a false approach to see the world in binary terms (male/female, gay/straight etc.): 'sex is fundamentally social. Individuals are born with bodies that produce biological responses to sexual stimuli, but it is society that determines which parts of the body and which pleasures and acts are considered sexual' (Taylor & Francis Group 2012).

There is also increasing evidence that there are risks in claiming a gay identity, in that it emphasises a false dichotomy between gay/straight, and also leaves less room for manoeuvre – claiming one's sexuality often depends on the social context (Kellinger and Cover, 2012):

> All queers have extensive experience with the closet, no matter how much of a sissy or tomboy we were as children, no matter how early we decided we are to be openly gay or lesbian. The closet is not a function of homosexuality in our culture, but of compulsory and presumptive heterosexuality. I may be publicly identified as gay, but in order for that identity to be acknowledged, I have to declare it on each new occasion. (Crimp, 1993: 305)

Perhaps one of the clearest summaries of queer theory is that offered by Len Moran who argues that, even when sexuality is not apparent, it is 'always in public', that heterosexuality is taken to be the norm[1] – and 'the very pinnacle of moral accomplishment' – all of which are identified by queer theory as 'part of a heteronormative regime' (Moran, 2012: 64-65).

For the future, as Peter Tatchell suggests:

> The evidence of considerable cross-over between gay and straight relations comes from research that records consciously recognised and admitted desires. At the level of unconscious feelings – where passions are often repressed, displaced, sublimated, projected and transferred – it seems probable that very few people are 100 percent straight or gay. Most are a mixture, even if they never mentally acknowledge or physically express both sides of the sexual equation.
>
> This picture of human sexuality is much more complex, diverse and blurred than the traditional simplistic binary image of hetero and homo, so loved by straight moralists and – equally significantly – by many lesbians and gay men. If sexual orientation has a culturally-influenced element of indeterminacy and

---

1   Since the 1980s, there has been considerable research into gender relations (Connell, 1987) and, particularly, the concept of 'hegemonic masculinity' (see Wikipedia, 2012k), that is, that most societies encourage men to 'embody a dominant version of masculinity', thereby privileging that over women and over men who do not embody this.

flexibility, then the present forms of homosexuality and heterosexuality are conditional. They are unlikely to remain the same in perpetuity. As culture changes, so will expressions of sexuality …

The vast majority of people will be open to the possibility of both opposite-sex and same-sex desires, regardless of whether they act upon them. They won't feel the need to label themselves (or others) as gay or straight because, in a future non-homophobic civilisation, no one will care who loves who. Love will transcend sexual orientation. (Tatchell, 2012)

The cultural sector's involvement in LGBT History Month and in LGBT Pride

This appendix shows examples of the wide range of work that the cultural sector has undertaken to celebrate LGBT History Month, celebrated in February each year; LGBT Pride, which is celebrated between April and October each year, depending on the location (see ILGA Europe, 2012); and International Coming Out Day, celebrated on 11 October.

The organisation Schools Out have particularly argued the importance of museums and galleries taking part (Fenwick, 2009).

Author/book promotions, book displays and booklists

Coventry Library

Coventry's Central Library proudly displayed the new books it had recently purchased to commemorate LGBT History Month 2012; which had been done in consultation with the city's LGBT community as part of a 'community buy' (Coventry LGBT, 2012).

Essex Libraries

Essex Libraries added a booklist to their reading ideas page for LGBT History Month 2012 (Essex Libraries, 2012).

Manchester Libraries

Manchester Libraries and the Lesbian and Gay Foundation celebrated 2012 International Coming Out Day by producing *Fifty Shades of Gay: The best in LGBT writing* (Manchester Library and Information Service, 2012).

Waltham Forest

For LGBT History Month in 2011, the North Chingford Reading Group (Waltham Forest) compiled a list of recommended reads (North Chingford Reading Group, 2011).

West Sussex Libraries

In 2012, West Sussex Libraries held an event with Stella Duffy and Jonathan Kemp; as well as having an evening with writer and alternative historian Rose Collis; and 'The lives and loves of the Bloomsbury Group in Sussex', a talk by Darren Clarke, from The Charleston Trust (West Sussex County Council, 2012).

Exhibitions

Jubilee Library Brighton

LGBT Exhibition for Holocaust Memorial Day 27 January:

> Called The Third Sex in the Third Reich, it traces the way Germany's Nazi Party changed the world for male and female homosexuals and transvestites, from the very beginning of its reign to well beyond the end.
>
> It has been compiled by Brighton Ourstory, Lesbian, Gay and Bisexual History Centre with the support of Brighton & Hove City Council's Equalities and Inclusion Unit. The exhibition includes poems written by members of Allsorts Youth Group, with the help of Queer Writing South, inspired by the famous 'First they came for...' poem by Pastor Martin Niemoller. (Zhooshbrighton. co.uk, 2012)

Barnsley Libraries & Archives

The library staff in the Barnsley area worked with the local LGBT Forum to have a large exhibition in the Central Library during LGBT History Month (Mann, 2012).

Camden and Islington

> With over 30 events this February [2012] the celebrations in Camden and Islington were great! Events this year were exciting and varied, including the Alternative Loudest Whispers exhibition featuring 11 LGBT artists; Sappho in Sainsbury's at the Petrie Museum; an exhibition of the original, artistically 'altered' books by Joe Orton at the Islington Museum; and discussions on homophobic and transphobic bullying at the Wiener Library. (Camden LGBT Forum, 2012

Coventry University Library

Coventry University Library organised 'Celebrating diversity: LGBT History Month Library Exhibition' in 2012 as one of their regular programme of diversity events (Coventry University, 2012).

Devon Record Office

The Intercom Trust, which supports gay, lesbian, bisexual, and trans-sexual people and communities throughout the South West, ... appointed, with funding from the Heritage Lottery Fund, a Heritage Project Co-ordinator for 18 months to research the histories of individual people and create collections of archival material. Although ... not easy, it [was] possible to start with a few notorious case studies, such as that of Mary Hamilton, who posed as a male doctor and was tried at Glastonbury in 1746. The hope is that other stories will emerge to fill in some of the gaps in the picture.

February 2008 [was] LGBT History Month, devoted to research into this hidden area of the history of the South West Peninsula. A travelling exhibition, '1967 and all that', [was] on display for a time at the Record Office in Exeter. (Devon Record Office, 2007: 1)

Surrey History Centre

LGBT History Month at Surrey History Centre, Woking – 7 February to 3 March 2012:

LGBT History Month takes place every year in February and celebrates the lives and achievements of the LGBT community. This is an opportunity to learn more about the histories of lesbian, gay, bisexual and trans people in Surrey and the UK.

This year's display features the finale of the 'LGBT on Tour', project which has focused on the impact of World War II and the holocaust on the LGBT community in Europe. Come and see what they discovered!

We'll also be featuring Hitler's notorious 'Black Book', which listed 2,800 prominent British citizens, many from the LGBT community, who were to be detained following Nazi invasion – find out who was on the hit list!

Throughout 2012 Surrey Heritage will be celebrating the lives of Surrey Heroes and for LGBT History Month you can learn more about Surrey's Gay 'heroes' including Sir Noel Coward, Sir John Gielgud, Sir Terence Rattigan and Denholm Elliott. Come and find out more about Surrey's LGBT past, present and future! (Surrey History Centre, 2012)

University of Leeds Stanley & Audrey Burton Gallery

Exhibition: 'Other Stories: Queering the University Art Collection', 27 February to 5 May 2012.

In February 2012, in celebration of LGBT History Month, the Stanley & Audrey Burton Gallery (University of Leeds) presented a special exhibition project, 'Other Stories: Queering the University Art Collection'. With support from the National Lottery through Arts Council England, artist Matt Smith was invited to create 'interventions' in the Gallery, inspired by the University's collection of materials relating to Edward Carpenter, Victorian writer, social campaigner and early gay rights activist. (Smith, M., 2012; The Stanley and Audrey Burton Gallery, 2012).

Events – organised by the cultural sector

Amgueddfa Cymru/National Museum Wales

Events have been run by Amgueddfa Cymru/National Museum Wales for the LGBT History months of 2011 and 2012 (in a number of their museums), and they also organised a stand at Cardiff Wales Mardi Gras in 2011 and 2012. Both these events are firm fixtures on Amgueddfa Cymru's calendar and will continue into the future (Jones, A., 2012).

English Heritage

'The Queens of Eltham Palace', the first public event specifically for LGBT History Month, was offered at an English Heritage site:

> From Edward II's relationship with Piers Gaveston to the Architects John Seely and Paul Paget, there is a rich LGBT history at Eltham Place. We will take you on a tour of the site and discover some of the historical characters with their stories. We will also look at the LGBT influences in the Art Deco movement of the 1930's [sic]. (Londongay, 2012)

Hampshire Libraries

As well as running a series of author talks for 2012 LGBT History Month, Hampshire organised a 'Living Library'[1] event at Winchester Discovery Centre (Coe 2012; Hampshire County Council, 2012a).

Lancashire

In 2011, Lancashire Archives hosted a training day for archivists and users of archives, 'Outing the Past: identifying, showcasing & celebrating the wealth of LGBT evidence in every archive' (Rooke, 2011) – this event was repeated in 2012.

---

1   The 'Living Library' is now called the 'Human Library': 'The Human Library is an international movement for social change, based around a concept that encourages us to challenge our prejudices through social contact ... Just like in a real library, a visitor to the Human Library can choose a Book from a range of titles. The difference is that Books are people! Once the Reader has chosen a Book they sit down with their Book and engage in a short respectful conversation' (Human Library UK, 2012).

Also in 2012, the Museum of Lancashire hosted a free evening event, 'Lancashire Later: Celebrating LGBT History Month' (Miller, S., 2012). Lancashire Library Service organised a series of events at Burnley, Lancaster and Leyland libraries (Irvine, 2012; Lancashire County Council, 2012).

Manchester Museum

In 2010, Manchester Museum hosted a day of workshops to celebrate LGBT History Month, 'Coming out of the Cabinet', run by postgraduate students at the School of Arts, Histories and Cultures at the University of Manchester (Welsh, 2010).

Events – taking part as a partner in wider events

Norfolk and Norwich Millennium Library

- Over 40 different stalls inside the Forum and outside on Theatre Plain. They include local support groups, major unions, national charities, and local craftspeople.
- Pride Film Festival in Fusion in the Forum: 30 minutes of LGBT films (looped throughout the day) from local and national filmmakers on Fusion, Europe's largest public access screen.
- Display in the library.
- Pride opening ceremony – just outside the Millennium Library on Millennium Plain.
- There will be a Rainbow Families story and craft sessions for children in the children's library between 10.30-12.00.
- Sew Gay will be holding a craft workshop in the library between 12.00-2.00.
- There will be a rest area on the second floor for disabled and elderly people attending Pride events.
- A mobile library van will be at Chapelfield Gardens for the Pride picnic, and taking part in the Pride parade from 2.00. (Holden, 2012)

Oral history

M-Shed, Bristol

M-Shed organised an oral history workshop on 25 February 2012: 'OutStories Bristol is looking for volunteers to gather the stories of LGBT people living in or associated with Bristol and the surrounding area. If you're interested, please come to our workshop arranged in conjunction with M-Shed' (LGBT Bristol, 2011).

Intergenerational projects

Age UK and ILC-UK

Age UK and the International Longevity Centre-UK ran intergenerational LGBT projects in Camden, Leicester and Stockport, in which groups of under-25s and over-50s worked together – the interviews recorded by the Leicester project were showcased at Leicester Central Library in February 2012 (ILC-UK, 2011; Kneale *et al.*, 2011; Rogers, E., 2012).

Appendix 3
The interviewees

I am immensely grateful to all those who volunteered to be interviewed. Each person is described in their own words.

Elizabeth L. Chapman

I fell into library work by accident after originally studying French, German and Italian and working as a translator – but quickly realised that I loved working in public libraries! I started researching the provision of LGBT-related fiction to children and young people in public libraries as part of my librarianship MA, impelled in part by my own identity as a bisexual woman, as well as by a more general interest in social inclusion and diversity. I am now engaged in doctoral research on the same topic at the University of Sheffield, where I also teach on the MA in Librarianship.

Rachel Hasted

I was born in 1953 and went to university 1972-1975. I took the Manchester University postgraduate diploma in museum studies (which specialised in decorative arts) in 1975-1976 and got my first job in a museum with Lancashire County Museum Service in September 1976. I came out at work in the early 1990s. I have worked at local and national level in museums, archives and the historic environment sector.

Jacky Logan

As soon as I was 15 and 3 months, in 1970, I started my first job as a Saturday Assistant at Earlsfield Library in Wandsworth. Forty-three years later, I am still in libraries.

I came out in my 30s and threw myself, amongst other things, into seeking better services for LGBT people.

I was treasurer of the Burning Issues Group for a number of years and even now lead a Lesbian Reading Group in Waltham Forest Libraries. Always in London, my role in libraries has been many and varied, including working as an Area Manager for Hackney Libraries, and a Children's Services Manager in Newham.

I am currently a Team Leader in Waltham Forest and a Reader Development Librarian in Havering.

I love working at the front face point-of-contact and am always amazed at the number of people who quote the library as a place where they found the courage to make changes and explore new paths in life.

Lorne

I was born female and grew up in East London in the 1980s and 1990s. I always felt like a boy, and in my teens I felt I had to assume the label 'lesbian' as the only vocabulary I was aware of that in some way described how I felt – though I never really felt comfortable with that label as I still secretly identified as a boy or young man. In my late teens I found out about transgender people and transsexualism. I began transitioning from female to male in my early 20s and have worked supporting young trans people and in the trans community for over 6 years since.

David Murray

My first job many, many years ago, was as a children's librarian in a London borough. I knew nothing really – but the story times with 50 toddlers, craft sessions with glue everywhere and a sense of being a valued part of that community left a lasting impression. Many, many years later, I've held a number of senior leadership roles – Executive Director in London Borough of Newham, Strategic Director Communities for Brighton & Hove – and the only constant throughout my career has been my link to public libraries. And I wouldn't have it any other way. It makes me proud and humble every day when I think of what libraries deliver to so many people in so many communities. And it's a privilege to be part of that.

Kathryn Rooke

I studied History as an undergraduate and eventually went on to Liverpool University, where I gained my Masters in Archives and Records Management in 2010. My first post was at Lancashire Record Office (now Lancashire Archives) and my first responsibility was to do 'something' for LGBT History Month. Two-and-a-half years on, we have built long-lasting relationships with groups and individuals in Lancashire who are working with Lancashire County Council's Cultural Services to improve and deliver a range of events and opportunities to learn more about LGBT history and heritage.

Adrian Whittle

I began working in libraries in 1978 in a small seaside town in the north east of England, the idea being it would be a six months' job until something 'more interesting' turned up. Thirty-five years later nothing more interesting has presented itself, and I have been lucky enough to have worked in London for 20 years and been a head of service in three different authorities. I suspect that, had I not taken the library assistant job in 1978, I might still be in that little seaside town now. I am extremely grateful for the opportunities libraries have given me and continue to believe in their horizon-widening capabilities for people who make use of them.

References

Aberdeen University, 1994. *Disadvantage in Rural Scotland*. York: Joseph Rowntree Foundation (Findings – Social Policy Research). [online] Available at: http://www.jrf.org.uk/sites/files/jrf/sp62.pdf [Accessed October 2012].

Action for Southern Africa, n.d. *The Anti-Apartheid Movement*. [online] Available at: http://www.actsa.org/page-1438-AAM.html [Accessed June 2012].

Adams, P., Berg, L., Berger, N., Duane, M., Neil, A.S. and Ollendorff, R., 1972. *Children's Rights: Towards the Liberation of the Child*. London: Panther Books.

Afridi, A. and Warmington, J., 2010. *Managing Competing Equality Claims: A Paper for the Equality and Diversity Forum*. London: Equality and Diversity Forum.

Agius, S. and Tobler, C., 2011. *Trans and Intersex People: Discrimination on the Grounds of Sex, Gender Identity and Gender Expression*. Brussels, Belgium: European Commission Directorate-General for Justice. [online] Available at: http://www.non-discrimination.net/content/media/Trans%20and%20intersex%20people.pdf [Accessed January 2013].

Ajamu, 2011a. *rukus!*. [online] Available at: http://rukus.org.uk/2011-2/ [Accessed May 2012].

Ajamu, 2011b. Celebrating a History. *Runnymede Bulletin*, June issue (366), p. 26. [online] Available at: http://www.runnymedetrust.org/uploads/bulletin/pdfs/366-BulletinSummer11W.pdf [Accessed November 2011].

Ajamu, 2012. Email to John Vincent. Sent 4 December 2012.

Ajamu, X., 2011. Engagement: Building Inclusive LGBT Communities, Creating a Right Ole Rukus!. In: *The London LGBT Voluntary and Community Sector Almanac*. Kairos in Soho, ed. London: Kairos in Soho, pp. 74-75. [online] Available at: http://www.kairosinsoho.org.uk/KISalmanacRGB.pdf [Accessed June 2012].

Ajamu, X., Campbell, T. and Stevens, M., 2009. Love and Lubrication in the Archives, or rukus!: A Black Queer Archive for the United Kingdom. *Archivaria*, Fall issue (68), 2009, pp. 271-294.

Albany Trust, 2012. *Welcome to Albany Trust*. [online] Available at: http://www.albanytrust.org/ [Accessed October 2012].

Aldrich, R. (ed.), 2006. *Gay Life and Culture: A World History*. London: Thames & Hudson.

Alexander, Z., 1982. *Library Services and Afro-Caribbean Communities*. London: Association of Assistant Librarians.

Alibhai-Brown, Y., 1994. The Great Backlash. In: *The War of the Words: The Political Correctness Debate*. S. Dunant, ed. London: Virago, pp. 55-75.

All in London, 2006. *'In Olden Days a Glimpse of Stocking'*. [online] Available at: http://www.allinlondon.co.uk/whats-on.php?event=10725 [Accessed October 2012].

Allen, J., Kerr, L., Rolph, A. and Chadwick, M., 1989. *Out on the Shelves: Lesbian Books into Libraries*. Newcastle-under-Lyme: AAL Publishing.

Alyson, S. (ed.), 1985. *Young, Gay and Proud*. Boston, Mass.: Alyson Publications.

American Library Association, 2012. *Gay, Lesbian, Bisexual and Transgender Round Table (GLBTRT)*. [online] Available at: http://www.ala.org/glbtrt/ [Accessed July 2012].

Anderson, E., 2009. *Inclusive Masculinity: The Changing Nature of Masculinities*. London: Routledge.

Anderson, M.J. and Gilmour, N., 2012. *Being out at Work: Exploring LGBT Women's Workplace Experience in the UK*. New York City: Evolved Employer. [online] Available at: http://www.evolvedemployer.com/media/2012/08/UKLGBTWomen-FINAL.pdf [Accessed November 2012].

Armstrong, L., 2006. *Do Personal and Institutional Anxieties within Sheffield Central Library and Norwich Millennium Library Affect the Promotion of Particular Genres (Black British/Asian and Gay/Lesbian Fiction)?* [Thesis] University of Sheffield, Sheffield. [online] Available at: http://dagda.shef.ac.uk/dispub/dissertations/2005-06/External/Armstrong_Laura_MALib.pdf [Accessed September 2011].

Arscott, K., 2011. Winterval: The Unpalatable Making of a Modern Myth. *Guardian 'comment is free'*. [online] Available at: http://www.guardian.co.uk/commentisfree/2011/nov/08/winterval-modern-myth-christmas [Accessed November 2011].

Arts Council of England, 1998. *Reading for Life: Conference Report*. Reading for Life, Warwickshire. London: Arts Council of England.

Arts Council England, ca. 2012. *Accreditation Scheme*. [online] Available at: http://www.artscouncil.org.uk/what-we-do/supporting-museums/accreditation-scheme/ [Accessed January 2013].

Ashby, R., 1987. Library Services to Gay and Lesbian People. *Assistant Librarian*, 80 (10), March, pp. 153-155.

Ashford, C., ca. 2011. The Long Legal Shadow of Section 28. *Freedom in a Puritan Age*. [online] Available at: http://www.freedominapuritanage.co.uk/?p=1814 [Accessed December 2011].

Aspinall, P.J., 2009. *Estimating the Size and Composition of the Lesbian, Gay, and Bisexual Population in Britain*. Manchester: Equality and Human Rights Commission (Research report 37). [online] Available at: http://www.equalityhumanrights.com/uploaded_files/research/research__37__estimatinglgbpop.pdf [Accessed July 2012].

Association of Labour Authorities, 1987. *It's the Way They Tell 'Em: Distortion, Disinformation and Downright Lies*. London: Association of Labour Authorities.

Aubrey, S., 1973. Queer Reading. *Librarians for Social Change* (4, Winter), p. 17.

Bailey, L., 2012. Trans Ageing: Thoughts on a Life Course Approach in Order to Better Understand Trans Lives. In: *Lesbian, Gay, Bisexual and Transgender Ageing : Biographical Approaches for Inclusive Care and Support.* R. Ward, I. Rivers and M. Sutherland, eds. London: Jessica Kingsley, pp. 51-66.

Baker, P. and Stanley, J., 2003. *Hello Sailor! The Hidden History of Gay Life at Sea.* London: Longman.

Baldwin, J., 1956. *Giovanni's Room.* New York: Dial Press.

Baldwin, J., 1957. *Giovanni's Room.* London: Michael Joseph.

Barker, M., Richards, C., Jones, R., Bowes-Catton, H., Plowman, T., Yockney, J. and Morgan, M., 2012. *Bisexuality Report: Bisexual Inclusion in LGBT Equality and Diversity.* Milton Keynes: Open University, Centre for Citizenship, Identity and Governance. [online] Available at: http://www8. open.ac.uk/ccig/files/ccig/The%20BisexualityReport%20Feb.2012_0.pdf [Accessed June 2012].

Barr, J., 1950. *Quatrefoil.* New York: Greenberg.

Barr, J., 1953. *Quatrefoil.* London: Vision.

Barriault, M., 2009. Archiving the Queer and Queering the Archives: A Case Study of the Canadian Lesbian and Gay Archives [CLGA]. In: *Community Archives: The Shaping of Memory.* J.A. Bastian and B. Alexander, eds. London: Facet (Principles and Practice in Records Management and Archives), pp. 97-108.

Barugh, J. and Woodhouse, R.G., 1987. *Public Libraries and Organisations Serving the Unemployed.* London: British Library (British Library Research Papers, 0269-9257).

BASIN course co-organiser, 2009. Email to John Vincent. Sent 19 June 2009.

Batten, R., 2006. *Rid England of This Plague.* London: Paradise Press.

Baveystock, Z., Tyack, N. and Little, K., ca. 2006. *Our Place in History at the Discovery Museum: A Case Study.* Newcastle upon Tyne: Tyne and Wear Museums.

Bawden, T., 2012. World of Business Is Intolerant of Gays, Says Ex-BP Chief Lord Browne. *The Independent* 'Business' 31 May 2012. p. 57.

BBC Home, 2006. *Tories' Gay Stance 'Was Wrong'.* [online]Available at: http:// news.bbc.co.uk/1/hi/uk_politics/4696236.stm [Accessed March 2013].

BBC Home, 2008a. *1957: Britons 'Have Never Had It So Good'.* BBC On This Day 1950-2005. [online] Available at: http://news.bbc.co.uk/onthisday/hi/ dates/stories/july/20/newsid_3728000/3728225.stm [Accessed June 2012].

BBC Home, 2008b. *1985: Riots in Brixton after Police Shooting.* On This Day 1950-2005. [online] Available at: http://news.bbc.co.uk/onthisday/hi/dates/ stories/september/28/newsid_2540000/2540397.stm [Accessed September 2012].

BBC News, 2000. *MSPs Abolish Section 28.* [online] Available at: http://news. bbc.co.uk/1/hi/scotland/800673.stm [Accessed November 2011].

BBC News, 2009. *PM Apology after Turing Petition.* [online] Available at: http:// news.bbc.co.uk/1/hi/8249792.stm [Accessed October 2012].

BBC News, 2010. *I Am Proud to Be Gay, Says Pop Star Ricky Martin.* [online] Available at: http://news.bbc.co.uk/1/hi/8594121.stm [Accessed October 2011].

BBC News Manchester, 2012. *Alan Turing Pardon Campaign Goes to House of Lords.* [online] Available at: http://www.bbc.co.uk/news/uk-england-manchester-18988608 [Accessed October 2012].

BBC News Stoke & Staffordshire, 2011. *Jamaican Lesbian Can Stay in the UK, Tribunal Rules.* [online] Available at: http://www.bbc.co.uk/news/uk-england-stoke-staffordshire-14047505 [Accessed January 2012].

BBC Sport, 2009. *Ex-Lion Gareth Thomas Reveals He Is Gay.* [online] Available at: http://news.bbc.co.uk/sport1/hi/rugby_union/welsh/8421956.stm [Accessed October 2011].

Beemyn, B., 2003. The Silence Is Broken: A History of the First Lesbian, Gay, and Bisexual College Student Groups. *Journal of the History of Sexuality*, 12(2 – Special issue: 'Sexuality and Politics since 1945'), April 2003, pp. 205-223.

Behr, A., 1990. Where Are We Now? Section 28: Two Years On. *Assistant Librarian*, 83(9), pp. 132-134.

The Ben Cohen StandUp Foundation, 2012. *The Ben Cohen StandUp Foundation.* [online] Available at: http://www.standupfoundation.com/ [Accessed January 2013].

Bennett, W., 1995. The Rise and Fall of Red Ted's Loony Lefties. *The Independent* 29 July 1995. [online] Available at: http://www.independent.co.uk/news/the-rise-and-fall-of-red-teds-loony-lefties-1593657.html [Accessed September 2012].

Berg, L., 1968. *Risinghill: Death of a Comprehensive School.* Harmondsworth: Penguin.

BFI. Screenonline, 2012. *Social Problem Films.* [online] Available at: http://www.screenonline.org.uk/film/id/1074067/index.html [Accessed October 2012].

Birmingham LGBT, 2011. *Before Stonewall 1930s-1950s.* [online] Available at: http://www.blgbt.org/?page_id=528 [Accessed October 2012].

Birmingham LGBT, 2012. *Gay Birmingham, Back to Back.* [online] Available at: http://www.blgbt.org/sample-page/gay-birmingham-back-to-back/ [Accessed January 2013].

Birmingham LGBT, 2013. *LGBT Heritage.* [online] Available at: http://www.blgbt.org/ [Accessed February 2013].

Birmingham LGBT Community Trust, 2008. *GLF National Conference.* [online] Available at: http://gaybirminghamremembered.co.uk/topics/GLF%20Nation al%20Conference [Accessed December 2012].

Birmingham Museum and Art Gallery, 2010. *Queering the Museum.* [Exhibition guide]. Birmingham: Birmingham Museum and Art Gallery.

Birmingham Museums and Art Gallery, 2010. *Queering the Museum.* [online] Available at: http://www.bmag.org.uk/news?id=128 [Accessed May 2012].

Blank, J., 1982. *The Playbook for Kids About Sex.* London: Sheba Feminist.

Bly, L. and Wooten, K. (eds), 2012. *Make Your Own History: Documenting Feminist and Queer Activism in the 21st Century.* Los Angeles, Calif.: Litwin Books.

Bookey, T., 2012. *Strange Bedfellows: Improving the Accessibility and Preservation of LGBTQ Archives through Partnership*. International Archives, Libraries, Museums and Special Collections Conference on the future of lesbian, gay, bisexual and trans histories 2012 (Amsterdam) 1-3 August 2012. [online] Available at: http://lgbtialms2012.blogspot.nl/2012/07/tamsin-bookey-strange-bedfellows.html#more [Accessed November 2012].

Bösche, S., 1983. *Jenny Lives with Eric and Martin*. London: Gay Men's Press.

Botcherby, S. and Creegan, C., 2009. *Moving Forward: Putting Sexual Orientation in the Public Domain*. Manchester: Equality and Human Rights Commission (Research summary 40). [online] Available at: http://www.equalityhumanrights.com/uploaded_files/research/research40_so_moving_forward.pdf [Accessed July 2012].

Bourn, G., 1994. *Invisibility: A Study of the Representation of Lesbian and Gay History and Culture in Social History Museums*. Unpublished MA dissertation.

Bradshaw, J., Kemp, P., Baldwin, S. and Rowe, A., 2004. *The Drivers of Social Exclusion: Review of the Literature for the Social Exclusion Unit in the Breaking the Cycle Series*. London: Office of the Deputy Prime Minister. [online] Available at: http://www.bris.ac.uk/poverty/downloads/keyofficialdocuments/Drivers%20of%20Social%20Exclusion.pdf [Accessed November 2012].

Bray, A., 1982. *Homosexuality in Renaissance England*. London: Gay Men's Press.

Brett, P., 1992. Politics and Public Library Provision for Lesbians and Gay Men in London. *International Journal of Information & Library Research*, 4(3), pp. 195-211.

Brettingham, M., 2008. Gay Education in Primaries Climbs Back into the Closet, *TES*, 18 October 2008. [online] Available at: http://www.tes.co.uk/article.aspx?storycode=6003864 [Accessed August 2012].

Breward, C., 2010. *From the Margins to the Core? Conference Reflections*. London: V&A Museum. [online] Available at: http://media.vam.ac.uk/vamembed/media/uploads/files/vanda_christopher_breward_conference_reflections.pdf [Accessed August 2012].

Brighton & Hove City Library Service, n.d. *Have You Been to the LGBT Section at the Library?*. [online] Available at: http://www.brighton-hove-rpml.org.uk/Libraries/Documents/LGBT%20consultation%20document[1].doc [Accessed October 2012].

Brighton Central Library, 1996a. *Gay Men out in Print*. 2nd edn. Brighton: Brighton Central Library.

Brighton Central Library, 1996b. *Lesbians out in Print*. 2nd edn. Brighton: Brighton Central Library.

Brighton Ourstory, 2001a. *A History of Lesbian & Gay Brighton – Chapter 2: An Underground World, 1900-67*. [online] Available at: http://www.brightonourstory.co.uk/brighton-s-history/a-history-of-lesbian-and-gay-brighton-chapter-2-an-underground-world-1900-67/ [Accessed July 2012].

Brighton Ourstory, 2001b. *A History of Lesbian & Gay Brighton – Chapter 3: Out of the Closet, 1967-87.* [online] Available at: http://www.brightonourstory. co.uk/brighton-s-history/a-history-of-lesbian-and-gay-brighton-chapter-3-out-of-the-closet-1967-87/ [Accessed July 2012].

Brighton Ourstory, 2012a. *Ourstory's History.* [online] Available at: http://www. brightonourstory.co.uk/ourstory-s-history/ [Accessed October 2012].

Brighton Ourstory, 2012b. *Ourstory's History: The Third Sex in the Third Reich.* [online] Available at: http://www.brightonourstory.co.uk/ourstory-s-history/ the-third-sex-in-the-third-reich/ [Accessed October 2012].

Brighton Ourstory, 2012c. *Gay Girls & Bachelor Boys.* [online] Available at: http://www.brightonourstory.co.uk/ourstory-s-history/gay-girls-and-bachelor-boys/ [Accessed October 2012].

Bristol City Council, 2012. *Out in the Workplace: Lesbian, Gay and Bisexual Employees' Experience of Working in the Public Sector.* Bristol: Bristol City Council. [online] Available at: http://www.bristol.gov.uk/sites/default/files/ documents/community_and_safety/equality_and_diversity/Out%20in%20 the%20work%20place%20-%20final.pdf [Accessed November 2012].

British Library, n.d. *Learning: Dreamers and Dissenters – Shrew.* [online] Available at: http://www.bl.uk/learning/histcitizen/21cc/counterculture/liberation/shrew/ shrew.htm [Accessed June 2012].

British Museum, 2012. *Grayson Perry: The Tomb of the Unknown Craftsman.* [online] Available at: http://www.britishmuseum.org/whats_on/exhibitions/ grayson_perry.aspx [Accessed November 2012].

British Museum, n.d.-a. *Explore/Same-Sex Desire and Gender.* [online] Available at: http://www.britishmuseum.org/explore/themes/same-sex_desire_and_gender/ introduction.aspx [Accessed November 2012].

British Museum, n.d.-b. *Warren Cup.* [online] Available at: http://www. britishmuseum.org/explore/highlights/highlight_objects/gr/t/the_warren_cup. aspx [Accessed November 2012].

Broch, E., 2012. Actors' Union Launches Initiative to Support LGBT Actors Coming Out. *Pink News,* 6 April 2012. [online] Available at: http://www. pinknews.co.uk/2012/04/06/actors-union-launches-initiative-to-support-lgbt-actors-coming-out/ [Accessed April 2012].

Brooke, S., 2011. *Sexual Politics: Sexuality, Family Planning, and the British Left from the 1880s to the Present Day.* Oxford: Oxford University Press.

Brown, A., 2011. How Queer 'Pack Rats' and Activist Archivists Saved Our History: An Overview of Lesbian, Gay, Bisexual, Transgender and Queer (LGBTQ) Archives, 1970-2008. In: *Serving LGBTIQ Library and Archives Users: Essays on Outreach, Service, Collections and Access.* E. Greenblatt, ed. Jefferson, North Carolina: McFarland & Company, pp. 121-135.

Brown, D.M., 2010. GLF Achievements. In: *Out of the Shadows: How London Gay Life Changed for the Better after the Act – a History of the Pioneering London Gay Groups and Organisations, 1967-2000.* T. Walton, ed. London: Bona Street Press, pp. 19-21.

Brown, E., 2002. *Rupert Croft-Cooke: Writer*. [online] Available at: http://www. croft-cooke.co.uk/ [Accessed December 2011].

Brown, H.G., 1963. *Sex and the Single Girl*. London: Frederick Muller.

Browne, J., Baron Browne of Madingley, 2012. *Inaugural Annual Lecture*. Arup's Connect Out group – the firm's Lesbian, Gay, Bisexual and Transgender (LGBT) network (London) 29 May 2012. Available at: http://www.arup.com/ Home/News/2012_05_May/29_May_2012_Lord_Browne_of_Madingley_ addresses_Arup_Connect_Out.aspx [Accessed June 2012].

Bryant, C., 2009. 25th Anniversary of the Raid on Gay's the Word. *Polari Magazine*, 15 August 2009. [online] Available at: http://www.polarimagazine. com/features/25th-anniversary-raid-gay%E2%80%99s-the-word-bookshop [Accessed August 2012].

Burning Issues Group, ca. 1997. [Survey Results]. Unpublished.

Burning Issues Group, 1999. The Burning Ground for LGBs. *Library Association Record*, 101(11), p. 660.

Burston, P., 2008. Tris Penna on Gay Magazines, *Time Out*, 29 January 2008. [online] Available at: http://www.timeout.com/london/gay/features/4161/Tris_ Penna_on_gay_magazines.html [Accessed July 2012].

Butt, G., 2005. *Between You and Me: Queer Disclosures in the New York Art World, 1948–1963*. Durham, North Carolina: Duke University Press.

Byrne, P., 1994. Pressure Groups and Popular Campaigns. In: *Twentieth-Century Britain: Economic, Social and Cultural Change*. P. Johnson, ed. London: Longman, pp. 442-459.

Calderdale Council, 2012. *Shibden Hall: Families at Shibden*. [online] Available at: http://www.calderdale.gov.uk/leisure/museums-galleries/shibden-hall/fami lies.html [Accessed January 2013].

Camden LGBT Forum, 2012. *Camden and Islington LGBT History Month 2012!*. [online] Available at: http://camdenlgbtforum.org.uk/2012/01/17/camden-and-islington-lgbt-history-month-2012-is-comming/ [Accessed May 2012].

Cameron, D., 2012. Foreword. *LGBT History Month Magazine* (March 2012), p. 4. [online] Available at: http://issuu.com/talentmedia/docs/lgbthistorymonth 2012?mode=window&pageNumber=2 [Accessed May 2012].

Cameron, F., 2010. Introduction. In: *Hot Topics, Public Culture, Museums*. F. Cameron and L. Kelly, eds. Newcastle upon Tyne: Cambridge Scholars Publishing, pp. 1-17.

Campaign for Homosexual Equality, 2012a. *Home Page*. [online] Available at: http://www.c-h-e.org.uk/index.htm [Accessed January 2013].

Campaign for Homosexual Equality, 2012b. *The History of CHE*. [online] Available at: http://www.c-h-e.org.uk/history.htm [Accessed November 2012].

Campaign for Nuclear Disarmament, ca. 2010. *The History of CND*. [online] Available at: http://www.cnduk.org/about/item/437 [Accessed June 2012].

Canadian Lesbian & Gay Archive, 2011. [online] Available at: http://www.clga.ca/ index.shtml [Accessed November 2011].

Cant, B., 1988. Introduction. In: *Radical Records: Thirty Years of Lesbian and Gay History, 1957-1987*. B. Cant and S. Hemmings, eds. London: Routledge, pp. 1-14.

Carmichael, J.V., 1998. Introduction: Makeover without a Mirror – a Face for Lesbigay Library History. In: *Daring to Find Our Names: The Search for Lesbigay Library History*. J.V. Carmichael, ed. New York: Greenwood Press, pp. 1-23.

Carpenter, H., 2010. *Leading Questions: Learning from the Reading and Libraries Challenge Fund*. London: Paul Hamlyn Foundation. [online] Available at: http://www.phf.org.uk/page.asp?id=762 [Accessed June 2011].

Carter, C., Cooper, R. and Wells, S., 1988. Power, Rule and Authority: A Report on the P.L.G. Weekend School 1988 at Nottingham. *Public Library Journal*, 3(5), pp. 107-109.

Carvel, J. and White, M., 2000. Section 28 Helps Bullies, Study Shows. *Guardian* 7 February 2000.

Chambers, R. and Cole, J., 2006. *Gender Spectrum: Gender, Sex and Life on the Other Side*. CILIP Diversity Group conference: 'Pride or Prejudice?' – How well are Libraries serving Lesbian, Gay, Bi- and Trans- Communities? (Manchester) 8 February 2006. [online] Available at: http://www.cilip.org.uk/get-involved/special-interest-groups/diversity/Documents/Genderlifeontheotherside_RChambers.ppt#256,1,Gender Spectrum [Accessed May 2012].

Changing Attitude, 2011. *Conference Hears How Uganda Is Generating LGBT Refugees*. [online] Available at: http://changingattitude.org.uk/archives/4003 [Accessed January 2012].

Chapman, E.L., 2007. *Provision of LGBT-Related Fiction to Children and Young People in Public Libraries*. [Thesis] University of Sheffield, Sheffield. [online] Available at: http://www.shef.ac.uk/polopoly_fs/1.128155!/file/Chapman_Elizabeth_MALib.pdf [Accessed January 2013].

Chapman, E.L., 2012a. *Full List of LGBT Fiction for Children and Young People Available in the UK as of Spring 2012*. Sheffield: University of Sheffield. [online] Available at: http://www.shef.ac.uk/polopoly_fs/1.164002!/file/LGBT_fiction_for_children_and_young_people_March_2012.xls [Accessed January 2013].

Chapman, E.L., 2012b. Email interview by John Vincent. 22 November 2012.

Chapman, E.L., 2012c. *LGBT Fiction for Children & Young People*. Sheffield: University of Sheffield. [online] Available at: http://www.shef.ac.uk/polopoly_fs/1.164000!/file/LGBT_fiction_for_children_and_young_people_recommended_list.pdf [Accessed January 2013].

Chapman, J. 2009. Cameron Apologises to Gays for Section 28: Law to Ban Promotion of Homosexuality in Schools Was Wrong, Says Tory Leader. *Mail Online* 2 July 2009. [online] Available at: http://www.dailymail.co.uk/news/article-1196924/Cameron-apologises-gays-Section-28-Maggies-law-ban-promotion-homosexuality-schools-wrong-says-Tory-leader.html [Accessed March 2013].

Chartham, R., 1969. *Sex and the over-Fifties*. London: Leslie Frewin.

City of London, 2011. *Events in October 2011: Young Hearts Run Free 2.* [online] Available at: https://www1.cityoflondon.gov.uk/Corporation/ LGNL_Services/Leisure_and_culture/Libraries/City_of_London_libraries/ Events+in+October2011.htm [Accessed August 2012].

City of London, 2012. *Our History – Ourselves.* [online] Available at: http://www. cityoflondon.gov.uk/events/Pages/event-detail.aspx?eventid=550 [Accessed January 2013].

Clews, C., 2012a. *1984: Lesbians and Gays Support the Miners – Part One.* [online] Available at: http://www.gayinthe80s.com/2012/09/10/1984-lesbians-and-gays-support-the-miners-part-one/ [Accessed October 2012].

Clews, C., 2012b. *1985: Lesbians and Gays Support the Miners – Part Two.* [online] Available at: http://www.gayinthe80s.com/2012/09/13/1985-lesbians-and-gays-support-the-miners-part-two/ [Accessed October 2012].

Clews, C., 2012c. *1984: The Trials of Gay's the Word.* [online] Available at: http://www.gayinthe80s.com/2012/10/01/1984-the-trials-of-gays-the-word/ [Accessed October 2012].

Clyde, L.A. and Lobban, M., 2001. A Door Half Open: Young People's Access to Fiction Related to Homosexuality. *School Libraries Worldwide*, 7(2), 1 pp. 7-30. [online] Available at: www.iasl-online.org/files/july01-clyde-lobban. pdf [Accessed October 2011].

Coard, B., 1971. *How the West Indian Child Is Made Educationally Subnormal in the British School System: The Scandal of the Black Child in Schools in Britain.* London: New Beacon for the Caribbean Education and Community Workers' Association.

Cochrane, K., 2010. Why It's Never Too Late to Be a Lesbian. *Guardian* (22 July 2010). [online] Available at: http://www.guardian.co.uk/lifeandstyle/2010/ jul/22/late-blooming-lesbians-women-sexuality [Accessed May 2012].

Coe, N., 2012. Email to John Vincent. Sent 24 July 2012.

Colwell, G.A., 1973. Censorship in Merton Public Libraries. *Librarians for Social Change* (1, Winter), pp. 25-27.

Committee on Homosexual Offences and Prostitution, 1957. *Report of the Committee on Homosexual Offences and Prostitution Presented to Parliament by the Secretary of State for the Home Department and the Secretary of State for Scotland, Etc [Chairman, Sir John Wolfenden]* London: HMSO.

Community Archives and Heritage Group, 2006a. *From History to Her Story.* [online] Available at: http://www.communityarchives.org.uk/page_id__14_ path__0p2p14p42p.aspx [Accessed October 2012].

Community Archives and Heritage Group, 2006b. *Women's Archive of Wales.* [online] Available at: http://www.communityarchives.org.uk/page_id__27_ path__0p2p14p42p.aspx [Accessed October 2012].

Community Archives and Heritage Group, 2007a. *Brighton Ourstory.* [online] Available at: http://www.communityarchives.org.uk/page_id__345_path__ 0p2p14p42p.aspx [Accessed October 2012].

Community Archives and Heritage Group, 2007b. *London LGBT Archive: rukus!*. [online] Available at: http://www.communityarchives.org.uk/page_id__430_path__0p2p14p42p.aspx [Accessed October 2012].

Community Archives and Heritage Group, 2007c. *LGBT Archives at Manchester Archives and Local Studies*. [online] Available at: http://www.community archives.org.uk/page_id__441_path__0p2p14p42p.aspx [Accessed October 2012].

Community Archives and Heritage Group, 2009. *Feministwebs Archive of Women and Girls' Youth Work*. [online] Available at: http://www.communityarchives. org.uk/page_id__877_path__0p2p14p42p.aspx [Accessed October 2012].

Condou, C., 2011. Why Is School Such a Hard Place to Be Gay? *Guardian* 10 November 2011. [online] Available at: http://www.guardian.co.uk/ society/2011/nov/10/school-hard-place-gay-bullying [Accessed November 2011].

Connell, R.W., 1987. *Gender and Power: Society, the Person and Sexual Politics*. Cambridge: Polity in association with Blackwell.

Cook, M., 2007a. Queer Conflicts: Love, Sex and War, 1914-1967. In: *A Gay History of Britain: Love and Sex between Men since the Middle Ages*. M. Cook, ed. Oxford: Greenwood World Publishing, pp. 145-177.

Cook, M., 2007b. From Gay Reform to Gaydar, 1967-2006. In: *A Gay History of Britain: Love and Sex between Men since the Middle Ages*. M. Cook, ed. Oxford: Greenwood World Publishing, pp. 179-214.

Cooper, D., 1994. *Sexing the City: Lesbian and Gay Politics within the Activist State*. London: Rivers Oram Press.

Cooper, D., 2005. *The Changing Politics of Lesbian and Gay Equality in Local Government 1990-2001*. Swindon: Economic and Social Research Council. [online] Available at: http://www.esrc.ac.uk/my-esrc/grants/R000239293/out puts/Read/4966303b-d607-4d1f-b513-f1747d5b318f [Accessed October 2012].

Cory, D.W., 1951. *The Homosexual in America: A Subjective Approach*. New York: Greenberg.

Coventry LGBT, 2012. *Coventry's LGBT History Month 2012*. [online] Available at: http://coventrylgbt.org.uk/index.php/lgbt-history-month/ [Accessed May 2012].

Coventry University, 2012. *Equality and Diversity: What's On*. [online] Available at: http://wwwm.coventry.ac.uk/equalitydiversity/events/Pages/Events.aspx [Accessed August 2012].

Cowan, K., 2006. *Monitoring: How to Monitor Sexual Orientation in the Workplace*. London: Stonewall (Workplace Guides). [online] Available at: http://www. stonewall.org.uk/at_work/research_and_guides/4907.asp [Accessed October 2012].

Cowen, T., Stella, F., Magahy, K., Strauss, K. and Morton, J., 2011. *Sanctuary, Safety and Solidarity: Lesbian, Gay, Bisexual, Transgender Asylum Seekers and Refugees in Scotland*. Glasgow: University of Glasgow. [online]

Available at: http://www.gla.ac.uk/media/media_195792_en.pdf [Accessed January 2012].

Cowley, J., 2011. *The Education Equality Curriculum Guide: Supporting Teachers in Tackling Homophobia in School*. Belfast: Cara-Friend/The Rainbow Project. [online] Available at: http://www.rainbow-project.org/assets/publications/the %20education%20equality%20curriculum%20guide.pdf [Accessed January 2012].

Creegan, C. and Lee, S., 2004. *Sexuality – the New Agenda: A Guide for Local Authorities on Engaging with Lesbian, Gay and Bisexual Communities*. London: Employers' Organisation for Local Government/Local Government Association.

Creegan, C. and Lee, S., 2007. *Sexuality – the New Agenda: A Guide for Local Authorities on Engaging with Lesbian, Gay and Bisexual Communities*. London: Improvement and Development Agency. [online] Available at: http://www.schools-out.org.uk/policy/docs/Sexuality%20-%20The%20New%20 Agenda.pdf [Accessed June 2012].

Crimp, D., 1993. Right on, Girlfriend!. In: *Fear of a Queer Planet: Queer Politics and Social Theory*. M. Warner, ed. 1993. Minneapolis: University of Minnesota Press (Cultural Politics Vol 6), pp. 300-320.

Crown Prosecution Service, 2009. *Policy for Prosecuting Cases of Homophobic and Transphobic Hate Crime*. London: Crown Prosecution Service. [online] Available at: http://www.cps.gov.uk/publications/prosecution/homophobic_ and_transphobic_hate_crime_leaflet.pdf [Accessed June 2012].

Crown Prosecution Service, 2012. *Hate Crime and Crimes against Older People Report 2010-2011*. London: Crown Prosecution Service, Equality and Diversity Unit. [online] Available at: http://www.cps.gov.uk/publications/ docs/cps_hate_crime_report_2011.pdf [Accessed June 2012].

Curran, S., 2012a. *The Museum through Queer Eyes: Bringing the 'Outsider' Narratives Inside*. International Archives, Libraries, Museums and Special Collections Conference on the future of lesbian, gay, bisexual and trans histories 2012 (Amsterdam) 1-3 August 2012. [online] Available at: http:// lgbtialms2012.blogspot.nl/2012/07/sean-curran-london-uk-museum-through. html [Accessed November 2012].

Curran, S., 2012b. Brave New World? LMA Conference. *towards queer.* [online] Available at: http://towardsqueer.blogspot.co.uk/2012/08/brave-new-world-lma-conference.html [Accessed October 2012].

Curry, A., 1997. *The Limits of Tolerance: Censorship and Intellectual Freedom in Public Libraries*. Lanham, Maryland: Scarecrow Press.

Daily Mail, 2007. Lord Montagu on the Court Case Which Ended the Legal Persecution of Homosexuals. *Daily Mail* 17 July 2007. [online] Available at: http://www.dailymail.co.uk/news/article-468385/Lord-Montagu-court-case-ended-legal-persecution-homosexuals.html [Accessed December 2011].

Daily Mail, 2011. Clarifications and Corrections. *Mail Online.* [online] Available at: http://www.dailymail.co.uk/home/article-2058830/Clarifications-corrections. html [Accessed November 2011].

Daily Mirror, 1986. Gays Whoop It up at Festival of 'Sin'. *Daily Mirror* 25 June 1986.

Davies, S. and Paine, C., 2004. Talking About Museums: The Insider's Voice. *Oral History*, 32(2), pp. 54-62.

Day, E., 2011. 'Why Was I Born Gay in Africa?'. *The Observer.* [online] Available at: http://www.guardian.co.uk/world/2011/mar/27/uganda-gay-lesbian-immigration-asylum [Accessed January 2012].

DCMS, 1999. *Libraries for All: Social Inclusion in Public Libraries – Policy Guidance for Local Authorities in England.* London: DCMS.

DCMS, 2001. *Libraries, Museums, Galleries and Archives for All: Co-Operating across the Sectors to Tackle Social Exclusion.* London: DCMS. [online] Available at: http://www.culture.gov.uk/PDF/libraries_archives_for_all.pdf [Accessed August 2009].

Debrett's, 2012. *The Baroness Knight of Collingtree, DBE.* [online] Available at: http://www.debretts.com/people/biographies/browse/k/996/(Joan%20 Christabel)%20Jill%20Knight+KNIGHT%20OF%20COLLINGTREE.aspx [Accessed February 2013].

Dedyna, K., 2012. UVic Now Has the Largest Transgender Archive in the World: 'Sex Is between Your Legs, Gender between Your Ears'. *Times Colonist* 31 October 2012. [online] Available at: http://www.timescolonist.com/ news/UVic+largest+transgender+archive+world/7474909/story.html [Accessed November 2012].

D'Emilio, J., 1991. Gay Politics and Community in San Francisco since World War II. In: *Hidden from History: Reclaiming the Gay and Lesbian Past.* M. Duberman, M. Vicinus and G. Chauncey, eds. London: Penguin Books Ltd, pp. 456-473.

Dennison, G., 1969. *The Lives of Children: The Story of the First Street School.* New York: Random House.

Department of Trade and Industry, 2003. *Final Regulatory Impact Assessment: Civil Partnership Act 2004.* London: DTI. [online] Available at: http:// webarchive.nationalarchives.gov.uk/+/http://www.berr.gov.uk/files/file23829. pdf [Accessed July 2012].

Devon County Council, n.d. *Libraries: LGBT.* [online] Available at: http://www. devon.gov.uk/index/cultureheritarge/libraries/libraries-lgbt.htm [Accessed October 2012].

Devon Record Office, 2007. Archives for All? *Devon Record Office Newsletter* (37), Autumn 2007. [online] Available at: http://www.devon.gov.uk/ autumn2007.pdf [Accessed October 2011].

Diane, ca. 2008. Diane. In: *Our Story Liverpool: Memories of Gay Liverpool.* Liverpool: Our Story Liverpool, 10-11.

Dick, S., n.d., ca. 2008. *Homophobic Hate Crime: The Gay British Crime Survey 2008*. London: Stonewall. [online] Available at: http://www.stonewall.org.uk/documents/revised_hate_crime_pdf_jane_2011_1.pdf [Accessed June 2012].

Dick, S., 2009. *Homophobic Hate Crimes and Hate Incidents*. Manchester: Equality and Human Rights Commission (Equality and Human Rights Commission research summary 38).

Dirs, B., 2012. *Boxer Orlando Cruz Dreams of Becoming First Gay World Champion*. [online] Available at: http://www.bbc.co.uk/sport/0/boxing/19925421 [Accessed October 2012].

DiVeglia, A.L., 2012. Accessibility, Accountability, and Activism. In: *Make Your Own History: Documenting Feminist and Queer Activism in the 21st Century*. L. Bly and K. Wooten, eds. Los Angeles, Calif.: Litwin Books, pp. 69-88.

Diversity Group, 2011. *Diversity Group at Umbrella – 12-13 July 2011*. [online] Available at: http://www.cilip.org.uk/get-involved/special-interest-groups/diversity/conferences/pages/default.aspx [Accessed October 2012].

Diversity in Heritage Group, 2011. *Lunch Time 'Talking Tables'*. [online] Available at: http://www.york.ac.uk/ipup/events/conferences/bmconf/talking-tables.pdf [Accessed January 2013].

Dixon, B., 1977a. *Catching Them Young 1: Sex, Race and Class in Children's Fiction*. London: Pluto Press.

Dixon, B., 1977b. *Catching Them Young 2: Political Ideas in Children's Fiction*. London: Pluto Press.

Donald, A., Bennett, K. and Leach, P., 2012. *Religion or Belief, Equality and Human Rights in England and Wales*. Manchester: Equality and Human Rights Commission (Research Report 84). [online] Available at: http://www.equalityhumanrights.com/uploadred_files/research/rr84_final_opt.pdf [Accessed November 2012].

Donnelly, M., 2005. *Sixties Britain: Culture, Society and Politics*. Harlow: Pearson Education.

Donovan, J., 1970. *I'll Get There: It Better Be Worth the Trip – a Novel*. London: Macdonald & Co.

Drury, I., 2011. Revealed: How RAF Tried to 'Cure' Lesbian Recruits. And Ordered Officers to Be on Lookout for Women Who Enjoyed Cricket, *Mail Online*, 16 April 2011. [online] Available at: http://www.dailymail.co.uk/news/article-1377494/RAF-tried-cure-lesbian-recruits.html [Accessed October 2012].

Dyer, C., 1998. CPS Rules out Obscenity Charge against University. *Guardian* 1 October 1998.

East Sussex County Council, n.d. *Lesbian, Gay, Bisexual and Transgender Books*. [online] Available at: http://www.eastsussex.gov.uk/libraries/booksfilmsmusic/books/goodreads/lgbtbooks/default.htm [Accessed October 2012].

Edinburgh Museums & Galleries, n.d. *Rainbow City*. [online] Available at: http://www.edinburghmuseums.org.uk/Venues/The-People-s-Story/Collections-(1)/Edinburgh-Life/Rainbow-City [Accessed May 2012].

Elbert, B., 1973. First Meeting of Gay Librarians Group. 5 September 1973. [Published letter] LSE – HCA/CHE/5/54.

Elbert, R.J., 1973a. [Letter]. *Assistant Librarian* June, p. 101.

Elbert, R.J., 1973b. Homosexual Equality [Letter]. *Library Association Record*, 75(6), June, p. 123.

Ellison, G. and Gunstone, B., 2009. *Sexual Orientation Explored: A Study of Identity, Attraction, Behaviour and Attitudes in 2009.* Manchester: Equality and Human Rights Commission (Research Report 35). [online] Available at: http://www.equalityhumanrights.com/uploaded_files/research/research35_so_ explored.pdf [Accessed June 2012].

Epstein, D. (ed.)., 1994. *Challenging Lesbian and Gay Inequalities in Education.* Buckingham: Open University Press.

Equality and Human Rights Commission, n.d. *Protected Characteristics: Definitions.* [online] Available at: http://www.equalityhumanrights.com/ advice-and-guidance/new-equality-act-guidance/protected-characteristics-definitions/ [Accessed November 2012].

Equality Commission for Northern Ireland, 2008. *Every Child an Equal Child: An Equality Commission Statement on Key Inequalities in Education and a Strategy for Intervention.* Belfast: Equality Commission for Northern Ireland. [online] Available at: http://www.equalityni.org/archive/pdf/ECkey inequalities.pdf [Accessed June 2012].

Equality Commission for Northern Ireland, 2012a. *Indicators of Equality of Opportunity and Good Relations in Education: Research Report.* Belfast: Equality Commission for Northern Ireland. [online] Available at: http://www. equalityni.org/archive/pdf/EveryChildIndicators_FinalMainReport250412. pdf [Accessed June 2012].

Equality Commission for Northern Ireland, 2012b. *Trans Memorial Day.* [online] Available at: http://www.equalityni.org/sections/default.asp?cms=News%5FP ress+Releases&cmsid=1_9&id=360&secid=1_1 [Accessed December 2012].

Equality Commission for Northern Ireland, 2012c. *Everyone Has the Right to Respect and Fair Treatment.* [online] Available at: http://www.equalityni.org/ sections/Default.asp?cms=News%5FNews&cmsid=1_2&id=348&secid=1_1 [Accessed September 2012].

Equality Network, 2012. *Stronger, Safer and Supported: Increasing LGBT Tolerance, Awareness and Service Provision in West Dunbartonshire.* Edinburgh: Equality Network. [online] Available at: http://www.lgbtwestdunbartonshire.com/ text%20docs%20info/Stronger+Safer+and+Supported.pdf [Accessed August 2012].

Eserin, A., 1973. [Letter]. *Library Association Record*, 75(10), October, p. 210.

Essex Libraries, 2012. *LGBT History Month Booklist.* [online] Available at: http://www.essex.gov.uk/Libraries-Archives/libraries/reading/Documents/ LGBT%20History%20Month.pdf [Accessed May 2012].

Fairbrother, P., 1998. Information Provision for Gay Users. *Community Librarian* (20), Spring, pp. 1-4.

Fairbrother, P., 2000. Section 28 – Speaking Out. *Impact*, 3(4), April 2000, pp. 52-53.

Fairweather, P., 2013. *Burnley LGBT*. Presentation at 'Brave New World?' Conference (London) 16 February 2013, [unpublished].

Feminist Archive North, 2006. *Appendix I – the Demands*. [online] Available at: http://www.feministarchivenorth.org.uk/chronology/appendixi.htm [Accessed August 2012].

Fenwick, T., 2009. Why Museums and Galleries Should Celebrate the Lives of LGBT People. *Museums Journal*, 109(12), December, p. 15.

Fenwick, T., ca. 2009. *Flights of Fancy: Report of the 7th LGBT History and Archives Conference at the London Metropolitan Archives, December 6th 2009*. [online] Available at: http://www.lgbthistorymonth.org.uk/documents/2010/FlightsofFancy.doc [Accessed August 2012].

Fenwick, T. and Sanders, S., 2012. Educating out Prejudice – Focusing on Homophobia and Transphobia. *Race Equality Teaching*, 30(2), pp. 15-18.

Fish, J., 2007. *Reducing Health Inequalities for Lesbian, Gay, Bisexual and Trans People – Briefings for Health and Social Care Staff*. [online] Available at: http://www.dh.gov.uk/en/Publicationsandstatistics/Publications/PublicationsPolicyAndGuidance/DH_078347 [Accessed January 2012].

Forced Migration Online, 2011. *Food and Nutrition*. [online] Available at: http://www.forcedmigration.org/research-resources/thematic/food-and-nutrition [Accessed February 2013].

Formby, E., 2011. *Tackling Homophobia and Transphobia in Settings Supporting Young People: What Are the Barriers and Facilitators? Findings from a South Yorkshire Study*. Sheffield: Sheffield Hallam University Centre for Education and Inclusion Research. [online] Available at: http://offlinehbpl.hbpl.co.uk/NewsAttachments/PYC/Homophobia%20full%20report.docx [Accessed November 2012].

Formby, E., 2012. *Solidarity but Not Similarity? LGBT Communities in the Twenty-First Century*. Sheffield: Sheffield Hallam University Centre for Education and Inclusion Research. [online] Available at: http://www.shu.ac.uk/_assets/pdf/ceir-LGBTcommunities-final-report-Nov2012.pdf?utm_source=LGF+weekly+bulletin&utm_campaign=416a7dea51-LGF_Weekly_Bulletin_12_18_2012&utm_medium=email [Accessed January 2013].

Foster, C., 2011. Your Homes Newcastle: Responding to Feedback to Improve LGB Inclusivity. *Equal Opportunities Review* (219), December, pp. 8-9.

Frost, S., 2007. SCHG Proud Heritage LGBT History Training Seminar, 14 December 2006, Leicester University. *SHCG News* (59), June 2007, pp. 14-15. [online] Available at: http://www.shcg.org.uk/domains/shcg.org.uk/local/media/downloads/SHCG59.pdf [Accessed November 2012].

Frost, S., 2010. Are Museums Doing Enough to Address LGBT History? *Museums Journal*, 111(1), January 2010, p. 19.

Fryer, P., 1984. *Staying Power: The History of Black People in Britain*. London: Pluto Press.

Fullwood, S.G., 2009. Always Queer, Always Here: Creating the Black Gay and Lesbian Archive in the Schomburg Center for Research in Black Culture. In: *Community Archives: The Shaping of Memory*. J.A. Bastian and B. Alexander, eds. London: Facet (Principles and Practice in Records Management and Archives), pp. 235-249.

Gage, C., 2010. *In All Our Colours: Lesbian, Bisexual and Trans Women's Services in the UK*. London: Women's Resource Centre. [online] Available at: http://www.wrc.org.uk/includes/documents/cm_docs/2010/l/2_lbt_report_design.pdf [Accessed June 2012].

Gallo, M.M., 2005. *Winds of Change: The Daughters of Bilitis and Lesbian Organizing*. [online] Available at: http://www.gerberhart.org/dob.html [Accessed July 2012].

Garnett, M., 2008. *From Anger to Apathy: The Story of Politics, Society and Popular Culture in Britain since 1975*. London: Vintage Books.

Gauntlett, D., ca. 2008. *Queer Theory*. [online] Available at: http://www.theory.org.uk/ctr-que1.htm [Accessed October 2012].

Gay and Grey in Dorset, 2006. *Lifting the Lid on Sexuality and Ageing: A Research Project into the Needs, Wants, Fears and Aspirations of Older Lesbians and Gay Men*. Bournemouth: Help and Care Development Ltd. [online] Available at: http://www.somerset.gov.uk/irj/go/km/docs/CouncilDocuments/SCC/Documents/Resources/Equality%20Documents/Gay_and_Grey_report.pdf [Accessed December 2012].

Gay and Lesbian Humanist Association, 1990. Lesbian Line Hit by Section 28. *Gay and Lesbian Humanist* Autumn. [online] Available at: http://www.pinktriangle.org.uk/glh/101/section28.html [Accessed December 2011].

Gay and Lesbian Humanist Association, 2009. *Humanism*. [online] Available at: http://www.galha.org/ [Accessed May 2012].

Gay Information, 1973. *Psychiatry and the Homosexual: A Brief Analysis of Oppression*. London: Gay Information (Gay Liberation pamphlet no.1).

Gay Left Collective, ca. 2007. *Gay Left*. [online] Available at: http://www.gayleft1970s.org/ [Accessed April 2012].

Gay Liberation Front, 1972. Union Tavern. *Come Together* (12), Spring. [online] Available at: http://www.bl.uk/learning/images/21cc/counterculture/large8677.html [Accessed December 2011].

Gay Liberation Front Manifesto Group, 1971. *Gay Liberation Front Manifesto*. Reprint, with new preface, 2010. London: Alan Wakeman. [online] Available at: http://www.awakeman.co.uk/Sense/Books/GLF%20Manifesto%201971.pdf [Accessed December 2011].

Gay Librarians Group, 1985. *Gay Librarians Group News Bulletin* (2), October 1985, LSE – HCA/CHE/13/43.

Gay Librarians Group, 1988. *Gay Librarians Group Clause 28 Newsletter* (2), April 1988, LSE – HCA/EPHEM/726.

Gay Police Association, 2010. *Gay Police Association*. [online] Available at: http://www.gay.police.uk/contact.html [Accessed February 2012].

Gay Rights at Work Committee, 1980. *Gays at Work*. London: Gay Rights at Work Committee.

GayWest, n.d.-a. *Welcome to GayWest*. [online] Available at: http://www.gaywest. org.uk/index.html [Accessed January 2013].

GayWest, n.d.-b. *GayWest Timeline*. [online] Available at: http://www.gaywest. org.uk/timeline.htm [Accessed January 2013].

Gendered Intelligence, 2012a. *Gendered Intelligence*. [online] Available at: http:// genderedintelligence.co.uk/ [Accessed November 2012].

Gendered Intelligence, 2012b. 2100 Animation. *I:Trans – Constructing Selves through Technology*. [online] Available at: http://itransblog.wordpress.com/ [Accessed November 2012].

Gender Matters, 2013. *Gender Matters [Home Page]*. [online] Available at: http:// www.gender-matters.org.uk/ [Accessed February 2013].

Gibbs, J., 2011. Seeking Sanctuary. *Runnymede Bulletin* (366), Summer, p. 7. [online] Available at: http://www.runnymedetrust.org/uploads/bulletin/ pdfs/366-BulletinSummer11W.pdf [Accessed August 2012].

Gilbert, J., 2007. The Proud Nation Survey Has Revealed a Shocking Reluctance of the Museum Sector to Integrate LGBT Material into Their Exhibitions. *Museums Journal*, 107(10), October, p. 19.

Gillan, A., 2003. Section 28 Gone. But Not Forgotten. *Guardian*. [online] Available at: http://www.guardian.co.uk/politics/2003/nov/17/uk.gayrights [Accessed November 2011].

Gender Identity Research and Education Society, 2012. *Information for Trans People, Their Families and the Professionals Who Care for Them*. [online] Available at: http://www.gires.org.uk/index.php [Accessed November 2012].

Gittings, B., 1998. Gays in Library Land: The Gay and Lesbian Task Force of the American Library Association: The First Sixteen Years. In: *Daring to Find Our Names: The Search for Lesbigay Library History*. J. V. Carmichael, ed. Westport, Conn/London: Greenwood Press, pp. 81-93.

GLADD, n.d. *The Gay and Lesbian Association of Doctors and Dentists*. [online] Available at: http://www.gladd.co.uk/ [Accessed February 2012].

Glasgow Libraries, 2010. *Book Discussion Groups*. [online] Available at: http:// www.glasgowlife.org.uk/libraries/books-reading/book-discussion-groups/ Pages/home.aspx [Accessed October 2012].

GLBTQ, 2006. *Glossary: Queer*. [online] Available at: http://www.glbtq.com/ glossary.php?id=17 [Accessed November 2012].

Gloucestershire Gay & Lesbian Community, 2012. *The History of the GGLC*. [online] Available at: http://www.gglc.co.uk/index.php?page=gglc-history [Accessed January 2013].

Golden Age of Detection Wiki, ca. 2006. *Spain, Nancy*. [online] Available at: http://gadetection.pbworks.com/w/page/7931556/Spain,%20Nancy [Accessed December 2011].

Goldthorp, J., 2006. *Alive but Not Kicking Enough! – Impact of Fiction on the Knowledge, Self Esteem and Well-Being of Women. In Particular Those Who*

Identify as Lesbian or Bisexual. CILIP Diversity Group conference: 'Pride or Prejudice?' – How well are Libraries serving Lesbian, Gay, Bi- and Trans-Communities? (Manchester) 8 February 2006. [online] Available at: http://www.cilip.org.uk/get-involved/special-interest-groups/diversity/conferences/pages/pastconferences.aspx [Accessed May 2012].

Goldthorp, J., 2007. Can Scottish Public Library Services Claim They Are Socially Inclusive of All Minority Groups When Lesbian Fiction Is Still So Inaccessible? *Journal of Librarianship and Information Science*, 39(4), December 2007, pp. 234-248.

Goldthorp, J., 2012. Where's Our Public Library Service? LGBT Fact or Fiction? In: *Out of the Ordinary: Representations of LGBT Lives*. I. Rivers and R. Ward, eds. Newcastle upon Tyne: Cambridge Scholars Publishing, pp. 29-42.

Gooch, B., 2011. *Shining the Light: 10 Keys to Becoming a Trans Positive Organisation*. London: Galop. [online] Available at: http://www.galop.org.uk/wp-content/uploads/2011/05/final-shine-report-low-res.pdf [Accessed August 2011].

Goodwillie, J., 1974. [Letter]. *Assistant Librarian* April, p. 68.

Gough, C. and Greenblatt, E. (ed.), 1990. *Gay and Lesbian Library Service*. London: McFarland.

Government Equalities Office, 2011. *Barriers to Employers in Developing Lesbian, Gay, Bisexual and Transgender-Friendly Workplaces*. London: Government Equalities Office (Research Findings no.2011/1). [online] Available at: http://webarchive.nationalarchives.gov.uk/+/http://www.homeoffice.gov.uk/publications/equalities/lgbt-equality-publications/workplace-equality/workplaceequalty-summary?view=Binary [Accessed August 2012].

Govier, D., 2007. *Community Archives and Local Studies Training Day*. [online] Available at: http://www.communityarchives.org.uk/page_id__406_path__0p3p37p.aspx [Accessed January 2013].

Grant, L. and Williams, H. (ed.), 2011. *Everything You Wanted to Know About Sexual Orientation Monitoring … But Were Afraid to Ask*. Manchester: NHS Northwest. [online] Available at: http://help.northwest.nhs.uk/somworkbook/SOM%20workbook.pdf [Accessed August 2012].

Grassroots Feminism, 2009. *Sappho (Magazine, 1972-1981)*. [online] Available at: http://www.grassrootsfeminism.net/cms/node/522 [Accessed October 2012].

Great Britain, 1967. *Sexual Offences Act 1967*. (c.60). HMSO.

Great Britain, 1988. *Local Government Act 1988*. (c.9). London: HMSO.

Great Britain. 2003. *Local Government Act 2003*. (Chapter 26). London: The Stationery Office. [online] Available at: http://www.legislation.gov.uk/ukpga/2003/26/pdfs/ukpga_20030026_en.pdf [Accessed March 2013].

Great Britain, 2010. *Equality Act 2010*. (Chapter 15). [online] Available at: http://www.legislation.gov.uk/ukpga/2010/15/pdfs/ukpga_20100015_en.pdf [Accessed November 2012].

Great Britain, 2013. *Marriage (Same Sex Couples) Bill.* (126/2012-2013). [online] Available at: http://www.publications.parliament.uk/pa/bills/cbill/2012-2013/0126/2013126.pdf [Accessed February 2013].

Greater London Council, 1974. *GLC Circular* (4), 15 October 1974.

Greater London Council/GLC Gay Working Party, 1985. *Changing the World: A London Charter for Gay and Lesbian Rights.* London: Greater London Council.

Greater Manchester NUT, 2012. *Prevalence of Homophobia Survey: Local Teachers Speak out About Homophobic Bullying Abuse of Our Children and Their Colleagues.* Manchester: National Union of Teachers. [online] Available at: http://www.schools-out.org.uk/research/docs/Gtr_Manchester_Prevalence_Hi-Res.pdf [Accessed November 2012].

Great Ormond Street Hospital for Children NHS Foundation Trust, 2007. *Sideroblastic Anaemia Information.* [online] Available at: http://www.gosh.nhs.uk/medical-conditions/search-for-medical-conditions/sideroblastic-anaemia/sideroblastic-anaemia-information/ [Accessed January 2013].

Green, A., 1994. *The Geography of Poverty and Wealth,1981 –1991.* York: Joseph Rowntree Foundation (Findings – Social Policy Research). [online] Available at: http://www.jrf.org.uk/sites/files/jrf/sp55.pdf [Accessed October 2012].

Greenblatt, E. (ed.), 2011a. *Serving LGBTIQ Library and Archives Users: Essays on Outreach, Service, Collections and Access.* Jefferson, North Carolina: McFarland & Company.

Greenblatt, E., 2011b. Selective Glossary of LGBTIQ Terms. In: *Serving LGBTIQ Library and Archives Users: Essays on Outreach, Service, Collections and Access.* E. Greenblatt, ed. Jefferson, North Carolina: McFarland & Company, pp. 5-6.

Grey, A., 1992. *Quest for Justice: Towards Homosexual Emancipation.* London: Sinclair Stevenson.

Group for Larger Local Authority Museums, 2000. *Museums and Social Inclusion, the GLLAM Report.* Leicester: Research Centre for Museums and Galleries. [online] Available at: http://www.le.ac.uk/ms/research/Reports/GLLAM.pdf [Accessed December 2009].

Guardian, 1978. Secret Customs List – Chancellor Challenged. *Guardian*, 14 December 1978.

Guasp, A., 2010. *Different Families: The Experience of Children with Lesbian and Gay Parents.* London: Stonewall. [online] Available at: http://www.stonewall.org.uk/at_school/education_for_all/quick_links/education_resources/4079.asp [Accessed January 2013].

Guasp, A., 2012. *The School Report: The Experiences of Gay Young People in Britain's Schools in 2012.* London: Stonewall. [online] Available at: http://www.stonewall.org.uk/documents/school_report_2012.pdf [Accessed January 2013].

Guasp, A., n.d. *The Teachers' Report: Homophobic Bullying in Britain's Schools.* London: Stonewall. [online] Available at: http://www.stonewall.org.uk/at_school/education_for_all/quick_links/education_resources/4003.asp [Accessed October 2012].

Guasp, A. and Dick, S., 2012. *Living Together: British Attitudes to Lesbian, Gay and Bisexual People in 2012*. London: Stonewall. [online] Available at: http://www.stonewall.org.uk/documents/living_together_2012.pdf [Accessed January 2013].

Guasp, A. and Kibirige, H., 2012. *One Minority at a Time: Being Black and Gay*. London: Stonewall. [online] Available at: http://www.stonewall.org.uk/documents/omt_final_report_low_res_pdf.pdf [Accessed August 2012].

Guinard, R., 1973. [Letter]. *Assistant Librarian*, September issue, pp. 154, 156.

Gundara, J., 1981. *Indian Women in Britain: A Study of Information Needs*. London: Polytechnic of North London, School of Librarianship (Occasional Publication No. 2).

Gunton, J., 1973. [Letter]. *Library Association Record*, 75(8), p. 168.

Hackney Leisure Services, 1984. *How Leisure Services Can Begin to Meet the Needs of Lesbians and Gay Men in Hackney: Report of the Director of Leisure Services to Hackney Leisure Services Committee, 13 Nov 1984*. London: Hackney Council.

Halberstam, J., 2005. *In a Queer Time and Place: Transgender Bodies, Subcultural Lives*. New York: New York University Press.

Hall, L., 2012. Lesley Hall: interview with John Vincent, 12 July 2012.

Hamer, E., 1996. *Britannia's Glory: A History of Twentieth-Century Lesbians*. London: Cassell.

Hamilton, A., 1995. Police and Customs Seize Gay Magazines and Videos. *Gay Times*, February issue, p. 31.

Hampshire County Council, 2012a. *Living Library: Winchester Discovery Centre*. Winchester: Hampshire County Council.

Hampshire County Council, 2012b. *Hantsweb: LGBT Fiction*. [online] Available at: http://www3.hants.gov.uk/library/booksandreading/recommended-reads/lgbt-fiction.htm [Accessed October 2012].

Hanckel, F. and Cunningham, J., 1976. Can Young Gays Find Happiness in YA Books? *Wilson Library Bulletin*, 50 (5) pp. 528-534.

Hansard, 1986. *Local Government Act 1986 (Amendment) Bill [H.L.]*. London: Hansard. [online] Available at: http://hansard.millbanksystems.com/lords/1986/nov/25/local-government-act-1986-amendment-bill [Accessed August 2012].

Hansen, J., 1970. *Fadeout*. New York: Harper & Row.

Hansen, J., 1972. *Fadeout*. London: Harrap.

Hansen, J., 2006. *The Complete Brandstetter*. London: No Exit Press.

Haringey Libraries, 1985. *Gay Pride 1985*. London: Haringey Libraries.

Hartley, C., 2012. Letter to John Vincent, 16 December 2012.

Harvey, J., 2006. *Consultation with the Lesbian, Gay, Bisexual & Transgender Community: The Brighton & Hove Experience*. CILIP Diversity Group conference: 'Pride or Prejudice?' – How well are Libraries serving Lesbian, Gay, Bi- and Trans- Communities? (Manchester) 8 February 2006. [online] Available at: http://www.cilip.org.uk/get-involved/special-interest-groups/

diversity/Documents/BrightonHoveExperienceJoHarvey.ppt#256,1, Consultation with the Lesbian, Gay, Bisexual & Transgender community [Accessed May 2012].

Hasted, R., 1996. *Lesbian Lifetimes: An Oral History Project for Croydon Museum Service*. Unpublished MA essay.

Hasted, R., 2012. Email interview by John Vincent, September 2012.

Hatzenbuehler, M.L., 2011. The Social Environment and Suicide Attempts in Lesbian, Gay, and Bisexual Youth. *Pediatrics*, 127(5), pp. 896-903.

Healy, E.M., 1998. [Letter]. *Community Librarian*, Autumn/Winter issue (21), p. 16.

Hemmings, S., 1980. Horrific Practices: How Lesbians Were Presented in the Newspapers of 1978. In: *Homosexuality: Power & Politics*. Gay Left Collective, ed. London: Allison and Busby, pp. 157-171.

Hendry, J., 1997. Freedom of Information: The Lesbian and Gay Issue. *Assistant Librarian*, 90(3), pp. 37-40.

Heritage Lottery Fund, 2011. *Welsh Pride – Celebrating LGBT Heritage in Wales*. [online] Available at: http://www.hlf.org.uk/news/Pages/WelshPride.aspx [Accessed May 2012].

Heritage Lottery Fund, 2012. *Schedule of Decisions under Delegated Powers to Head of HLF West Midlands 25 June 2012*. Birmingham: Heritage Lottery Fund. [online] Available at: http://www.hlf.org.uk/aboutus/decisionmakers/committees/Documents/DDecisionsJunWM.pdf [Accessed February 2013].

The Highland Council/Comhairle na Gàidhealtachd, 2012. *Services for LGBT Communities*. [online] Available at: http://www.highland.gov.uk/leisureandtourism/libraries/referenceandlocalhistory/services-for-LGBT-communities.htm [Accessed October 2012].

Hill, J. (ed.), 1971. *Books for Children: The Homelands of Immigrants*. London: Institute of Race Relations.

Hill, N., 2012. *Pink Guide to Adoption for Lesbians and Gay Men* 2nd edn. London: British Association for Adoption & Fostering. [online] Available at: http://www.baaf.org.uk/bookshop/book_pinkguide [Accessed September 2012].

Hills, J., 1995. *Inquiry into Income and Wealth. Volume 2: a summary of the evidence*. York: Joseph Rowntree Foundation.

Hipperson, S., n.d. *Greenham Common Women's Peace Camp 1981 – 2000*. [online] Available at: http://www.greenhamwpc.org.uk/ [Accessed October 2012].

Holden, J., 2012. ''Norwich Pride''. Email to John Vincent. Sent 24 July 2012.

Holt, J.C., 1969a. *The Underachieving School*. Harmondsworth: Penguin.

Holt, J.C., 1969b. *How Children Fail*. Harmondsworth: Penguin.

Holt, J.C., 1972. *Freedom and Beyond*. Harmondsworth: Penguin.

Home Office, 2001a. *Community Cohesion: A Report of the Independent Review Team Chaired by Ted Cantle*. London: Home Office. [online] Available at:

http://image.guardian.co.uk/sys-files/Guardian/documents/2001/12/11/communitycohesionreport.pdf [Accessed August 2012].

Home Office, 2001b. *Building Cohesive Communities: A Report of the Ministerial Group on Public Order and Community Cohesion.* London: Home Office. [online] Available at: http://www.communities.gov.uk/documents/communities/pdf/buildingcohesivecommunities.pdf [Accessed August 2012].

Home Office, 2010. *Working for Lesbian, Gay, Bisexual and Transgender Equality.* London: Home Office. [online] Available at: http://www.homeoffice.gov.uk/publications/equalities/lgbt-equality-publications/lgbt-work-plan?view=Binary [Accessed May 2012].

Home Office, 2011a. *Tackling Homophobia and Transphobia in Sport: The Charter for Action.* London: Home Office. [online] Available at: http://www.homeoffice.gov.uk/publications/equalities/lgbt-equality-publications/sports-charter?view=Binary [Accessed May 2012].

Home Office, 2011b. *Working for Lesbian, Gay, Bisexual and Transgender Equality: Moving Forward.* London: Home Office. [online] Available at: http://www.homeoffice.gov.uk/publications/equalities/lgbt-equality-publications/lgbt-action-plan?view=Binary [Accessed May 2012].

Home Office, 2011c. *Advancing Transgender Equality: A Plan for Action.* London: Home Office. [online] Available at: http://www.homeoffice.gov.uk/publications/equalities/lgbt-equality-publications/transgender-action-plan?view=Binary [Accessed January 2012].

Home Office, 2012a. *Hate Crimes, England and Wales 2011/12.* [online] Available at: http://www.homeoffice.gov.uk/publications/science-research-statistics/research-statistics/crime-research/hate-crimes-1112/ [Accessed November 2012].

Home Office, 2012b. *Historic Convictions for Consensual Acts to Be Deleted.* [online] Available at: http://www.homeoffice.gov.uk/media-centre/news/historic-convictions [Accessed November 2012].

Home Office, ca. 2012. *Lesbian, Gay, Bisexual and Transgender People and the Law.* [online] Available at: http://www.homeoffice.gov.uk/equalities/lgbt/lgbt-law/ [Accessed May 2012].

Homotopia, 2012. *Homotopia.* [online] Available at: http://www.homotopia.net/ [Accessed August 2012].

Houlbrook, M., 2005. *Queer London: Perils and Pleasures in the Sexual Metropolis, 1918-1957.* Chicago, Ill/London: University of Chicago Press.

House, C., 1986. Gay Sex Book Is 'Vice Lure' – Police Chief Hits at Peril in Libraries. *Sunday Mirror* 26 October 1986.

House of Lords, 1986. *Local Government Act 1986 (Amendment Bill) 1986-87 [HL].*

House of Lords, 1999. *Hansard House of Lords Debate, 6 Dec 1999.* vol 607, col 1102. [online] Available at: http://www.parliament.the-stationery-office.co.uk/pa/ld199900/ldhansrd/vo991206/text/91206-10.htm [Accessed December 2011].

House of Lords Debate, 1988. vol 493, cols 585-643. [online] Available at: http://hansard.millbanksystems.com/lords/1988/feb/16/local-government-bill-1 [Accessed October 2012].

Howes, K., 1993. *Broadcasting It: An Encyclopaedia of Homosexuality on Film, Radio and TV in the UK 1923-1993*. London: Cassell.

Howes, R., 2011. *Gay West: Civil Society, Community and LGBT History in Bristol and Bath, 1970 to 2010*. Bristol: SilverWood Books.

Howes, R., 2012. *Voluntary Action and the LGBT Movement*. [online] Available at: http://www.vahs.org.uk/2012/02/lgbt-howes/ [Accessed October 2012].

Hoyle, J., 1973. [Letter]. *Library Association Record*, 75(8), August, p. 168.

Hsu, A., 2011. Gay Asylum Seekers Flee to Live, While UKBA Plays Dumb in Miming Ignorance. *Migration Pulse*. [online] Available at: http://www.migrantsrights.org.uk/migration-pulse/2011/gay-asylum-seekers-flee-live-while-ukba-plays-dumb-miming-ignorance [Accessed September 2011].

Human Library UK, 2012. *The Human Library*. [online] Available at: http://humanlibraryuk.org/home/what-is-human-library/ [Accessed August 2012].

Humphreys, B., 2002. The Law That Dared to Lay the Blame. *Gay and Lesbian Humanist* (Summer 2002). [online] Available at: http://www.pinktriangle.org.uk/glh/214/humphreys.html [Accessed May 2012].

Humphreys, L., 1970. *Tearoom Trade*. Chicago, Ill.: Aldine.

Hunt, R. and Fish, J., 2008. *Prescription for Change: Lesbian and Bisexual Women's Health Check 2008*. London: Stonewall. [online] Available at: http://www.stonewall.org.uk/documents/prescription_for_change_1.pdf [Accessed November 2011].

Hunt, R. and Jensen, J., 2007. *The School Report: The Experiences of Young Gay People in Britain's Schools*. London: Stonewall. [online] Available at: http://www.stonewall.org.uk/documents/school_report.pdf [Accessed October 2012].

Hunt, R. and Jensen, J., ca. 2007. *The Experience of Young Gay People in Britain's Schools*. London: Stonewall. [online] Available at: http://www.stonewall.org.uk/at_school/education_for_all/quick_links/education_resources/4004.asp [Accessed October 2011].

Hunt, R. and Valentine, G., [2011]. *Love Thy Neighbour: What People of Faith Really Think About Homosexuality*. London: Stonewall. [online] Available at: http://www.stonewall.org.uk/documents/love_thy_neighbour.pdf [Accessed July 2011].

Hutton, W., 1995. *The State We're In*. London: Jonathan Cape.

Hyde, H.M., 1970. *The Other Love: An Historical and Contemporary Survey of Homosexuality in Britain*. London: Heinemann.

ILC-UK, 2011. *Bridging the Gap: Exploring the Potential for Bringing Older and Younger LGBT People Together*. London: ILC–UK. [online] Available at: http://www.ilcuk.org.uk/files/Report.pdf [Accessed May 2012].

ILGA Europe, 2012. *Calendar of European Pride Events*. [online] Available at: http://ilga-europe.org/home/issues/assembly_prides/pride_events_in_europe/ calendar [Accessed August 2012].

ILGA Europe and AGE Platform Europe, 2012. *Equality for Older Lesbian, Gay, Bisexual, Trans and Intersex People in Europe: A Joint Policy Paper by Age Platform Europe and the European Region of the International Lesbian, Gay, Bisexual, Trans and Intersex Association*. Brussels, Belgium: ILGA Europe. [online] Available at: http://www.ilga-europe.org/media_library/euro_letter/2012/ november/diversity/joint_policy_age_and_sogi [Accessed January 2013].

Imperial War Museums, n.d. *Hidden Histories*. [online] Available at: http://www. youtube.com/playlist?list=PL54F4B26A37FE219B&feature=plcp [Accessed November 2012].

Institute for the Public Understanding of the Past, 2012. *Cultural Equalities Now: A British Museum Conference in Collaboration with IPUP and DHG, Friday 9th December 2011 at the Stevenson Lecture Theatre, British Museum – Resources*. [online] Available at: http://www.york.ac.uk/ipup/events/ conferences/bm-equality.html [Accessed January 2013].

Intercom Trust, 2007. *The Cedar Project*. [online] Available at: http://www. intercomtrust.org.uk/cedar/index.htm [Accessed October 2012].

Internet Movie Database, n.d. *Biography for John Gielgud*. [online] Available at: http://www.imdb.com/name/nm0000024/bio [Accessed December 2011].

Intersex Society of North America, 2008. *What Is Intersex?*. [online] Available at: http://www.isna.org/faq/what_is_intersex [Accessed November 2012].

Irvine, G., 2012. Email to John Vincent. Sent 15 January 2012.

Islington Council, 1996. *Strength and Pride*. London: Islington Council.

Islington Libraries, 1985. *Being Gay: A Book List*. London: Islington Libraries.

Jeater, M., 2008. *Curating the Outside Edge Exhibition at the Museum in Docklands*. [online] Available at: http://www.mymuseumoflondon.org.uk/blogs/blog/ curating-the-outside-edge-exhibition-at-the-museum-in-docklands/ [Accessed May 2012].

Jeffreys, S., 2003. *Unpacking Queer Politics: A Lesbian Feminist Perspective*. Cambridge: Polity.

Jennings, R., 2007. *Lesbian History of Britain: Love and Sex between Women since 1500*. Oxford: Greenwood World Publishing.

Jespersen, S., 1982. Positive Action: Women in Libraries Second Annual Conference. *Librarians for Social Change*, 10(1), 3-14, pp. 19-22.

Jivani, A., 1997. *It's Not Unusual: A History of Lesbian and Gay Britain in the Twentieth Century*. London: Michael O'Mara Books.

John, E., 2011. I Want Zachary to Grow up in a World without Homophobia. *Guardian* 4 November 2011. [online] Available at: http://www.guardian. co.uk/commentisfree/2011/nov/04/homophobia-bullying-elton-john?dm_ i=FBX,LF20,21Z939,1QJBM,1 [Accessed January 2012].

Johnson, M., 2007. *GLBT Controlled Vocabularies and Classification Schemes.* [online] Available at: http://www.ala.org/glbtrt/popularresources/vocab [Accessed February 2013].

Jones, A., 2012. Email to John Vincent. Sent 24 July 2012.

Jones, O., 2012. Homophobia: When 'Coming out' Ends, Equality Will Be Total. *The Independent* 'Opinion', p. 17.

Jongh, N. de, 1977. Magazine Alleges Discrimination. *Guardian* 21 August 1977.

Jongh, N. de, 1992. *Not in Front of the Audience: Homosexuality on Stage.* London: Routledge.

Joseph Rowntree Foundation, 2012. *A Better Life: Old Age, New Thoughts.* [online] Available at: http://betterlife.jrf.org.uk/ [Accessed February 2012].

The Justin Campaign, 2011. *Interview – Anton Hysen.* [online] Available at: http://www.thejustincampaign.com/interview-antonhysen.htm [Accessed November 2011].

Kaczorowski, C., 2008. *Gay, Lesbian, and Queer Studies.* [online] Available at: http://www.glbtq.com/social-sciences/gay_lesbian_queer_studies,2.html [Accessed November 2012].

Kaur, R., 2005. *Unearthing Our Past: Engaging with Diversity at the Museum of London (Consultancy for Reassessing What We Collect Phase II).* London: Museum of London. [online] Available at: http://www.museumoflondon. org.uk/NR/rdonlyres/A138DFA6-9B14-4E8C-9F53-D47DA649415D/0/ Raminder.rtf [Accessed October 2012].

Kellinger, J.J. and Cover, R., 2012. Cross-Generational Risks of Ascribing and Employing 'Queer', 'Gay and Lesbian' or Even 'Straight'. In: *Passing/Out: Sexual Identity Veiled and Revealed.* D.R. Cooley and K. Harrison, eds. Farnham, Surrey: Ashgate, pp. 105-135.

Kempson, E. and Dee, M. (eds), 1987. *A Future Age : A Practical Handbook for Librarians Working with Older Adults.* Newcastle-under-Lyme: Association of Assistant Librarians.

Kenric., 2010. *About Us.* [online] Available at: http://www.kenric.org/About.html [Accessed October 2012].

Keogh, P., Reid, D. and Weatherburn, P., 2006. *Lambeth LGBT Matters: The Needs and Experiences of Lesbians, Gay Men, Bisexuals and Trans Men and Women in Lambeth.* London: Sigma Research. [online] Available at: http://www.sigmaresearch.org.uk/files/report2006c.pdf [Accessed March 2012].

Kerr, S., 2011. Burgess, Guy Francis De Moncy (1911–1963). In: *Oxford Dictionary of National Biography.* Oxford: Oxford University Press. [online] Available at: http://www.oxforddnb.com/view/article/37244 [Accessed September 2012].

Kester, N.G. (ed.), 1997. *Liberating Minds: The Stories and Professional Lives of Gay, Lesbian, and Bisexual Librarians and Their Advocates.* Jefferson, North Carolina: McFarland & Company.

Kneale, D., Serra, V., Bamford, S.-M. and Diener, L., 2011. *Celebrating Intergenerational Diversity: An Evaluation of Three Projects Working with Younger and Older Lesbian, Gay, Bisexual and Transgender People.* London:

ILC–UK. [online] Available at: http://www.ilcuk.org.uk/files/Report_1.pdf [Accessed May 2012].

Knightley, P., 2011. *The Cambridge Spies.* [online] Available at: http://www.bbc.co.uk/history/worldwars/coldwar/cambridge_spies_01.shtml [Accessed September 2012].

Knocker, S., 2012. *Perspectives on Ageing: Lesbians, Gay Men and Bisexuals.* York: Joseph Rowntree Foundation. [online] Available at: http://www.jrf.org.uk/sites/files/jrf/ageing-lesbians-bisexuals-gay-men-summary.pdf [Accessed February 2012].

Knowles, J.J., 2009. *An Investigation into the Relationship between Gay Activism and the Establishment of a Gay Community in Birmingham, 1967-97.* [Thesis] University of Birmingham. [online] Available at: http://etheses.bham.ac.uk/686/1/KnowlesMPhil10.pdf [Accessed December 2012].

Kollman, K. and Waites, M., 2011. United Kingdom: Changing Political Opportunity Structures, Policy Success and Continuing Challenges for Lesbian, Gay and Bisexual Movements. In: *Lesbian and Gay Movement and the State: Comparative Insights into a Transformed Relationship.* M. Tremblay, D. Paternotte and C. Johnson, eds. Farnham, Surrey: Ashgate, pp. 181-195.

Koskovich, G., 2008. Lesbian, Gay, Bisexual and Transgender Archives and Libraries in the United States, *LGBTQ America Today: An Encylopedia*, Vol. 2. Westport, Conn: Greenwood Press, pp. 684-692.

Kulii, B.T., 2012. Lorde, Audre, *The Concise Oxford Companion to African American Literature.* Oxford: Oxford University Press. [online] Available at: http://www.oxfordreference.com/view/10.1093/acref/9780195138832.001.0001/acref-9780195138832-e-363?rskey=oxqz8F&result=335&q= [Accessed February 2013].

LAGAR, 2012. *Lesbian and Gay Archives Roundtable.* [online] Available at: http://www2.archivists.org/groups/lesbian-and-gay-archives-roundtable-lagar [Accessed October 2012].

LAGNA, 2012. *1967 and All That.* [online] Available at: http://www.lagna.org.uk/exhibitions/1967-and-all-that [Accessed October 2012].

Lahusen, K.T., ca. 2001. *Barbara Gittings (1932-): Independent Spirit.* [online] Available at: http://www.williamapercy.com/wiki/images/Barbara_gittings.pdf [Accessed July 2012].

Lambeth Amenity Services, 1987a. *Stories and Poems by and About Lesbian Women: A Booklist.* London: Lambeth Amenity Services.

Lambeth Amenity Services, 1987b. *Creative Writing by and About Gay Men: A Booklist.* London: Lambeth Amenity Services.

Lambeth Environmental Services, 1994. *Library Service Policy Guidelines.* Revised ed. London: Lambeth Environmental Services.

Lancashire County Council, 2012. *Your Lancashire: LGBT History Month.* [online] Available at: http://www.lancashire.gov.uk/corporate/web/?siteid=6463&pageid=38519 [Accessed November 2012].

Landerson, L., 1974. Psychiatry and Homosexuality: New 'Cures'. In: *The Radical Therapist*. Radical Therapist & Rough Times Collective, ed. Harmondsworth: Penguin, pp. 166-170.

Latimer, J., 2006. *What Is a Community Archive?*. [online] Available at: http://www.communityarchives.org.uk/page_id__32_path__0p1p73p.aspx [Accessed October 2012].

Learner, S., 2012. Call for More LGBT Training for Care Home Staff after Gay Resident Attempts Suicide, *carehome.co.uk*, 6 November 2012. [online] Available at: http://www.carehome.co.uk/news/article.cfm/id/1558312/call-for -more-lgbt-training-for-care-home-staff-after-a-lesbian-tries-to-commit-sui cide-in-a-care-home?fb_action_ids=10152249792950085&fb_action_ types=og.likes&fb_aggregation_id=288381481237582 [Accessed January 2013].

Lehmann, J., 1976. *In the Purely Pagan Sense*. London: Blond and Briggs.

Lehmann, J., 1985. *In the Purely Pagan Sense*. London: GMP.

Leitch, D., 1996. Obituary: John Vassall. *The Independent*, 9 December 1996. [online] Available at: http://www.independent.co.uk/news/obituaries/obituary-john-vassall-1313796.html [Accessed February 2013].

Lesbian Advocacy Services Initiative, n.d. *Coming Out*. [online] Available at: http://www.lasionline.org/the-issues/coming-out.html [Accessed May 2012].

Lesbian Herstory Archives, 2012. *Welcome to the Lesbian Herstory Archives*. [online] Available at: http://www.lesbianherstoryarchives.org/ [Accessed December 2012].

Lesbians in Libraries, 1986. *Lesbians in Libraries Newsletter*. October 1986.

Lesbians in Libraries, 1989. An Introduction to Books for Lesbian History Studies. In: *Not a Passing Phase: Reclaiming Lesbians in History 1840-1985*. Lesbian History Group, ed. London: The Women's Press.

Levin, A.K., 2012. Unpacking Gender: Creating Complex Models for Gender Inclusivity in Museums. In: *Museums, Equality and Social Justice*. R. Sandell and E. Nightingale, eds. London: Routledge (Museum Meanings), pp. 156-168.

LfSC, 1972. *Librarians for Social Change*, Winter issue (1).

LGBT Bristol, 2011. *LGBT History Month 2012 Programme*. [online] Available at: http://lgbtbristol.org.uk/2012/01/12/lgbt-history-month/ [Accessed May 2012].

LGBT Excellence Centre, 2011. *LGBT History Month Cymru a Roaring Sucess!!!*. [online] Available at: http://lgbtec.org.uk/lgbt-history-month-cymru [Accessed May 2012].

LGBT Excellence Centre, 2012a. *Libraries*. [online] Available at: http://lgbtec. org.uk/page/libraries [Accessed February 2012].

LGBT Excellence Centre, 2012b. *About Us*. [online] Available at: http://lgbtec. org.uk/page/about-us [Accessed February 2012].

LGBT Excellence Centre, 2012c. *Welsh Pride*. [online] Available at: http://lgbtec. org.uk/welsh-pride [Accessed August 2012].

LGBT History Month, 2007. *Let's Pretend! – Fifth Annual LGBT History and Archives Conference.* [online] Available at: http://lgbthistorymonth.org.uk/ the-blog/conference/let%E2%80%99s-pretend-fifth-annual-lgbt-history-and-archives-conference/ [Accessed October 2012].

LGBT History Month, 2012. *Black History Month LGBT Event.* [online] Available at: http://lgbthistorymonth.org.uk/featured-right/black-history-month-lgbt-event/ [Accessed October 2012].

LGBT Network Stoke-on-Trent & North Staffordshire, ca. 2011. *Community Consultation Survey.* [online] Available at: http://www.gaystoke.org.uk/ default.asp?Id=216&sC=page62 [Accessed August 2012].

LGBT Youth Scotland, 2012. *Life in Scotland for LGBT Young People: Education Report.* Edinburgh: LGBT Youth Scotland. [online] Available at: https:// www.lgbtyouth.org.uk/files/documents/Life_in_Scotland_for_LGBT_Young_ People_-_Education_Report_NEW.pdf [Accessed November 2012].

LGBT Youth Scotland, ca. 2012. *LGBT History Month Scotland.* [online] Available at: http://www.lgbthistory.org.uk/ [Accessed May 2012].

Librarians for Social Change Collective, 1974. *Librarians for Social Change Feminist Group Issue.* (5).

Librarians for Social Change Collective, 1975. *Sexual Politics: A Basic Reading List.* London: Release Publications.

LibrariesWest, 2010. *LibrariesWest Annual Report 2009–10.* Bridgwater: LibrariesWest. [online] Available at: http://www.somerset.gov.uk/irj/go/ km/docs/CouncilDocuments/SCC/Documents/Community/Libraries/ LibrariesWest%20Annual%20Report%202010.pdf [Accessed May 2012].

Library Association, 1988. Prohibition of Promotion of Homosexuality: Section 28 of the Local Government Act 1988 – Brief by the Library Association. In: *Out on the Shelves: Lesbian Books into Libraries.* J. Allen, L. Kerr, A. Rolph and M. Chadwick, eds. Newcastle-under-Lyme: AAL Publishing, pp. 71-75.

Library Association London and Home Counties Branch, 1986. *Branchlines* (3), December, p. 4.

Liddiard, M., 2004. Changing Histories: Museums, Sexuality and the Future of the Past. *Museum and Society*, 2(1), pp. 15-29. [online] Available at: http://www2. le.ac.uk/departments/museumstudies/museumsociety/documents/volumes/ liddiard.pdf [Accessed May 2012].

Liddington, J, n.d. *Who Was Anne Lister?.* [online] Available at: http://www. jliddington.org.uk/annelister.html [Accessed November 2012].

Lindley, D., 1973. [Letter]. *Library Association Record*, 75(9), 182.

Lindsay, J., 1979. *Radical Librarianship.* Brighton: Librarians for Social Change.

Lindsay, J., 2003. The Big ISsues. *Information for Social Change*, Winter issue (18). [online] Available at: http://www.libr.org/isc/articles/18-Lindsay-1.html [Accessed August 2012].

Lindsay, J., 2005. John McKay – Obituary. *Update*, 4(3), p. 47.

Littauer, D., 2013a. Belarus: No Gay Rights Groups Allowed Here. *Gay Star News* 14 February 2013. [online] Available at: http://www.gaystarnews.com/

article/belarus-no-gay-rights-groups-allowed-here140213 [Accessed February 2013].

Littauer, D., 2013b. Macedonia Local Elections Whip up Anti-Gay Hate. *Gay Star News* 5 February 2013. [online] Available at: http://www.gaystarnews. com/article/macedonia-local-elections-whip-anti-gay-hate050213 [Accessed February 2013].

Little, J., 1982. Women in Libraries: The First Eighteen Months. And the Future. *Librarians for Social Change*, 10(1).

Living Memory Association, ca. 2010. *Reminiscence and Oral History in Edinburgh*. [online] Available at: http://www.livingmemory.org.uk/ [Accessed May 2012].

Lobban, M. and Clyde, L.A., 1996. *Out of the Closet and into the Classroom: Homosexuality in Books for Young People* 2nd edn. Port Melbourne (Australia): ALIA/Thorpe.

Local Government Association, 2001. *Supporting Inclusive Communities – Lesbians, Gay Men and Local Democracy: Guidelines for Local Authorities*. London: LGA Publications.

Locke, T.G., 1973. [Letter]. *Library Association Record*, 75(10), p. 210.

Logan, J., 2013. Email interview by John Vincent, 8 February 2013.

London Borough of Hackney, 1995. *Lesbian & Gay Booklist & Resource Guide*. London: London Borough of Hackney.

Londongay, 2012. LGBT History Month. *London [Gay London Travel]*. [online] Available at: http://gaylondontravel.com/blog/?p=2332 [Accessed April 2012].

London Lesbian & Gay Switchboard, 2009. *London Lesbian & Gay Switchboard*. [online] Available at: http://www.llgs.org.uk/ [Accessed December 2011].

London Lesbian Line, 1987. *Women Like Us*. London: London Lesbian Line.

London Metropolitan Archives, 2005. *'Changing the World' Twenty Years On*. London: London Metropolitan Archives. [online] Available at: http://www. lgbthistorymonth.org.uk/documents/ChangingTheWorld.doc [Accessed October 2012].

London Metropolitan Archives, 2008. *Curiouser and Curiouser. : The Sixth Annual LGBT History and Archives Conference*. London: London Metropolitan Archives. [online] Available at: http://www.communityarchives.org.uk/ documents/Poster.pdf [Accessed August 2012].

London Metropolitan Archives, 2009. *Flights of Fancy: The Seventh Annual LGBT History and Archives Conference*. London: London Metropolitan Archives. [online] Available at: http://217.154.230.218/NR/rdonlyres/B71498 85-7F9D-448C-B740-C29131098737/0/LGBT09FLIERPrintversion.pdf [Accessed August 2012].

London Metropolitan Archives, 2010. *Young Hearts. Run Free: The Eighth Annual LGBT History and Archives Conference*. London: London Metropolitan Archives. [online] Available at: http://www.exploringsurreyspast.org.uk/ assets/userfiles/News/LGBT2_reduced.pdf [Accessed August 2012].

London Metropolitan Archives, 2011a. *Resist. Action. Change*. London: London Metropolitan Archives. [online] Available at: http://217.154.230.218/NR/rdon lyres/2A12109E-BDB1-44C8-AB18-8E6C9451DBA0/0/FINALLGBT_ Flyer_2011.pdf [Accessed August 2012].

London Metropolitan Archives, 2011b. *Lesbian, Gay, Bisexual and Transgender (LGBT) Community Archives at London Metropolitan Archives*. London: London Metropolitan Archives. [online] Available at: http://www.cityoflondon. gov.uk/things-to-do/archives-and-city-history/london-metropolitan-archives/ Documents/visitor-information/25%20Lesbian,%20gay,%20bisexual,%20 transgender%20(LGBT)%20community%20archives%20at%20London%20 Metropolitan%20Archives.pdf [Accessed August 2012].

London Metropolitan Archives, 2012. *LGBT Creative Writing Workshops*. London: London Metropolitan Archives. [online] Available at: http://www. cityoflondon.gov.uk/things-to-do/archives-and-city-history/london-metro politan-archives/news-and-events/Documents/LGBT%20Creative%20 Writing%20Workshops%202012.pdf [Accessed August 2012].

London School of Economics and Political Science, 2011. *Hall-Carpenter Archives*. [online] Available at: http://www2.lse.ac.uk/library/archive/hold ings/lesbian_and_gay_archives.aspx [Accessed November 2011].

Lorne, 2012. Email interview by John Vincent, 26 October 2012.

Lukenbill, B., 2002. Modern Gay and Lesbian Libraries and Archives in North America: A Study in Community Identity and Affirmation. *Library Management*, 23(1/2), pp. 93-100.

Lyddon, D, n.d. *The 1984–85 Miners' Strike*. TUC History Online. [online] Available at: http://www.unionhistory.info/timeline/1960_2000_Narr_ Display_2.php?Where=NarTitle+contains+'The+1984-85+Miners+Strike'+ [Accessed September 2012].

Lynch, B., 2012. *Whose Cake Is It Anyway? A Collaborative Investigation into Engagement and Participation in 12 Museums and Galleries in the UK*. London: Paul Hamlyn Foundation. [online] Available at: http://www.phf.org. uk/page.asp?id=1417 [Accessed February 2013].

McClenahan, S., 2012. *Multiple Identity; Multiple Exclusions and Human Rights: The Experiences of People with Disabilities Who Identify as Lesbian, Gay, Bisexual and Transgender People Living in Northern Ireland*. Belfast: Disability Action. [online] Available at: http://www.disabilityaction.org/fs/ doc/publications/final-report-on-the-rainbow-disability-action-work-v1-2.pdf [Accessed December 2012].

McCormack, M., 2012. *The Declining Significance of Homophobia: How Teenage Boys Are Redefining Masculinity and Heterosexuality*. New York: Oxford University Press, Inc (Sexuality, Identity and Society Series).

McFarnon, L., 2011. Brixton Riots – in Pictures. *The Independent*. [online] Available at: http://www.independent.co.uk/life-style/history/brixton-riots-- in-pictures-2266287.html [Accessed September 2012].

McIntyre, D., 2007. What to Collect? Museums and Lesbian, Gay, Bisexual and Transgender Collecting. *International Journal of Art and Design Education*, 26(1), pp. 48-53.

MacKeith, L. and Osborne, K., 2003. *Embracing Cultural Diversity and Social Inclusion: South West Museums*. Taunton: South West Museums Libraries and Archives Council.

McSmith, A., 2011. *No Such Thing as Society*. London: Constable.

Madden, E., 2012. *The Irish Queer Archive: Institutionalization and Historical Narrative*. International Archives, Libraries, Museums and Special Collections Conference on the future of lesbian, gay, bisexual and trans histories 2012 (Amsterdam) 1-3 August 2012. [online] Available at: http://lgbtialms2012. blogspot.nl/2012/07/ed-madden-irish-queer-archive.html [Accessed November 2012].

Manchester City Council. Communities and Neighbourhoods, 2005. *Manchester Community Engagement Toolkit*. Manchester: Manchester City Council. [online] Available at: http://www.manchester.gov.uk/downloads/download/172/community_engagement_toolkit [Accessed October 2012].

Manchester City Council. Libraries. Archives and Local Studies, 2011. *LGBT Source Guide: About This Guide*. [online] Available at: http://www.manchester.gov.uk/info/448/archives_and_local_studies/520/lgbt_source_guide/1 [Accessed November 2011].

Manchester Library and Information Service, 2012. 50 Shades of Gay: Manchester Libraries and the Lesbian and Gay Foundation Celebrate International Coming Out Day. *Manchester Lit List*. [online] Available at: http://www.manchesterlitlist.blogspot.co.uk/2012/10/50-shades-of-gay-manchester-libraries.html [Accessed January 2013].

Mann, W., 2012. Email to John Vincent. Sent 24 July 2012.

Mapplethorpe, R. and Danto, A.C., ca. 1992. *Mapplethorpe, Essay by Arthur C. Danto*. New York: Random House.

Marquand, D., 2004. *Decline of the Public: The Hollowing-out of Citizenship*. Cambridge: Polity Press.

Marr, A., 2007. *A Swansong to 'Olde Britain'*. [online] Available at: http://news.bbc.co.uk/1/hi/magazine/6676967.stm [Accessed November 2012].

Marshall, M.R., 1981. *Libraries and the Handicapped Child*. London: Deutsch.

Marston, B.J., 1998. Archivists, Activists, and Scholars: Creating a Queer History. In: *Daring to Find Our Names: The Search for Lesbigay Library History*. J. V. Carmichael, ed. Westport, Conn/London: Greenwood Press, pp. 135-152.

Martin, H.J. and Murdock, J.R., ca. 2007. *Serving Lesbian, Gay, Bisexual, Transgender, and Questioning Teens: A How-to-Do-It Manual for Librarians*. New York/London: Neal–Schuman.

Marwick, A., 1968. *Britain in the Century of Total War: War, Peace and Social Change*. London: The Bodley Head.

Mason, A. and Palmer, A., 1996. *Queer Bashing: A National Survey of Hate Crimes against Lesbians and Gay Men*. London: Stonewall.

Mason-John, V. and Khambatta, A., 1993. *Lesbians Talk: Making Black Waves*. London: Scarlet Press.

Medway Council, 2012. *LGBTQ: Lesbian, Gay, Bi-Sexual, Transgender and Questioning (LGBTQ) Resources*. [online] Available at: http://www.medway. gov.uk/leisureandculture/libraries/lovetoread/lgbtq.aspx [Accessed October 2012].

Merseyside Maritime Museum, 2012. *Hello Sailor! Gay Life on the Ocean Wave*. [online] Available at: http://www.liverpoolmuseums.org.uk/maritime/ exhibitions/gaylife/ [Accessed August 2012].

Metcalf, H. and Rolfe, H., 2011. *Barriers to Employers in Developing Lesbian, Gay, Bisexual and Transgender-Friendly Workplaces*. London: National Institute of Economic and Social Research. [online] Available at: http://webarchive. nationalarchives.gov.uk/+/http://www.homeoffice.gov.uk/publications/ equalities/lgbt-equality-publications/workplace-equality/workplaceequality-fullreport?view=Binary [Accessed August 2012].

Miles, N., 2011. *How to Engage Gay People in Your Work*. London: Stonewall. [online] Available at: http://www.stonewall.org.uk/documents/ engagementforwebsite.pdf [Accessed January 2013].

Miller, O., 2011. LGBT Progress in Scotland – Are We There Yet? *So So Gay*, 16 September 2011. [online] Available at: http://sosogay.org/2011/opinion-lgbt-progress-in-scotland-are-we-there-yet/ [Accessed January 2012].

Miller, S., 2012. *Lancashire Later: Celebrating LGBT History Month*. [online] Available at: http://www.lgbtdevelopment.org.uk/consortium2/node/152 [Accessed November 2012].

Mills, R., 2010. Queer Is Here? Lesbian, Gay, Bisexual and Transgender Histories and Public Culture. In: *Gender, Sexuality and Museums: A Routledge Reader*. A.K. Levin, ed. London: Routledge, pp. 80-88.

Milner, D., 1975. *Children and Race*. Harmondsworth, Middlesex: Penguin Books.

Montgomery, A. and Behr, A., 1988. Significant Others. *Assistant Librarian*, 81(11), pp. 164-168.

Mooney, D., 2012. *Pink Brick: Lesbian, Gay, Bisexual & Trans Histories of the University of Liverpool*. Liverpool: University of Liverpool. [online] Available at: http://www.liv.ac.uk/media/livacuk/lgbthistory/pdf/PINK-BRICk-LGBT-Histories-TIMELINE.pdf [Accessed November 2012].

Moore, A.L., 2011. The History of the GLBT Round Table. In: *Serving LGBTIQ Library and Archives Users: Essays on Outreach, Service, Collections and Access* E. Greenblatt ed. Jefferson, North Carolina: McFarland & Company, pp. 319-323.

Moran, L.J., 2012. To Be Judged 'Gay'. In: *Out of the Ordinary: Representations of LGBT Lives*. I. Rivers and R. Ward, eds. Newcastle upon Tyne: Cambridge Scholars Publishing, pp. 61-75.

Moynihan, M., 2009. Donal Óg Gets '100%' Backing from Cork Colleagues, *Irish Examiner* (19 October 2009). [online] Available at: http://www.irishexaminer. com/sport/donal-og-gets-100-backing-from-cork-colleagues-103675.html [Accessed May 2012].

Muddiman, D., Durrani, S., Dutch, M., Linley, R., Pateman, J. and Vincent, J., 2000a. *Open to All? The Public Library and Social Exclusion. Volume 1: Overview and conclusions.* London: Resource (Library and Information Commission Research Report 84). [online] Available at: http://www.seapn.org.uk/content_files/files/ota_volume_1_final_version_sept_211.doc [Accessed 10 July 2009].

Muddiman, D., Durrani, S., Dutch, M., Linley, R., Pateman, J. and Vincent, J., 2000b. *Open to All? The Public Library and Social Exclusion. Volume 2: Survey, case studies and methods.* London: Resource (Library and Information Commission Research Report 85).

Muddiman, D., Durrani, S., Dutch, M., Linley, R., Pateman, J. and Vincent, J., 2000c. *Open to All? The Public Library and Social Exclusion. Volume 3: Working Papers.* London: Resource (Library and Information Commission Research Report 86).

Munisi, S.E., 1973a. [Letter]. *Library Association Record*, 75(8), pp. 167-168.

Munisi, S.E., 1973b. [Reply to Letters]. *Library Association Record*, 75(10), p. 210.

Munt, S.R., 2013. *The Mood of History.* Brave New World? (London) 16 February 2013, [unpublished].

Murray, D., ca. 1997. Burning Issues Group – Working Towards Quality Library Services for Lesbians and Gay Men. March 1997. [Published letter].

Murray, D., 2012. Email interview by John Vincent, 23 November 2012.

Museum of London., ca. 1999. *Pride & Prejudice : Lesbian and Gay London.* Capital Concerns. [online] Available at: http://www.museumoflondon.org.uk/archive/exhibits/pride/index.htm [Accessed May 2012].

Museum of London, 2005a. *The LGBT Community in London.* [online] Available at: http://www.museumoflondon.org.uk/Collections-Research/Research/Your-Research/RWWC/Themes/1161/ [Accessed August 2012].

Museum of London, 2005b. *Re-Assessing What We Collect.* [online] Available at: http://www.museumoflondon.org.uk/Collections-Research/Research/Your-Research/RWWC/ [Accessed August 2012].

Museum of London, 2006. *Queer Is Here.* [online] Available at: http://www.museumoflondon.org.uk/Explore-online/Past/QueerIsHere.htm [Accessed October 2012].

Museum of Science & Industry, 2012. *Behind the Scene: Stories from Manchester's LGBT Communities.* [online] Available at: http://www.mosi.org.uk/whats-on/behind-the-scene.aspx?utm_source=LGF+weekly+bulletin&utm_campaign=6ee4cc1b6e-Weekly_Bulletin_08_07_2012&utm_medium=email [Accessed August 2012].

Museums Journal, 1999. Embrace the Socially Excluded. *Museums Journal* 'Comment' July issue, p. 14.

National AIDS Trust, 1999. *Are Health Authorities Failing Gay Men?: HIV Prevention Spending in England 1997/98.* London: National AIDS Trust.

The National Archives, 2011. *Your Archives: Lesbian, Gay, Bisexual and Transgender (LGBT) History in the National Archives: Identified Documents by Theme.* [online] Available at: http://yourarchives.nationalarchives.gov. uk/index.php?title=Lesbian,_Gay,_Bisexual_and_Transgender_(LGBT)_ History_in_The_National_Archives:_Identified_documents_by_theme [Accessed November 2011].

The National Archives, 2013. *Gay and Lesbian History.* [online] Available at: http://www.nationalarchives.gov.uk/records/research-guides/gay-lesbian.htm [Accessed February 2013].

National Council on Archives, 2001a. *Archives in the Regions: An Overview of the English Regional Archive Strategies.* Sheffield: National Council on Archives.

National Council on Archives, 2001b. *Taking Part: An Audit of Social Inclusion Work in Archives.* Sheffield: The National Council on Archives. [online] Available at: http://www.ncaonline.org.uk/materials/takingpart.pdf [Accessed 21 September 2009].

National Museums Liverpool, 2012. *Sudley House: Hitched – Wedding Clothes and Customs.* [online] Available at: http://www.liverpoolmuseums.org.uk/ sudley/exhibitions/hitched/ [Accessed November 2012].

National Portrait Gallery, n.d. (2007)-a. *Gay Icons: Exhibition.* [online] Available at: http://www.npg.org.uk/gayicons/exhib.htm [Accessed October 2012].

National Portrait Gallery, n.d. (2007)-b. *Gay Icons: Selectors.* [online] Available at: http://www.npg.org.uk/gayicons/select.htm [Accessed October 2012].

National Portrait Gallery, 2012. *Family Album.* [online] Available at: http://www. npg.org.uk/beyond/exhibitions/partnership/past/family-album.php [Accessed October 2012].

Nectoux, T.M. (ed.), 2011. *Out Behind the Desk: Workplace Issues for LGBTQ Librarians.* Duluth, Minnesota: Library Juice Press.

Neild, L., 2007. A City Blazes in Front of the Whole World. *Liverpool Daily Post* 9 July 2007. [online] Available at: http://www.liverpooldailypost.co.uk/ liverpool-culture/liverpool-special-features/2007/07/09/a-city-blazes-in-front-of-the-whole-world-64375-19429599/ [Accessed September 2012].

The Network, 2013. *LGBT.* [online] Available at: https://www.jiscmail.ac.uk/cgi-bin/webadmin?A0=LGBT [Accessed January 2013].

New Manchester Walks, 2012. *Alan Turing – Tortured Genius of the Computer Age.* [online] Available at: http://www.newmanchesterwalks.com/walks-tours/science/alan-turing-tortured-genius-of-the-computer-age-2/ [Accessed October 2012].

News of the World, 1950. He Killed Man Who Dressed as a Woman. *News of the World* 26 November 1950.

NHS Norfolk, 2010. *Research Report: Lesbian, Gay & Bisexual in Norfolk Today – Findings of Consultation with Lesbian, Gay & Bisexual Residents.* Norwich: NHS Norfolk. [online] Available at: http://www.norfolk.nhs.uk/

sites/default/files/LGB%20Survey%202010%20-%20Final%20Report.pdf [Accessed January 2013].

NHS Northwest Health Equality Library Portal, 2009. *Everything You Wanted to Know About Sexual Orientation Monitoring. But Were Afraid to Ask*. [online] Available at: http://help.northwest.nhs.uk/somworkbook/what_monitoring.php [Accessed August 2012].

Nicolson, A., 1998. Obscenity Case the Police Cannot Win. *Sunday Telegraph* 8 March 1998, p. 6.

Nightingale, E. and Sandell, R., 2012. Introduction. In: *Museums, Equality and Social Justice*. R. Sandell and E. Nightingale, eds. London: Routledge, pp. 1-9.

Noble, M. and Smith, G., 1994. *Increasing Polarisation between Better-Off and Poorer Neighbourhoods in Oldham and in Oxford*. York: Joseph Rowntree Foundation (Findings – Social Policy Research). [online] Available at: http://www.jrf.org.uk/sites/files/jrf/sp56.pdf [Accessed October 2012].

Norman, M., 1998. *Out on Loan*. [Thesis] University of Brighton, Brighton.

North Chingford Reading Group, 2011. *LGBT History Month Reading List*. Walthamstow: Waltham Forest Library and Information Services.

Northamptonshire Libraries and Information Service, 1999. *Northamptonshire's Coming out on the Shelves*. [Press Release]. Northamptonshire Libraries and Information Service.

NUS, 2012. *Out in Sport: LGBT Students' Experiences of Sport*. London: National Union of Students. [online] Available at: http://www.nus.org.uk/Global/NUS%20Cards/Out%20in%20Sport%20web.pdf [Accessed November 2012].

Ofsted, 2012a. *Exploring the School's Actions to Prevent Homophobic Bullying: Briefing for Section 5 Inspection*. Manchester: Ofsted. [online] Available at: http://www.ofsted.gov.uk/resources/briefings-and-information-for-use-during -inspections-of-maintained-schools-and-academies-january-201?dm_i=FBX, S8A7,21Z939,2AJST,1 [Accessed November 2012].

Ofsted, 2012b. *A Whole-School Approach to Tackling Homophobic Bullying and Ingrained Attitudes: Stoke Newington School and Sixth Form*. Manchester: Ofsted. [online] Available at: http://www.ofsted.gov.uk/resources/good-practice -resource-whole-school-approach-tackling-homophobic-bullying-and- ingrained-attitudes-st [Accessed November 2012].

Ofsted, 2012c. *No Place for Bullying: How Schools Create a Positive Culture and Prevent and Tackle Bullying*. Manchester: Ofsted. [online] Available at: http://www.ofsted.gov.uk/resources/no-place-for-bullying [Accessed November 2012].

Old Bailey Proceedings Online, 2012. *Homosexuality*. [online] Available at: http://www.oldbaileyonline.org/static/Gay.jsp [Accessed August 2012].

Ollendorff, R., 1972. The Rights of Adolescents. In: *Children's Rights: Towards the Liberation of the Child*. London: Panther Books Ltd, pp. 97-134.

ONE National Gay & Lesbian Archives, 2011. *Welcome*. [online] Available at: http://www.onearchives.org/ [Accessed November 2011].

Onlywomen Press, ca. 2011. *Onlywomen Press*. [online] Available at: http://www.onlywomenpress.com/index.html [Accessed April 2012].

Opening the Book, ca. 2006a. *Branching out – Archive*. [online] Available at: http://www.openingthebook.com/archive/branching-out/frontpage.asp [Accessed August 2011].

Opening the Book, ca. 2006b. *Branching out – Archive – Gay and Lesbian Writing*. [online] Available at: http://www.openingthebook.com/archive/branching-out/page2.asp?idno=407 [Accessed August 2011].

Oram, A., 2011. Going on an Outing: The Historic House and Queer Public History. *Rethinking History*, 15(2), June 2011, pp. 189-207.

Oram, A., 2012a. Email to John Vincent. Sent 23 March 2012.

Oram, A., 2012b. Sexuality in Heterotopia: Time, Space and Love between Women in the Historic House. *Women's History Review*, 21(4), pp. 533-551.

Oscar Wilde Bookshop, 2009. *The Oscar Wilde Bookshop*. [online] Available at: http://www.oscarwildebooks.com/Home.html [Accessed July 2012].

OurStory Scotland, 2012. *Storytelling*. [online] Available at: http://www.ourstoryscotland.org.uk/storytelling/index.htm [Accessed October 2012].

OurStory Scotland, n.d.-a. *Becoming Visible: Exhibition of Gay, Lesbian, Bisexual and Transgender History in Scotland*. [online] Available at: http://www.ourstoryscotland.org.uk/exhibitions/becomingVisible/tour.htm [Accessed October 2012].

OurStory Scotland, n.d.-b. *The Origins of Ourstory Scotland*. [online] Available at: http://www.ourstoryscotland.org.uk/heritage/assocSupp/storyOSS.htm [Accessed October 2012].

OutHistory, 2008. *Harry Hay: Founding the Mattachine*, Part 2. [online] Available at: http://www.outhistory.org/wiki/Harry_Hay:_Founding_the_Mattachine,_part_2 [Accessed July 2012].

OutHistory, 2012. *Harry Hay: Founding the Mattachine Society, 1948-1953*. [online] Available at: http://www.outhistory.org/wiki/Harry_Hay:_Founding_the_Mattachine_Society,_1948-1953 [Accessed July 2012].

Out in the City, 2012. The Next Generation. *Out in the City* (70), October 2012, pp. 37-39.

OutRage! 2012. *Outrage!*. [online] Available at: http://outrage.org.uk/ [Accessed January 2012].

Oyekanmi, B., 2011. Black, Gay and Proud. *Runnymede Bulletin* Summer issue (366), pp. 8-9. [online] Available at: http://www.runnymedetrust.org/uploads/bulletin/pdfs/366-BulletinSummer11W.pdf [Accessed November 2011].

Park, J., 2011. Ben Daniels Rejects Rupert Everett's Advice for Aspiring Gay Actors Not to Come Out. *Pink News*. [online] Available at: http://www.pinknews.co.uk/2011/07/16/ben-daniels-rejects-rupert-everetts-advice-for-aspiring-gay-actors-not-to-come-out/?utm_source=feedburner&utm_medium=feed&utm_campaign=Feed%3A+Pinknews+%28Pink+News%29&utm_content=Bloglines [Accessed August 2011].

Park, J., 2012. Joe McElderry Victim of 'Twitter Homophobia', Again, *Pink News*, 25 April 2012. [online] Available at: http://www.pinknews.co.uk/2012/04/25/joe-mcelderry-victim-of-twitter-homophobia-again/ [Accessed April 2012].

Parkinson, R., 2012. *A 'Great Unrecorded History': Presenting LGBT History in a Museum for the World.* International Archives, Libraries, Museums and Special Collections Conference on the future of lesbian, gay, bisexual and trans histories 2012 (Amsterdam) 1-3 August 2012. [online] Available at: http://lgbtialms2012.blogspot.nl/2012/08/richard-parkinson-british-museum-london.html#more [Accessed November 2012].

Pateman, J., 2012. Email to John Vincent. Sent 13 June 2012.

Patterson, C., 2013. Why It's Time for Galleries to Dump the Jargon. *The Independent* 5 February 2013. [online] Available at: http://www.independent.co.uk/arts-entertainment/art/features/why-its-time-for-galleries-to-dump-the-jargon-8480622.html [Accessed February 2013].

Pearlman, D., 1982. *No Choice: Library Services for the Mentally Handicapped.* London: Library Association.

Peters, F., 1951. *Finistère.* New York: Farrar, Strauss & Co.

Petry, M., 2004. *Hidden Histories: 20th Century Same Sex Male Lovers in the Visual Arts.* London: Artmedia Press.

Petry, M., 2007. Hidden Histories: The Experience of Curating a Male Same Sex Exhibition and the Problems Encountered. *International Journal of Art and Design Education*, 26(1) February, pp. 19-128.

Pettinger, T., 2012. *Causes of Boom and Bust Cycles.* [online] Available at: http://www.economicshelp.org/blog/5030/economics/causes-of-boom-and-bust-cycles/ [Accessed February 2013].

Pettis, R.M., 2009. *Libraries and Archives.* GLBTQ. [online] Available at: http://www.glbtq.com/social-sciences/libraries_archives.html [Accessed January 2013].

Phibbs, H., 2009. Councils Should NOT Be Spending Your Money on Promoting Homosexuality, *Mail Online.* [online] Available at: http://www.dailymail.co.uk/debate/article-1197038/HARRY-PHIBBS-Councils-NOT-spending-money-promoting-homosexuality.html [Accessed December 2011].

Phillips, T., 2009. Foreword. In: *Beyond Tolerance: Making Sexual Orientation a Public Matter.* London: Equality and Human Rights Commission. [online] Available at: http://www.equalityhumanrights.com/uploaded_files/research/beyond_tolerance.pdf [Accessed October 2011].

Phillpott, M., 2012. Nine and a Half Years: The Impact of London Metropolitan Archives LGBT History and Archives Conference. *History SPOT: IHR Digital: Seminars and Research Training Blog.* [online] Available at: http://ihrprojects.wordpress.com/2012/04/04/nine-and-a-half-years-the-impact-of-london-metropolitan-archives-lgbt-history-and-archives-conference/ [Accessed November 2012].

Pimblett, J., 2012. *Looking Back: Looking Forward – London Metropolitan Archives: LGBT History and Archives Conference 2003-2012.* International

Archives, Libraries, Museums and Special Collections Conference on the future of lesbian, gay, bisexual and trans histories 2012 (Amsterdam) 1-3 August 2012. [online] Available at: http://lgbtialms2012.blogspot.nl/2012/08/looking-back-looking-forward.html#more [Accessed November 2012].

Pinfold, C., 2013. Germany: Poll Finds That 26% of Voters Would Not Back a Gay Chancellor. *Pink News* 13 February 2013. [online] Available at: http://www.pinknews.co.uk/2013/02/13/germany-poll-finds-that-26-of-voters-would-not-back-a-gay-chancellor/ [Accessed February 2013].

Pink News, 2012. Liverpool: Two-Year Project on Life of April Ashley Launched. *Pink News* 27 July 2012. [online] Available at: http://www.pinknews.co.uk/2012/07/27/liverpool-two-year-project-on-life-of-april-ashley-launched/?utm_source=feedburner&utm_medium=feed&utm_campaign=Feed%3A+Pinknews+%28Pink+News%29 [Accessed August 2012].

Pittman, G., 2011. *Social Environment Linked to Gay Teen Suicide Risk*. [online] Available at: http://www.reuters.com/article/2011/04/18/us-gay-teen-suicide-idUSTRE73H1GV20110418 [Accessed October 2011].

Porter, D. and Prince, D., 2010. *50 Years of Queer Cinema: 500 of the Best GLBTQ Films Ever Made*. New York: Blood Moon Productions.

Porter, K. and Weeks, J. (ed.), 1991. *Between the Acts: Lives of Homosexual Men 1885-1967*. London: Routledge.

Portsmouth City Council, 2012. *Reading Groups in Portsmouth*. [online] Available at: http://www.portsmouth.gov.uk/learning/12449.html [Accessed October 2012].

Powell, V., 1998. University in Mapplethorpe Obscenity Row. *Gay Times* April, p. 46.

Powell, V. and Richardson, C., 1997. Lessons to Be Learned. *Gay Times* February, pp. 46-50.

Powell, V. and Richardson, C., 1999. How Did They Get Away with Murder? *Gay Times* April, pp. 36-42.

Power, L., 1995. *No Bath but Plenty of Bubbles: An Oral History of the Gay Liberation Front, 1970–1973*. London: Cassell.

Pride in our Past, 2012a. *News: National Award for 'Pride in Our Past' – Most Inspirational Community Archive*. [online] Available at: http://prideinourpast.wordpress.com/ [Accessed August 2012].

Pride in our Past, 2012b. *Welcome to the Plymouth LGBT History Archive*. [online] Available at: http://plymlgbtarchive.org.uk/ [Accessed August 2012].

Prudames, D., 2004. *Hidden Histories – Gay Art at the New Art Gallery in Walsall*. [online] Available at: http://www.culture24.org.uk/art/art22239 [Accessed October 2012].

Pursglove, G. and Brownjohn, A., 2009. James Kirkup – Obituary. *Guardian* 16 May 2009. [online] Available at: http://www.guardian.co.uk/books/2009/may/16/obituary [Accessed May 2012].

Quirke, D., 1974. GLG Meeting at CHE Annual Conference. 4 May 1974. [Published letter] LSE – HCA/EPHEM/125.

Rainbow Reading Group, 2012. *Rainbow Reading Group.* [online] Available at: http://www.rainbowreadinggroup.org.uk/index.htm [Accessed October 2012].

Rais, G., 1986. 'Sin Week Disgrace' to Hackney. *Daily Telegraph* 24 June 1986.

Rechy, J., 1963. *City of Night.* New York: Grove Press.

Rees, D., 1982. *The Milkman's on His Way.* London: Gay Men's Press.

Renault, M., 1944. *The Friendly Young Ladies.* London: Longmans, Green.

Renault, M., 1953. *The Charioteer.* London: Longman.

Renault, M., 1956. *The Last of the Wine.* London: Longmans, Green & Co.

Renault, M., 1963. *The Last of the Wine.* London: New English Library (Four Square Books).

Reuben, D.R., 1969. *Everything You Always Wanted to Know About Sex, but Were Afraid to Ask, Explained by David R. Reuben.* New York: D. McKay Co.

Reuben, D.R., 1970. *Everything You Always Wanted to Know About Sex. But Were Afraid to Ask (Explained by David R. Reuben).* London/New York: W H Allen.

Reynolds, P., 2011. Welcome from Pat Reynolds. In: *Surrey Heritage: Discovering, Preserving, Celebrating.* Woking: Surrey County Council, p. 3. [online] Available at http://www.surreycc.gov.uk/__data/assets/pdf_file/0007/177316/Surrey-Heritage-Discovering-Preserving-Celebrating.pdf [Accessed September 2013].

Richardson, C., 1995. 'Homosexual Panic' Defence Succeeds Again. *Gay Times* November issue, p. 30.

Rimmerman, C.A., 2008. *The Lesbian and Gay Movements: Assimilation or Liberation?* Philadelphia: Westview Press (Dilemmas in American Politics).

Robinson, L., 2003. Carnival of the Oppressed: The Angry Brigade and the Gay Liberation Front. *University of Sussex Journal of Contemporary History* (6), August. [online] Available at: http://www.sussex.ac.uk/history/research/usjch/pastissues [Accessed December 2011].

Rogers, A., 2012. 'In This Our Lives': Invisibility and Black British Gay Identity. In: *Out of the Ordinary: Representations of LGBT Lives.* I. Rivers and R. Ward, eds. Newcastle upon Tyne: Cambridge Scholars Publishing, pp. 43-59.

Rogers, E., 2012. Different Age, Similar Struggle. *Children & Young People Now* (7-20 February 2012), pp. 22-23.

Rolph, A., 1984. The Power of Women in Libraries. In: *Women and Librarianship.* J. Shuter, ed. Bradford: MCB University Press (Library Management, 5 (4)).

Rolph, A., 2000. The Life and Times of LiL: Lesbians in the Library. In: *Gendering Library History.* E. Kerslake and N. Moody, eds. Liverpool: Media Critical and Creative Arts, Liverpool John Moores University/Association for Research in Popular Fictions, pp. 196-207.

Rooke, K., 2011. *Outing the Past!.* [online] Available at: http://www.lancashire.gov.uk/corporate/web/?siteid=4528&pageid=36870&e=e [Accessed November 2012].

Rooke, K., 2012. *Outing the Past: Identifying, Showcasing and Celebrating the Wealth of LGBT Evidence in Every Archive* [presentation] Our History – Ourselves (London) 8 December 2012.

Rooke, K., 2013. Email interview by John Vincent, 19 February 2013.

Roszak, T., 1970. *The Making of a Counter Culture: Reflections on the Technocratic Society and Its Youthful Opposition*. London: Faber.

Rouse, B., 2010. Official Statistics Reveal UK Gay, Lesbian and Bisexual Population. *The Independent* 23 September 2010. [online] Available at: http://www.independent.co.uk/news/uk/home-news/official-statistics-reveal-uk-gay-lesbian-and-bisexual-population-2087829.html [Accessed November 2012].

rukus! Federation, 2011. *rukus!*. [online] Available at: http://rukus.org.uk/rukus/ [Accessed November 2011].

Runnymede Trust, 2012. *The Struggle for Race Equality: An Oral History of the Runnymede Trust, 1968-1988 – Broadwater Farm Inquiry*. [online] Available at: http://www.runnymedetrust.org/histories/race-equality/105/broadwater-farm-inquiry.html [Accessed September 2012].

Rush, A, n.d.-a. *Queer Heritage – a Timeline: The 1950s*. [online] Available at: http://www.aaronsgayinfo.com/timeline/Ftime50.html [Accessed November 2012].

Rush, A., n.d.-b. *Queer Heritage – a Timeline: The 1960s*. [online] Available at: http://www.aaronsgayinfo.com/timeline/Ftime60.html [Accessed November 2012].

Saini, A., 2008. *The Fight to Be Out*. [online] Available at: http://www.bbc.co.uk/london/content/articles/2007/02/12/lgbt_exhibition_feature.shtml [Accessed August 2012].

Sampson, K., 2012. I Walked One Way. The Less Fortunate Walked Another. *The Observer* 'Comment' 16 September, p. 31.

Sandbrook, D., 2011. *State of Emergency – the Way We Were: Britain, 1970-1974*. London: Penguin Books.

Sandbrook, D., n.d. *Sixties Britain: A Social and Cultural Revolution? Introduction*. [online] Available at: http://www.nationalarchives.gov.uk/education/topics/sixties-britain.htm [Accessed November 2012].

Sandell, R., 2001. Preface. In: *Museums, Society, Inequality*. R. Sandell, ed. London: Routledge (Museum Meanings), pp. xvii-xix.

Sandell, R. (ed.), 2002. *Museums, Society, Inequality*. London: Routledge.

Sandell, R., 2012. Museums and the Human Rights Frame. In: *Museums, Equality and Social Justice*. R. Sandell and E. Nightingale, eds. London: Routledge (Museum Meanings), pp. 195-215.

Sandell, R. and Frost, S., 2010. A Persistent Prejudice. In: *Hot Topics, Public Culture, Museums*. F. Cameron and L. Kelly, eds. Newcastle upon Tyne: Cambridge Scholars Publishing, pp. 150-174.

Sandell, R., Dodd, J. and Jones, C., 2010. *An Evaluation of Sh[out] – the Social Justice Programme of the Gallery of Modern Art, Glasgow 2009-2010*. Leicester: Research Centre for Museums and Galleries. [online] Available at: http://www2.le.ac.uk/departments/museumstudies/rcmg/projects/sh-out/An%20evaluation%20of%20shOUT.pdf [Accessed May 2012].

Sanders, S., 2012a. 'LGBT History Month 2012 Report'. Email to John Vincent. Sent 9 May 2012.

Sanders, S., 2012b. Comment: The Story of LGBT History Month, *Pink News* (31 January 2012). [online] Available at: http://www.pinknews.co.uk/2012/01/31/comment-the-story-of-lgbt-history-month/ [Accessed May 2012].

Sanderson, T., 1993. 'Media Watch' Column. *Gay Times* April issue.

Sanderson, T., 1995. *Mediawatch: The Treatment of Male and Female Homosexuality in the British Media*. London: Cassell.

Savin-Williams, R.C., 2005. *The New Gay Teenager*. London: Harvard University Press.

Savin-Williams, R.C., 2009. How Many Gays Are There? It Depends. In: *Contemporary Perspectives on Lesbian, Gay, and Bisexual Identities*. D.A. Hope, ed. New York; London: Springer (Nebraska Symposium on Motivation, No.54), pp. 5-41.

Schifferes, S., 2004. *The Trade Unions' Long Decline*. [online] Available at: http://news.bbc.co.uk/1/hi/business/3526917.stm [Accessed September 2012].

Schools Out, ca. 2011. *Schools Out*. [online] Available at: http://www.schools-out.org.uk/ [Accessed December 2011].

Science Museum, 2012. *Codebreaker – Alan Turing's Life and Legacy*. [online] Available at: http://www.sciencemuseum.org.uk/visitmuseum/galleries/turing [Accessed August 2012].

Scottish Executive, 1999. *Social Justice ... a Scotland Where Everyone Matters*. Edinburgh: Scottish Executive. [online] Available at: http://www.scotland.gov.uk/Resource/Doc/158142/0042789.pdf [Accessed June 2011].

Scottish Transgender Alliance, n.d.-a. *Cross-Dressing People*. [online] Available at: http://www.scottishtrans.org/Page/Cross_dressing_People.aspx [Accessed July 2012].

Scottish Transgender Alliance, n.d.-b. *Androgyne People*. [online] Available at: http://www.scottishtrans.org/Page/Androgyne_People.aspx [Accessed July 2012].

Scottish Transgender Alliance, n.d.-c. *Transgender Umbrella*. [online] Available at: http://www.scottishtrans.org/Transgender_Umbrella.aspx [Accessed July 2012].

Seidel, H., 1998. The 'Invisibles': Lesbian Women as Library Users. *Progressive Librarian* (14), Spring. [online] Available at: http://pacificreference.pbworks.com/f/The+_Invisibles_.pdf [Accessed October 2011].

Seidman, S., Fischer, N. and Meeks, C. (ed.), 2011. *Introducing the New Sexuality Studies*. 2nd ed. Abingdon, Oxon: Routledge.

SEMLAC, 2005. *Social Inclusion Strategy 2005-2007*. Winchester: South East Museum, Library & Archive Council.

Senate Historical Office, ca. 2005. *Biographical Directory of the United States Congress*. [online] Available at: http://bioguide.congress.gov/scripts/biodisplay.pl?index=m000315 [Accessed November 2012].

Sheffield Archives and Local Studies, 2010. *Good Practice in Working with LGBT Communities: Sheffield Archives and Local Studies*. [online] Available at:

http://www.seapn.org.uk/content_files/files/good_practice_in_working_with_ lgbt_communities.doc [Accessed October 2012].

Sheffield Libraries Archives and Information, 2009. *Sources for the Study of the History of Lesbian, Gay, Bisexual and Trans Communities*. Sheffield: Sheffield Libraries, Archives and Information. [online] Available at: https://www. sheffield.gov.uk/libraries/archives-and-local-studies/research-guides/lesbian-and-gay-sources.html [Accessed January 2013].

Sheila, ca. 2008. Sheila. In: *Our Story Liverpool: Memories of Gay Liverpool*. Liverpool: Our Story Liverpool, pp. 4-5.

Shopland, N., 2012. Email to John Vincent. Sent 24 July 2012.

Simsova, S., 1982. *Library Needs of the Vietnamese in Britain*. London: Polytechnic of North London, School of Librarianship and Information Studies (Research Report 10).

Simsova, S. and Chin, W.T., 1982. *Library Needs of Chinese in London*. London: Polytechnic of North London, School of Librarianship and Information Studies (British Library Research and Development Reports No. 5718 / Research Report – Polytechnic of North London. School of Librarianship and Information Studies No. 9).

Sinfield, A., 1999. *Out on Stage: Lesbian and Gay Theatre in the Twentieth Century*. New Haven, Conn; London: Yale University Press.

SINTO, 2011. *SINTO the Information Partnership: Welcome*. [online] Available at: http://extra.shu.ac.uk/sinto/Index.html [Accessed May 2012].

Smart, D., 2012. Daniel Smart. In: *Out in the Workplace: Lesbian, Gay and Bisexual Employees' Experience of Working in the Public Sector*. Bristol City Council, ed. Bristol: Bristol City Council, p. 8. [online] Available at: http:// www.bristol.gov.uk/sites/default/files/documents/community_and_safety/ equality_and_diversity/Out%20in%20the%20work%20place%20-%20final. pdf [Accessed November 2012].

Smith, A.M., 1990. A Symptomology of an Authoritarian Discourse: The Parliamentary Debates on the Prohibition of the Promotion of Homosexuality. *New Formations*, 10 (Spring 1990), pp. 41-65. [online] Available at: http:// www.amielandmelburn.org.uk/collections/newformations/10_41.pdf [Accessed April 2012].

Smith, D., 2012. *Sex, Lies & Politics: Gay Politicians in the Press*. Brighton/ Portland, Oregon/Vaughan, Ontario: Sussex Academic Press.

Smith, D.J., 1977. *Racial Disadvantage in Britain: The PEP Report*. Harmondsworth, Middlesex: Penguin Books.

Smith, G., Bartlett, A. and King, M., 2004. Treatments of Homosexuality in Britain since the 1950s—an Oral History: The Experience of Patients. *BMJ*, pp. 328-427. [online] Available at: http://www.bmj.com/content/328/7437/427 [Accessed October 2012].

Smith, K., 2012. *Queering the Handling Collection at the Geffrye Museum*. [online] Available at: http://untoldlondon.org.uk/articles/read/queering_the_ handling_collection_at_the_geffrye_museum [Accessed January 2013].

Smith, M., 2012. *Other Stories: Queering the University Art Collection*. Leeds: The Stanley & Audrey Burton Gallery.

Social Exclusion Unit, 1998. *Bringing Britain Together: A National Strategy for Neighbourhood Renewal. Cm 4045*. London: The Stationery Office.

Social Exclusion Unit, 2001a. *National Strategy for Neighbourhood Renewal: Policy Action Team Audit: A Report by the Social Exclusion Unit*. London: Cabinet Office.

Social Exclusion Unit, 2001b. *Preventing Social Exclusion: A Report by the Social Exclusion Unit*. London: Cabinet Office. [online] Available at: http://webarchive.nationalarchives.gov.uk/+/http://www.cabinetoffice.gov.uk/media/cabinetoffice/social_exclusion_task_force/assets/publications_1997_to_2006/preventing.pdf [Accessed May 2012].

Social Trends, 2010. Social Trends through the Decades. *Social Trends*, 40 p. xxxiii. [online] Available at: http://www.palgrave-journals.com/st/journal/v40/n1/full/st20104a.html#The-1970s [Accessed January 2013].

Somerset, J., 2011. Doing It Together: LGBT Mentoring in West Yorkshire. *Equal Opportunities Review* (219), December, pp. 13-15.

Sparrow, A., 2013. MPs Vote in Favour of Gay Marriage. *Guardian Politics Live*. [online] Available at: http://www.guardian.co.uk/politics/blog/2013/feb/05/gay-marriage-debate-politics-live-blog [Accessed February 2013].

Spencer, C., 1996. *Homosexuality: A History*. London: Fourth Estate.

Sport England, 2012. *New Charter Tackles Homophobia in Sport*. [online] Available at: http://www.sportengland.org/about_us/our_news/new_charter_tackles_homophobia.aspx [Accessed August 2012].

Stafford, J.M., 1993. The Need for Gay Lessons. *Gay and Lesbian Humanist* Spring. [online] Available at: http://www.pinktriangle.org.uk/glh/123/lessons.html [Accessed December 2011].

The Stanley and Audrey Burton Gallery, 2012. *Press Release: University of Leeds Art Collection 'Queer-Ied' by Artist Matt Smith for LGBT History Month. Exhibition: 'Other Stories: Queering the University Art Collection', 27 February – 5 May 2012*. [online] Available at: http://www.york.ac.uk/media/modernstudies/documents/Press%20Release%20-%20Other%20Stories.pdf [Accessed May 2012].

Stiff, D., 2010. *Gay Surrey's IDAHO Event, 17 May 2010, the Talbot Inn, Ripley*. Woking: Surrey Heritage.

Stones, R., 1988. 13 Other Years: The Other Award 1975-1987. *Books for Keeps*, 53 (November), p. 22.

Stones, R., 1994. I Din Do Nuttin… To Gregory Cool. *Books for Keeps*, 88 (September), p. 5.

Stonewall, 2000a. The Legality of Section 28. *Impact*, 3(4), pp. 50-52.

Stonewall, 2000b. Section 28 – Speaking Out. *Impact*, 3(4), pp. 52-53.

Stonewall, 2003. *Profiles of Prejudice: Detailed Summary of Findings*. London: Stonewall. [online] Available at: http://www.stonewall.org.uk/documents/profiles.doc [Accessed May 2012].

Stonewall, ca. 2010. *Unseen on Screen: Gay People on Youth TV*. London: Stonewall. [online] Available at: http://www.stonewall.org.uk/documents/ unseen_on_screen_web_final.pdf [Accessed November 2011].

Stonewall, 2011a. *History of Lesbian, Gay and Bisexual Equality*. [online] Available at: http://www.stonewall.org.uk/at_home/history_of_lesbian_gay_ and_bisexual_equality/default.asp [Accessed January 2012].

Stonewall, 2011b. *Lesbian, Gay & Bisexual People in Later Life*. London: Stonewall. [online] Available at: http://www.stonewall.org.uk/documents/lgb_ in_later_life_final.pdf [Accessed October 2011].

Stonewall, 2011c. *Gay People Are Stereotypes, Jokes or Almost Invisible on Youth TV*. [online] Available at: http://www.stonewall.org.uk/media/current_ releases/4510.asp [Accessed November 2011].

Stonewall, 2012. *Stonewall's Diversity Champions Programme*. [online] Available at: http://www.stonewall.org.uk/at_work/diversity_champions_programme/ default.asp [Accessed August 2012].

Stonewall, ca. 2012a. *Everyone Is Included*. London: Stonewall. [online] Available at: http://www.stonewall.org.uk/documents/everyone_is_included_2012.pdf [Accessed January 2013].

Stonewall, ca. 2012b. *Diversity Champions Programme*. London: Stonewall.

Stonewall, 2013. *Immigration, Asylum and International*. [online] Available at: http://www.stonewall.org.uk/at_home/immigration_asylum_and_international/ default.asp [Accessed January 2013].

Storr, A., 1964. *Sexual Deviation*. Harmondsworth: Penguin Books.

Strom, M.G. (ed.), 1977. *Library Services to the Blind and Physically Handicapped*. Metuchen/London: Scarecrow Press.

Sullivan, J, n.d. *Audre Lorde (1934-1992)*. Modern American Poetry. [online] Available at: http://www.english.illinois.edu/maps/poets/g_l/lorde/lorde.htm [Accessed February 2013].

Summerskill, B., 2012a. Introduction. In: *Gay and Bisexual Men's Health Survey*. A. Guasp, ed. London: Stonewall, p. 3. [online] Available at: http://www. healthylives.stonewall.org.uk/includes/documents/cm_docs/2012/g/gay-and- bisexual-mens-health-suvey.pdf [Accessed May 2012].

Summerskill, B., 2012b. Introduction. In: *The School Report: The Experiences of Gay Young People in Britain's Schools in 2012*. A. Guasp, ed. London: Stonewall, p. 1. [online] Available at: http://www.stonewall.org.uk/documents/ school_report_2012.pdf [Accessed January 2013].

Summerskill, C., 2012. *Gateway to Heaven: Fifty Years of Lesbian and Gay Oral History*. London: Tollington Press.

Sunday Pictorial, 1955. The Squalid Truth: MP in Spy Sensation. *Sunday Pictorial* 25 September 1955, p. 1.

Surrey Heritage, 2011a. *Exploring Surrey's Past: Out, Loud and Proud Receive a Heart of Equality Award*. [online] Available at: http://www. exploringsurreyspast.org.uk/themes/subjects/diversity/lgbt_youth_project/ award [Accessed October 2011].

Surrey Heritage, 2011b. *LGBT Bibliography*. Woking: Surrey County Council, Surrey History Centre. [online] Available at: http://www.exploringsurreys past.org.uk/assets/userfiles/PDFs/LGBT_Month_Bibliog_2011.pdf [Accessed October 2011].

Surrey Heritage, ca. 2011. *Exploring Surrey's Past: Diversity*. [online] Available at: http://www.exploringsurreyspast.org.uk/themes/subjects/diversity [Accessed October 2011].

Surrey Heritage, n.d. *Exploring Surrey's Past: Gay Surrey Archives*. [online] Available at: http://www.exploringsurreyspast.org.uk/themes/subjects/divers ity/gay_surrey_archives [Accessed November 2012].

Surrey History Centre, 2012. *Exploring Surrey's Past: News – LGBT (Lesbian Gay Bisexual Trans) History Month 2012*. [online] Available at: http://www. exploringsurreyspast.org.uk/news/001016.html [Accessed August 2012].

Sylla, J., 2011. Double Struggle to Belong. *Runnymede Bulletin* (366, Summer), p. 12. [online] Available at: http://www.runnymedetrust.org/uploads/bulletin/ pdfs/366-BulletinSummer11W.pdf [Accessed November 2011].

Takács, J., 2006. *Social Exclusion of Young Lesbian, Gay, Bisexual and Transgender (LGBT) People in Europe*. Brussels, Belgium: ILGA-Europe.

Tameside Metropolitan Borough, 2012. *The Tameside Citizen: Services for Lesbian, Gay, Bisexual and Transgender People (LGBT)*. [online] Available at: http://www.tameside.gov.uk/libraries/gay [Accessed October 2012].

Tatchell, P., 2010. The Gay Liberation Front's Social Revolution. *Guardian* 12 October 2010. [online] Available at: http://www.guardian.co.uk/commentisfree/ 2010/oct/12/gay-liberation-front-social-revolution [Accessed December 2011].

Tatchell, P., 2012. Comment: Future Sex – Beyond Gay and Straight, *Pink News* (10 January 2012). [online] Available at: http://www.pinknews.co. uk/2012/01/10/comment-future-sex-beyond-gay-and-straight/?utm_source =feedburner&utm_medium=feed&utm_campaign=Feed%3A+Pinknews+%2 8Pink+News%29&utm_content=Bloglines [Accessed May 2012].

Tate, 2012. *Civil Partnerships? Queer and Feminist Curating*. [online] Available at: http://www.tate.org.uk/whats-on/tate-modern/conference/civil-partnerships- queer-and-feminist-curating [Accessed November 2012].

Tatler, 2012. Where Are All the Lesbians? London's Loveliest, Liveliest Lesbians Tell It Like It Is. *Tatler*, August issue. [online] Available at: http://www.tatler. com/magazine [Accessed July 2012].

Taylor, W., 1999. *Jerome*. Dunedin (New Zealand): Longacre Press.

Taylor & Francis Group, 2012. *Introducing 'the New Sexuality Studies' Second Edition*. [online] Available at: http://cw.routledge.com/textbooks9780415781 268/explore.asp [Accessed January 2012].

Thatcher, M., 1987. *Speech to Conservative Party Conference*. Conservative Party Conference (Blackpool) October 1987, Margaret Thatcher Foundation. [online] Available at: http://www.margaretthatcher.org/speeches/display document.asp?docid=106941 [Accessed December 2011].

Thistlethwaite, P., 1990. The Lesbian Herstory Archives. In: *Gay and Lesbian Library Service*. C. Gough and E. Greenblatt, eds. London: McFarland, pp. 61-64.

Thistlethwaite, P., 1995. The Lesbian and Gay Past: An Interpretive Background. *Gay Community News*. Winter issue, pp. 10-11, 24.

Thorp, A. and Allen, G., 2000. *The Local Government Bill [HL]: The 'Section 28' Debate: Bill 87 of 1999-2000*. London: House of Commons (Research Paper 00/47). [online] Available at: http://www.google.co.uk/url?sa=t&rct=j&q=&e src=s&frm=1&source=web&cd=1&ved=0CEoQFjAA&url=http%3A%2F%2 Fwww.parliament.uk%2Fbriefing-papers%2FRP00-47.pdf&ei=LZEzUP3cGs aW0QXx1YH4BQ&usg=AFQjCNEkR7uliJoMUjsiBcZmkah5VFsMMQ&si g2=ALn2p7IF_cq7ok_ZjAcQoA [Accessed August 2012].

Tibbles, A., 2012. Hello Sailor! How Maritime Museums Are Addressing the Experience of Gay Seafarers. *International Journal of Heritage Studies*, 18(2), pp. 160-173.

Tingle, R., 1986. Straining Sexual Tolerance. *Daily Telegraph*, 17 December 1986.

Tobias, A., 1999. Everything You Never Wanted to Know. *Advocate*, 20 July 1999, p. 63. [online] Available at: http://books.google.co.uk/books?id=o2QEA AAAMBAJ&pg=PA63&lpg=PA63&dq=david+reuben+everything+you+al ways+wanted+%2B+gay&source=bl&ots=_Ab1n7RI0c&sig=c02ONky-OR 9R23NHb-XEOSWq10Q&hl=en&sa=X&ei=-rcXUaCCMoyU0Q WyoYGYAw&ved=0CFsQ6AEwBg#v=onepage&q=david%20reuben%20 everything%20you%20always%20wanted%20%20%2B%20gay&f=false [Accessed February 2013].

Townsend, P., 1979. *Poverty in the United Kingdom: A Survey of Resources and Standards of Living*. Harmondsworth: Penguin.

Trades Union Congress, 1994. *Lesbian and Gay Rights at Work : A TUC Charter for Equality of Opportunity*. London: Trades Union Congress.

Traies, J., 2012. 'Women Like That': Older Lesbians in the UK. In: *Lesbian, Gay, Bisexual and Transgender Ageing : Biographical Approaches for Inclusive Care and Support*. R. Ward, I. Rivers and M. Sutherland, eds. London: Jessica Kingsley, pp. 67-82.

Traies, J.E., 2009. *'Now You See Me': The Invisibility of Older Lesbians*. [Thesis] University of Birmingham, Birmingham. [online] Available at: http://etheses. bham.ac.uk/497/1/Traies09MPhil.pdf [Accessed July 2012].

Traynor, I., 2009. Anti-Gay, Climate Change Deniers: Meet David Cameron's New Friends. *Guardian*, 3 June 2009. [online] Available at: http://www.guardian. co.uk/politics/2009/jun/02/david-cameron-alliance-polish-nationalists [Accessed February 2013].

Tseliou, M.-A., 2011. *Subverting the (Hetero)Normative Museum*. 1st Global Conference: Gender and Love (Oxford). [online] Available at: http://www. inter-disciplinary.net/wp-content/uploads/2011/08/tseliougpaper.pdf [Accessed November 2012].

Turner, A.W., 2010. *Rejoice! Rejoice! Britain in the 1980s*. London: Aurum Press.

Turock, B.J., 1982. *Serving the Older Adult : A Guide to Library Programs and Information Sources*. New York/London: Bowker.

UK Black Pride, 2011. *UK Black Pride*. [online] Available at: http://www. ukblackpride.org.uk/ [Accessed November 2011].

UK Intersex Association, n.d. *The United Kingdom Intersex Association*. [online] Available at: http://www.ukia.co.uk/index.htm#list [Accessed January 2013].

UK Lesbian & Gay Immigration Group, n.d. *Asylum Overview*. [online] Available at: http://www.uklgig.org.uk/asylum.htm [Accessed January 2012].

UNISON, 2007. *Workforce Monitoring for Sexual Orientation and Gender Identity*. London: UNISON. [online] Available at: http://www.unison.org.uk/ acrobat/B3155.pdf [Accessed October 2012].

Unravelled, 2012. *Unravelling. Nymans*. [online] Available at: http://www. unravelled.org.uk/nymans.html [Accessed January 2013].

Untold London, 2011. *Write Queer London 2012 Is on Its Way*. [online] Available at: http://untoldlondon.org.uk/articles/read/write_queer_london_2012_is_on_ its_way [Accessed August 2012].

Untold London, 2012. *LGBT Events*. [online] Available at: http://untoldlondon. org.uk/community/LGBT [Accessed August 2012].

Vaknin, J., 2009. *Lesbian and Gay Newsmedia Archive*. [online] Available at: http://www.communityarchives.org.uk/page_id__936_path__0p2p14p42p. aspx [Accessed October 2012].

Valentine, G. and McDonald, I., 2004. *Understanding Prejudice: Attitudes Towards Minorities*. London: Stonewall. [online] Available at: http://www.stonewall. org.uk/documents/pdf_cover__content.pdf [Accessed February 2010].

Valentine, G., Skelton, T. and Butler, R., 2003. *Towards Inclusive Youth Policies and Practices: Lessons from Young Lesbians, Gay Men and D/Deaf People*. Leicester: The National Youth Agency.

Valentine, S., Vincent, J. and Whitehead, P., 2002. Making the Best of Consortium Purchasing. *The Network Newsletter*, February issue (5), pp. 4-7. [online] Available at: http://www.seapn.org.uk/content_files/files/newsletter_ns_5.doc [Accessed August 2012].

Vanegas, A., 2002. Representing Lesbians and Gay Men in British Social History Museums. In: *Museums, Society, Inequality*. R. Sandell, ed. London: Routledge, pp. 98-109.

Vasagar, J., 2012. Gay–Straight Alliance Club Confronts Homophobia at North London School. *Guardian*, 2 March 2012. [online] Available at: http://www. guardian.co.uk/education/2012/mar/02/gay-straight-alliance-homophobia-school [Accessed November 2012].

Vaswani, R., 2000. Inclusion Is the Key for the 'Post-Museum'. *Museums Journal*, May issue, p. 13.

Victoria and Albert Museum, 2010. *From the Margins to the Core? Conference Programme*. [online] http://media.vam.ac.uk/vamembed/media/uploads/files/ vanda_margins_to_core_3day_prog.pdf [Accessed August 2012].

Victoria and Albert Museum, 2012. *LGBTQ Histories at the V&A*. [online] Available at: http://www.vam.ac.uk/content/articles/l/lgbtq-histories-at-the-v-and-a/ [Accessed May 2012].

Vidal, G., 1948. *The City and the Pillar*. New York: E.P. Dutton & Co.

Vidal, G., 1949. *The City and the Pillar*. London: John Lehmann.

Vincent, J., 1976. Bias in Children's Books. *Assistant Librarian*, 69(4), pp. 68-70.

Vincent, J., 1986a. *An Introduction to Community Librarianship*. Sheffield: Association of Assistant Librarians (AAL Pointers: 3).

Vincent, J., 1986b. Censorship and Selection in Public Libraries. In: *Fiction in Libraries*. J. Dixon, ed. London: Library Association, pp. 127-134.

Vincent, J., 1999. Lesbians, Bisexuals, Gay Men and Transgendered People [Working Paper 5]. In: *Open to All? The Public Library and Social Exclusion. Volume 3: Working Papers*, D. Muddiman, S. Durrani, M. Dutch, R. Linley, J. Pateman and J. Vincent, eds. London: Resource, pp. 62-86.

Vincent, J., 2000a. Political Correctness [Working Paper 14]. In: *Open to All? The Public Library and Social Exclusion*. Vol. 3: Working Papers, D. Muddiman, S. Durrani, M. Dutch, R. Linley, J. Pateman and J. Vincent, eds. London: Resource, pp. 350-361.

Vincent, J., 2000b. Join up to Tackle Exclusion. *Public Library Journal* 'Ideas into Action', 15(1),p. 23.

Vincent, J., 2006. *LGBT People and Libraries – How Well Do We Do?* CILIP Diversity Group conference: 'Pride or Prejudice?' – How well are Libraries serving Lesbian, Gay, Bi- and Trans- Communities? (Manchester) 8 February 2006, CILIP. [online] Available at: http://www.cilip.org.uk/get-involved/special-interest-groups/diversity/Documents/JohnVincentKeynote06.pdf [Accessed May 2012].

Vincent, J., 2009. Public Library Provision for Black and Minority Ethnic Communities – Where Are We in 2009? *Journal of Librarianship and Information Science*, 41(3), pp. 137-147.

Vincent, J. and Hardie, R., 2000. *'Clause 28' and Its Effects*. Nadderwater, Exeter: The Network.

Walker, A., 1997. Introduction: The Strategy of Inequality. In: *Britain Divided: The Growth of Social Exclusion in the 1980s and 1990s*. A. Walker and C. Walker, eds. London: CPAG, pp.1-13.

Walker, A. and Walker, C. (ed.), 1987. *The Growing Divide – a Social Audit 1979-1987*. London: CPAG.

Walker, H., 2012. Lesbianism – the Love That's Fair Game for All. *The Independent*, 'Opinion'. 7 July 2012, p. 42.

Walker, T., 2012. Sexuality: A Frank and Moving Statement. *The Independent*, 5 July 2012, p. 26.

Wallace, W., 2000. I Hated School. You Have to Put on an Act Every Day. *Times Education Supplement*, 3 March 2000, pp. 8,10.

Walter, A. (ed.), 1980. *Come Together: The Years of Gay Liberation (1970-73)*. London: Gay Men's Press.

Walton, T. (ed.), 2010. *Out of the Shadows: How London Gay Life Changed for the Better after the Act – a History of the Pioneering London Gay Groups and Organisations, 1967-2000*. London: Bona Street Press.

Warburton, J., 1998. How Serious Is Your Commitment to Your Lesbian and Gay Readers? *Community Librarian*, Spring issue (20), pp. 6-9.

Warwick, I., Chase, E., Aggleton, P. and Sanders, S., 2004. *Homophobia, Sexual Orientation and Schools: A Review and Implications for Action*. London: Department for Education and Skills (Research Report 594).

Warwick University. Department of History, 2010. *Homophobia and Sport*. [online] Available at: http://www2.warwick.ac.uk/fac/arts/history/atoz/think ingaloud/podcasts/homophobia/ [Accessed January 2012].

Watney, S., 1987. *Policing Desire: Pornography, Aids and the Media*. Minneapolis: University of Minnesota Press.

Watts, A., 1969. [Review]. *San Francisco Chronicle*.

Watts, L., 2011. Interview: Joe McElderry on the X Factor, Coming out and Winning Popstar to Operastar, *Pink News*, 19 December 2011. [online] Available at: http://www.pinknews.co.uk/2011/12/19/interview-joe-mcelderry-on-the-x-factor-coming-out-and-winning-popstar-to-operastar/ [Accessed April 2012].

Weatherall, P., 2012. Email to John Vincent. Sent 23 November 2012.

Weeks, J., 1990. *Coming Out: Homosexual Politics in Britain from the Nineteenth Century to the Present*. Revised edn. London: Quartet.

Weeks, J., 1991. *Against Nature: Essays on History, Sexuality and Identity*. London: Rivers Oram.

Welch, D., 1944. When I Was Thirteen. *Horizon*, April 1944, pp. 250-265.

Welch, D., 1948. *Brave and Cruel, and Other Stories*. London: Hamish Hamilton.

Wellcome Library, 2012. *Sex: Archival Sources in the Wellcome Library*. [online] Available at: http://library.wellcome.ac.uk/doc_WTL039946.html [Accessed August 2012].

Welsh, S.T., 2010. Coming out of the Cabinet. *ManCultural*. [online] Available at: http://mancultural.wordpress.com/2010/02/11/coming-out-of-the-cabinet/ [Accessed November 2012].

Welsh, S.T., 2012. Email to John Vincent. Sent 4 December 2012.

Werz, M. and Conley, L., 2012. *Climate Change, Migration, and Conflict: Addressing Complex Crisis Scenarios in the 21st Century*. Washington, DC: Center for American Progress. [online] Available at: http://www.american progress.org/wp-content/uploads/issues/2012/01/pdf/climate_migration.pdf [Accessed February 2013].

West, D.J., 1960. *Homosexuality*. London: Pelican.

West Sussex County Council, 2012. *LGBT History Month*. Chichester: West Sussex County Council.

West Yorkshire Archive Service, n.d.-a. *Nowthen: Home*. [online] Available at: http://nowthen.php5.truth.posiweb.net/ [Accessed January 2013].

West Yorkshire Archive Service, n.d.-b. *Nowthen: LGBT Archive.* [online] Available at: http://nowthen.php5.truth.posiweb.net/collections/lgbt-archive/about-the-project [Accessed January 2013].

Whittle, A., 2013. Email interview by John Vincent, 14 January 2013.

Whittle, S., Turner, L. and Al-Alami, M., 2007. *Engendered Penalties: Transgender and Transsexual People's Experiences of Inequality and Discrimination.* London: Press for Change. [online] Available at: http://www.pfc.org.uk/pdf/EngenderedPenalties.pdf [Accessed December 2012].

Wikipedia, 2011a. *'Round the Horne'.* [online] Available at: http://en.wikipedia.org/wiki/Round_the_Horne [Accessed February 2012].

Wikipedia, 2011b. *International Day against Homophobia and Transphobia.* [online] Available at: http://en.wikipedia.org/wiki/International_Day_Against_Homophobia_and_Transphobia [Accessed October 2011].

Wikipedia, 2011c. *Michael Pitt-Rivers.* [online] Available at: http://en.wikipedia.org/wiki/Michael_Pitt-Rivers [Accessed December 2011].

Wikipedia, 2011d. *Edward Douglas-Scott-Montagu, 3rd Baron Montagu of Beaulieu.* [online] Available at: http://en.wikipedia.org/wiki/Edward_Douglas-Scott-Montagu,_3rd_Baron_Montagu_of_Beaulieu [Accessed December 2011].

Wikipedia, 2011e. *Sunday Mirror.* [online] Available at: http://en.wikipedia.org/wiki/Sunday_Mirror [Accessed December 2011].

Wikipedia, 2011f. *Section 28.* [online] Available at: http://en.wikipedia.org/wiki/Section_28 [Accessed December 2011].

Wikipedia, 2011g. *London Lesbian and Gay Centre.* [online] Available at: http://en.wikipedia.org/wiki/London_Lesbian_and_Gay_Centre#cite_note-0 [Accessed August 2012].

Wikipedia, 2011h. *Beverley Nichols.* [online] Available at: http://en.wikipedia.org/wiki/Beverley_Nichols [Accessed December 2011].

Wikipedia, 2012a. *Esme Langley.* [online] Available at: http://en.wikipedia.org/wiki/Esme_Langley [Accessed July 2012].

Wikipedia, 2012b. *John Wolfenden, Baron Wolfenden.* [online] Available at: http://en.wikipedia.org/wiki/John_Wolfenden,_Baron_Wolfenden [Accessed May 2012].

Wikipedia, 2012c. *The City and the Pillar.* [online] Available at: http://en.wikipedia.org/wiki/The_City_and_the_Pillar [Accessed January 2013].

Wikipedia, 2012d. *Timeline of LGBT History in Britain.* [online] Available at: http://en.wikipedia.org/wiki/Timeline_of_LGBT_history_in_Britain#cite_note-MINER1-44 [Accessed October 2012].

Wikipedia, 2012e. *John Vassall.* [online] Available at: http://en.wikipedia.org/wiki/John_Vassall [Accessed February 2013].

Wikipedia, 2012f. *Godfrey Winn.* [online] Available at: http://en.wikipedia.org/wiki/Godfrey_Winn [Accessed February 2012].

Wikipedia, 2012g. *Mary Whitehouse.* [online] Available at: http://en.wikipedia.org/wiki/Mary_Whitehouse [Accessed May 2012].

Wikipedia, 2012h. *Community Charge*. [online] Available at: http://en.wikipedia. org/wiki/Community_Charge [Accessed September 2012].

Wikipedia, 2012i. *Sanford Berman*. [online] Available at: http://en.wikipedia.org/ wiki/Sanford_Berman [Accessed February 2013].

Wikipedia, 2012j. *David Wilshire*. [online] Available at: http://en.wikipedia.org/ wiki/David_Wilshire [Accessed.

Wikipedia, 2012k. *Hegemonic Masculinity*. [online] Available at: http:// en.wikipedia.org/wiki/Hegemonic_masculinity [Accessed February 2013].

Wikipedia, 2012l. *John Giffard, 3rd Earl of Halsbury*. [online] Available at: http:// en.wikipedia.org/wiki/John_Giffard,_3rd_Earl_of_Halsbury [Accessed.

Wikipedia, 2012m. *Alan Turing*. [online] Available at: http://en.wikipedia.org/ wiki/Alan_Turing [Accessed October 2012].

Wikipedia, 2012n. *Malcolm Sinclair, 20th Earl of Caithness*. [online] Available at: http://en.wikipedia.org/wiki/Malcolm_Sinclair,_20th_Earl_of_Caithness.

Wikipedia, 2012o. *John Browne, Baron Browne of Madingley*. [online] Available at: http://en.wikipedia.org/wiki/John_Browne,_Baron_Browne_of_Madingley [Accessed June 2012].

Wikipedia, 2013. *Economic History of the United Kingdom*. [online] Available at: http://en.wikipedia.org/wiki/Economic_history_of_the_United_Kingdom #1960.E2.80.931979:_the_Sixties_and_Seventies [Accessed January 2013].

Wildeblood, P., 1955. *Against the Law*. London: Weidenfeld & Nicolson.

Williams, H., 2011a. The Day I Came Out: Simon Callow. *The Independent Magazine*, 17 December 2011, pp. 21, 23.

Williams, H., 2011b. The Day I Came Out: Stella Duffy. *The Independent Magazine*, 17 December 2011, p. 29.

Wilson, K. and Birdi, B., 2008. *The Right 'Man' for the Job? The Role of Empathy in Community Librarianship*. Sheffield: Department of Information Studies, University of Sheffield. [online] Available at: http://www.shef.ac.uk/content/1/ c6/07/85/14/AHRC%202006-8%20final%20report%2004.08.pdf   [Accessed July 2011].

Winchester, O., 2012a. Oliver Winchester: interview by John Vincent, 3 July 2012.

Winchester, O., 2012b. A Book with Its Pages Always Open?. In: *Museums, Equality and Social Justice*. R. Sandell and E. Nightingale, eds. London: Routledge (Museum Meanings), pp. 142-155.

Wintemute, R., 1995. Sexual Orientation Discrimination. In: *Individual Rights and the Law in Britain*. C. McCrudden and G. Chambers, eds. Oxford: Oxford University Press for the Law Society, pp. 491-533.

Wolverhampton City Council, 2011. *LGBT Reading Group*. [online] Available at: http://www.wolverhampton.gov.uk/leisure_culture/libraries/reading/LGBT+ Reading+Group.htm [Accessed October 2012].

Women in Libraries, 1987. *Women and Language: Proceedings of the Women in Libraries 7th Annual Conference*. Wolsey Hall, Cheshunt, Herts. 10 October 1987. London: Women in Libraries.

Women's Resource Centre, 2010. *Trans*. London: Women's Resource Centre (Lesbian, Bisexual and Trans Women's Services in the UK: Briefing 2). [online] Available at: http://www.wrc.org.uk/includes/documents/cm_docs/2011/t/trans_updated_apri_2011.pdf [Accessed June 2012].

Women's Resource Centre, 2012. *Women's Resource Centre*. [online] Available at: http://www.wrc.org.uk/ [Accessed November 2012].

Wood, G.W., 2011. *Out & About: Mapping LGBT Lives in Birmingham*. Birmingham: Birmingham LGBT. [online] Available at: http://blgbt.org/downloads/outandaboutreportfinalweb.pdf [Accessed August 2012].

World Health Organization, 2012. *Gender*. [online] Available at: http://www.who.int/topics/gender/en/ [Accessed November 2012].

Wright, B.C., 1987. *Library Services to UK Penal Establishments : A Comparative Study*. London: Library Association, Prison Libraries Group.

Wright, L., 1999. The Stonewall Riots 1969 – A Turning Point in the Struggle for Gay and Lesbian Liberation. *Socialism Today* July issue (40). [online] Available at: http://socialistalternative.org/literature/stonewall.html [Accessed December 2011].

Young, I., n.d. *The Paperback Explosion: How Gay Paperbacks Changed America*. [online] Available at: http://www.ianyoungbooks.com/GayPbks/Paperbacks.htm [Accessed November 2012].

Young, L., 2005. *Our Lives, Our Histories, Our Collections*. [online] Available at: http://www.museumoflondon.org.uk/Collections-Research/Research/Your-Research/RWWC/Essays/Essay2/ [Accessed October 2012].

Younge, G., 2007. 'I'm Not Just That Big Gay Bloke'. *Guardian* 28 June 2007. [online] Available at: http://www.guardian.co.uk/world/2007/jun/28/usa.americansports [Accessed October 2011].

YouthNet, 2003. *Shout: The Needs of Young People in Northern Ireland Who Identify as Lesbian, Gay, Bisexual and or Transgender*. Belfast: YouthNet. [online] Available at: http://www.youthnetni.org.uk/Site/29/Documents/shout%20pdf.pdf [Accessed June 2012].

Zhooshbrighton.co.uk, 2012. LGBT Exhibition for Holocaust Memorial Day January 27th. *The Zhoosh! Brighton Blog.* [online] Available at: http://blog.zhooshbrighton.co.uk/2012/01/26/brighton-hove-libraries-services-celebrate-lgbt-history-month-2012/ [Accessed May 2012].

Zieman, K., 2009. Youth Outreach Initiatives at the Canadian Lesbian and Gay Archives. *Archivaria Fall issue* (68), pp. 311-317.

Index